COMPLEX PTSD

FROM SURVIVING TO THRIVING
A GUIDE AND MAP FOR RECOVERING
FROM CHILDHOOD TRAUMA

Pete Walker

Author of *The Tao of Fully Feeling*

"Pete Walker's new book is an invaluable, comprehensive resource for anyone with a childhood history of trauma. This book is certain to benefit clients and clinicians alike."

- Julie Scheinman, M.A., MFT

Testimonials about Pete Walker's first book, *The Tao of Fully Feeling*, and his website: www.pete-walker.com

I am writing from Survivors of Abuse Recovering (S.O.A.R.) Society, located in Canada. We would like to include "13 Steps for Managing Flashbacks" in our resource manual.

I found myself. I found myself in your words. It's as if you had unzipped me, stepped inside my traumatized inner self, meandered around a bit, come back outside, and wrote about what you discovered inside of me. For the first time in my life.......and I'm in my fifties now........I don't feel defective......or crazy.......or "weird".......or even unlovable. – D.M.

I sat in the San Francisco Airport reading your book (in the washroom, shaking and weeping) to get the courage to go the next leg of the trip. It helped me so much just to know that you live in that area-strange when I haven't even met you! Your website and book are invaluable to me. – A. R.

I want to thank you so much for all the help you have given me (and all the people I've passed your website link onto since finding out about it). Your understanding of emotional flashbacks has made an enormous difference in my life. I've gone from being smashed about by huge waves to having a surfboard on which I can ride at least some of them, and even if I fall off into it, I know it won't last forever. – J, New Zealand

Thank you for all of your educational information with regards to PTSD and abandonment. I have finally found something that I have tried to explain to therapists for years. Every single piece of information is exactly what I experience from my PTSD and attachment depression. – A

I thank you on a personal and professional level. Your articles on healing from CPTSD have excited me and validated me both. I will be a better therapist now, and heal further in my own life. — D

Your article will be one of my regular handouts now to my clients. Needless to say I feel this information and the way you articulate it is a life saver! — L.P

How impactful all you have written has been for me and how much healing I have found in the pages of your website. Like the authors you note in your article on bibliotherapy - I was convinced you would have empathy for me had I the occasion to meet you - and here, in this moment, that belief is powerfully actualized. — J.S.

I have been labeled and diagnosed with everything from panic disorder to separation anxiety and attachment disorder, bipolar disorder, generalized anxiety, etc. Then I found a therapist who said I had PTSD from long-term emotional abuse from my father and emotional neglect from my mother and that's when things really started to click. I feel like everything I have been reading from this website is the final piece to the puzzle that I have been searching for in my journey. It is indeed very empowering and liberating. — A.M.

I'm a long way into my own recovery process now and have recently reached a point of wanting to look back and celebrate how far I've come. Your words were just what I needed to see at this time. I feel really seen and understood and appreciated. What a gift. — P.

After a degree in psychology, training in counseling and decades of therapy this is the first time I've read something that describes my internal state! — F.K.

I've been working with your book for a few years, and for the first time in my life I'm able to be myself and feel a full range of feelings - and my kids are starting to flower due to this hard work. So thank you. — N.A.

I wanted to extend my gratitude for all the information you have made available on complex PTSD. Clearly the best resource on the internet. — J.C.

I found your online articles about 5 years ago, and have consistently come back to them as I work through Complex PTSD with a wonderful therapist. Your words are sturdy and compassionate and direct and I now find life worth living again. P.S. I keep a copy of 13 Steps/Flashback in my purse. — P.B.

This is and will always be a historic day in my life; simply from stumbling onto your articles. Twelve years of huge wastes of treatment time suffering. You've nailed it. I'm talking van der Kolk could learn from you. I've always hated the psych chatter of how great it is to be able to put a name to this or that or blah, blah. But I stand converted. It is absolutely a miracle to know emotional flashbacks 'fit' the 'thing'. — M.

I've read your articles many many times. Particularly on abandonment depression, you have given me hope to refrain from committing suicide. Thank you so much for taking the time to write these exceptional articles on the internet. I cannot thank you enough. — T.M., N. Ireland

I just finished your book. It is powerful and gentle. I am starting your book over now and am using a highlighter as I go through it again. You invite the reader into a warm therapeutic relationship as you write. A beautiful, beautiful book! Thank you — A. R.

I wanted to thank you for sharing your work on your website. It was exactly what I needed to get an area of my life unstuck! Your work is insightful, your suggestions are doable, and most importantly they resulted in achieving the gentle shifts most needed to change my life. — L.K.

Your articles have offered more insight and hope to me as a CPTSD sufferer, than any other, and I am grateful for this and would like to share this knowledge with others. Please could we have permission to publish your articles on www.ptsdforum.org .

Reading your article was like the clouds clearing up and the sun coming out. I'm not crazy, I'm not stupid, I'm not broken forever. I just have emotional flashbacks and *it's not my fault*. — M.L.

I've never read something that helped me gain such personal insight and clarity to my own life experience. After years of working with coaches, healers, and therapists, I've never been able to 'pinpoint' what exactly was happening in my own internal processing. I never clearly fit in any 'box' or diagnosis... that is, until now. It is such a relief to read these articles and know that what I struggle with 'makes sense' based on my difficult life (and childhood) experiences. And it's an even greater relief to recognize that there are ways to approach and manage this in a positive way. — R.T.

I don't think it would be an understatement to tell you that your work has possibly saved my life as well as my fiancé's life. We both have complex PTSD and had both pretty much given up on life. Your material has allowed us to understand what is happening to us. It has really opened my eyes. — M. M.

You are a gift to me and thousands of people who have suffered like me and who struggle to find their anger (it's coming!), self-protection, self-sorrowing, growth. I am re-building, re-parenting myself. — L.K., U.K.

I just re-read your book and underlined almost the whole thing. I have gotten so much from your web-site and now the book. Three years plus into therapy, I am amazed at how much I have changed. It blows my mind when I read the fawning stuff now, and realize that I don't really do that anymore. — A.

I have been to counseling, psychologists, psychiatrists, spiritual help, you name it; I have tried it. I have many self-help books and online resources. They all give me some helpful information, but, your article gave me more than anything ever has. — J. T.

I have been working in the field of counseling education for 12 years, and I can honestly say, I have never found information and theory such as this before. — C.M., Asst. Professor of Counseling Psychology

I felt compelled to write and thank you for your article on complex PTSD. Reading it has for the first time allowed me to cry real tears from the depths of my body for the pain and loss I experienced on my life journey so far. — M.

COMPLEX PTSD

FROM SURVIVING TO THRIVING

Pete Walker

COMPLEX PTSD: FROM SURVIVING TO THRIVING

AN AZURE COYOTE BOOK / 2013
www.pete-walker.com
First Edition

Cover Art: Pete Walker

DEDICATION

To my wife, Sara Weinberg To my son, Jaden Michael Walker.

You both show me on a daily basis that I have escaped my parents' legacy of contempt, that I can nurture our family with love and kindness and that I am ongoingly healed by the love and kindness that you generously shower upon me.

I also dedicate this book to those who on a regular basis were verbally and emotionally abused at the dinner table, and I pray that this book will help you heal any damage that was done to you and your relationship with food.

And the day came
When the risk to remain
Closed tightly in a bud
Became more painful
Than the risk it took
To Blossom

— Anais Nin

When inward tenderness
Finds the secret hurt,
Pain itself will crack the rock
And, Ah! Let the soul emerge.

— Rumi

We are all of us exceedingly complex creatures and do ourselves a service in regarding ourselves as complex. Otherwise, we live in a dream world of nonexistent, simplistic black-and-white notions which simply do not apply to life.

— Theodore Rubin

COMPLEX PTSD:
FROM SURVIVING TO THRIVING

TABLE OF CONTENTS

ACKNOWLEDGEMENTS

I am grateful to all my lovely clients who, over the last three decades, honored me with their brave vulnerability and authenticity. Their stories verified to me that there is an epidemic of poor parenting, and their inspiring work proved to me that the effects of it could be largely overcome.

I am also grateful to the readers of my first book and to my website respondents whose generous feedback greatly alleviated my performance anxiety about writing another book and putting my words out there for public viewing. Their overwhelmingly positive support ameliorates the fear that my words will be used as weapons against me as they so often were in childhood.

I am grateful to my good friend Bill O'Brien who gave me invaluable editorial assistance.

I am grateful to all those writers listed in the Bibliography, and those unlisted, whose ideas have fertilized my mind and helped me to write this book.

I am grateful to my friends in recovery with whom I have shared the process of mutual commiseration. We have aided each other greatly in our journeys of recovery.

DISCLAIMER

I am not an academic expert on Complex PTSD [Cptsd]. I have read and studied a great deal, but by no means exhaustively, and I do not make it a point to religiously keep up with all the latest developments. What I bring to the table here is almost 30 years of treating trauma survivors in individual and group settings. What I describe here is a pragmatic, multidimensional approach to recovering based on what I have seen work with my clients, my loved ones and myself.

INTRODUCTION

If you're in immediate distress, please turn to chapter 8, and read the list of 13 steps for reducing Cptsd fear and stress.

Forty years ago, I was riding on a train in India travelling from Delhi to Calcutta. I was at the end of a failed, yearlong spiritual quest in India. Instead of enlightenment, my salvation fantasy had only netted me despair and amoebic dysentery. The latter cost me thirty pounds of flesh, and left me looking like an emaciated monk.

Even worse was the absolute loss of the hope that had been inflamed by reading Walt Whitman's "Song of the Open Road." This hope had supported me through five years of world travel after I was unceremoniously kicked out of my family home.

But, back to the train. I was sitting in my cramped second class seat with the untouchables, chickens and goats, reading an English version of an Indian newspaper. The paper informed me that my destination, Calcut

ta, was now inundated with 100,000 refugees from Bangladesh who had just fled their flood–swamped homes. They were all apparently sleeping on the downtown streets in the recesses beneath the protruding second floors of all the buildings that lined the streets.

I came in late at night and sure enough, sleeping bodies wrapped in sheets, shoulder to shoulder, lined the streets everywhere. I checked into a twenty cents-a-night hotel that a fellow traveler had told me about. I slept unevenly, dreading the sight that I would behold the next morning. How would I handle viewing masses of desperate people, especially when I had nothing to give? I doubted that I even had enough money to make it to Australia where I could hopefully replenish my wallet.

When I finally nudged myself down the stairs late the next morning, I was aghast at the transformed scene on the streets. Sheets had been spread out like picnic blankets and each hosted happy families. Little portable stoves produced meals and cups of tea. People bantered with incredible vitality and enthusiasm, and children...children [this was the part that emblazoned on my memory] crawled all over their parents, especially their fathers in affectionate playful gymnastics that their fathers seemed to love as much as they did.

I was flooded with a mélange of feelings unlike anything I'd ever experienced before - a strange cocktail of relief, delight and anxiety. The anxiety I wouldn't understand until ten years later when I realized that envy had been percolating below the surface of my awareness.

I was deeply envious of this gorgeous buffet of familial love that I had never experienced or even witnessed before. The family sitcoms – even the syrupy sweet ones - that I had watched growing up came nowhere near creating such an authentic, tactile representation of healthy bonding and attachment.

When I realized what this was years later as an anthropology and social work student, I positively flashed back to other non-industrial countries where I had seen similar scenes on a less grand level: Morocco, Thailand, Bali, and an Aboriginal reserve in Australia.

These memories also viscerally informed me about the kind of relational love I had never seen in my own or my friends' families. As I digested this experience over the years and used it to overcome my denial about what I had missed out on as a child, I began the decades long quest that has lead me to write this book as well as *The Tao of Fully Feeling,* which precedes it. The Tao of Fully Feeling is a companion to this book and elaborates many of the foundational principles of this book.

This book then is my hopeful effort to create a map that you can follow to heal the wounds that come from not enough childhood love. If I am a bit repetitive at times about issues like shrinking the critic and grieving the losses of childhood, it is my attempt to find different ways to emphasize the great importance of engaging these themes of recovery work over and over again. If you find yourself lost and not sure of how to get back onto the map, these themes will always be key portals for reentry.

I sometimes recommend that readers view the table of contents and start with whatever headings most strike a chord. Although the book is laid out in a somewhat linear fashion, everyone's journey of recovering is different, and journeys can be initiated in a variety of ways.

Journeys of recovering may begin when a death or great loss brings up an emotional storm that opens up a hidden reservoir of childhood pain; or when a friend shares something about his or her recovery process that strikes a chord; or when a book or TV show triggers a more serious consideration of what really happened in childhood; or when something gets "opened up" in couple's therapy; or when a healing crisis in the form of panic attacks or a nervous breakdown requires some outside help; or when the self-medicating strategies developed to soothe depression and anxiety get out of control and also require outside help.

I hope that readers will be able to use this book as a textbook for recovering, and that certain sections will call you back or forward to them repeatedly, as over time and with effective work, certain themes continue to take on ever deepening meaning.

In this vein, you will find that the Table of Contents is quite comprehensive, and sometimes the best way to use this book is to browse through it and then read the sections and chapters that most capture your interest.

Moreover, this is not a one size fits all formula for recovering. Depending on the specific pattern of your childhood trauma, some of the advice contained herein may be less relevant or even irrelevant to you. Please then focus on the material that seems applicable and helpful to you.

———•——

I also hope this map will guide you to heal in a way that helps you become an unflinching source of kindness and self-compassion for yourself, and that out of that journey you will find at least one other human being who will reciprocally love you well enough in that way.

Finally I have illustrated this work with many real life examples. All names and identifying information have been changed to protect client confidentiality.

PART 1

AN OVERVIEW OF RECOVERING

CHAPTER 1

THE JOURNEY OF RECOVERING FROM CPTSD

I wrote this book from the perspective of someone who has Complex Post-Traumatic Stress Disorder [Cptsd], and who has experienced a great reduction of symptoms over the years. I also wrote it from the viewpoint of someone who has discovered many silver linings in the long, windy, bumpy road of recovering from Cptsd. I have also seen this type of recovering in a number of my friends and many long term clients.

First, the good news about Cptsd. It is a learned set of responses, and a failure to complete numerous important developmental tasks. This means that it is environmentally, not genetically, caused. In other words, unlike most of the diagnoses it is confused with, it is neither inborn nor characterological. As such, it is learned. It is not inscribed in your DNA. It is a disorder caused by nurture [or rather the lack of it] not nature.

This is especially good news because what is learned can be unlearned and vice versa. What was not provided by your parents can now be provided by yourself and others.

Recovery from Cptsd typically has important self-help and relational components. The relational piece can come from authors, friends, partners, teachers, therapists, therapeutic groups or any combination of these. I like to call this *reparenting by committee.*

I must emphasize, however, that some survivors of Cptsd-engendering families were so thoroughly betrayed by their parents, that it may be a long time, if ever, before they can trust another human being enough to engage in relational healing work. When this is the case, pets, books and online therapeutic websites can provide significant relational healing.

This book describes a multimodal treatment approach to Cptsd. It is oriented toward the most prevalent kind of Cptsd, the kind that comes from growing up in a severely abusive and/or neglectful family. In this vein, the book describes a journey of healing the damage that occurs when you suffer traumatizing abuse and abandonment. Traumatizing abuse and abandonment can occur on verbal, emotional, spiritual, and/or physical levels. Moreover, sexual abuse is especially traumatizing.

I believe that we have an epidemic of traumatizing families. Current estimates posit that one in three girls and one in five boys are sexually abused before they enter adulthood, and recent statistics from The Kim Foundation report that 26% of Americans over 18 have been diagnosed with a mental disorder.

When abuse or neglect is severe enough, any one category of it can cause the child to develop Cptsd. This is true even in the case of emotional neglect if both parents collude in it, as we will see in chapter 5. When abuse and neglect is multidimensional, the severity of the Cptsd worsens accordingly.

Definition of Complex PTSD

Cptsd is a more severe form of Post-traumatic stress disorder. It is delineated from this better known trauma syndrome by five of its most common and troublesome features: emotional flashbacks, toxic shame, self-abandonment, a vicious inner critic and social anxiety.

Emotional flashbacks are perhaps the most noticeable and characteristic feature of Cptsd. Survivors of traumatizing abandonment are extremely susceptibility to painful emotional flashbacks, which unlike ptsd do not typically have a visual component.

Emotional flashbacks are sudden and often prolonged regressions to the overwhelming feeling-states of being an abused/abandoned child. These feeling states can include overwhelming fear, shame, alienation, rage, grief and depression. They also include unnecessary triggering of our fight/flight instincts.

It is important to state here that emotional flashbacks, like most things in life, are not all-or-none. Flashbacks can range in intensity from subtle to horrific. They can also vary in duration ranging from moments to weeks on end where they devolve into what many therapists call a regression.

Finally, a more clinical and extensive definition of Cptsd can be found on p. 121 of Judith Herman's seminal book, *Trauma and Recovery*.

An Example of an Emotional Flashback

As I write this I recall the first emotional flashback I was ever able to identify, although I did not identify it until about ten years after it occurred. At the time of the event, I was living with my first serious partner. The honeymoon phase of our relationship came to a screeching halt when she unexpectedly started yelling at me for something I no longer recall.

What I do most vividly recall was how the yelling felt. It felt like a fierce hot wind. I felt like I was being blown away – like my insides were being blown out, as a flame on a candle is blown out.

Later, when I first heard about auras, I flashed back to this and felt like my aura had been completely stripped from me.

At the time itself, I also felt completely disoriented, unable to speak, respond or even think. I felt terrified, shaky and very little. Somehow, I finally managed to totter to the door and get out of the house where I eventually slowly pulled myself together.

As I said earlier, it took me ten years to figure out that this confusing and disturbing phenomenon was an intense emotional flashback. Some years later, I came to understand the nature of this type of regression. I realized it was a flashback to the hundreds of times my mother, in full homicidal visage, blasted me with her rage into terror, shame, dissociation and helplessness.

Emotional flashbacks are also accompanied by intense arousals of the fight/flight instinct, along with hyperarousal of the sympathetic nervous system, the half of the nervous system that controls arousal and activation. When fear is the dominant emotion in a flashback the person feels extremely anxious, panicky or even suicidal. When despair predominates, a sense of profound numbness, paralysis and desperation to hide may occur.

A sense of feeling small, young, fragile, powerless and helpless is also commonly experienced in an emotional flashback, and all symptoms are typically overlaid with humiliating and crushing toxic shame.

Toxic Shame: The Veneer of an Emotional Flashback

Toxic shame, explored enlighteningly by John Bradshaw in *Healing The Shame That Binds,* obliterates a Cptsd survivor's self-esteem with an overwhelming sense that he is loathsome, ugly, stupid, or fatally flawed. Overwhelming self-disdain is typically a flashback to the way he felt when suffering the contempt and visual skewering of his traumatizing parent. Toxic shame can also be created by constant parental neglect and rejection.

Early in my career I worked with David, a handsome, intelligent man who was a professional actor. One day David came to see me after an unsuccessful audition. Beside himself, he burst out: "I never let on to anyone, but I know that I'm really very ugly. It is so stupid that I'm trying to be an actor when I'm so painful to look at." I will never forget how shocked and disbelieving I felt at first, that such a handsome person could feel ugly, but further exploration brought me understanding.

David's childhood was characterized by broad spectrum abuse and neglect. He was the last and unwanted child of a large family, and his alcoholic father repeatedly attacked and looked at him with disgust. To make matters worse, his family imitated his father and frequently humiliated him with heavy doses of contempt. His older brother's favorite gibe, accompanied by a nauseated grimace, was "I can't stand sight of you. You make me want to vomit!"

Toxic shame *can* obliterate your self-esteem in the blink of an eye. In an emotional flashback you can regress instantly into feeling and thinking that you are as worthless and contemptible as your family perceived you. When you are stranded in a flashback, toxic shame devolves into the intensely painful alienation of the abandonment mélange - a roiling morass of shame, fear and depression.

The *abandonment mélange* is the fear and toxic shame that surrounds and interacts with the abandonment depression. The *abandonment depression* itself is the deadened feeling of helplessness and hopelessness that afflicts traumatized children.

Toxic shame also inhibits us from seeking comfort and support. In a reenactment of the childhood abandonment we are flashing back to, we often isolate ourselves and helplessly surrender to an overwhelming feeling of humiliation.

If you are stuck viewing yourself as worthless, defective, or despicable, you are probably in an emotional flashback. This is typically also true when you are lost in self-hate and virulent self-criticism. Immediate help for managing emotional flashbacks can be found at the beginning of chapter 8 which lists 13 practical steps for resolving flashbacks.

Numerous clients and respondents to my website tell me that the concept of *emotional flashback* brings them a great sense of relief. They report that for the first time they are able to make some sense of their troubled lives. A common comment has been "Now I understand why all the psychological and spiritual approaches I have pursued had so few answers for me." Many also note feeling freed from a shaming list of misdiagnoses that have been given to them by themselves or others. This in turn has aided them in ridding themselves of the self-destructive habit of amassing evidence of their own defectiveness or craziness. Many also report a quantum leap in their motivation to challenge the learned habits of self-hate and self-disgust.

List of Common Cptsd Symptoms

Survivors may not experience all of these. Varying combinations are common. Factors affecting this are your 4F type and your childhood abuse/neglect pattern.

Emotional Flashbacks
Tyrannical Inner &/or Outer Critic
Toxic Shame
Self-Abandonment
Social anxiety
Abject feelings of loneliness and abandonment
Fragile Self-esteem
Attachment disorder
Developmental Arrests
Relationship difficulties
Radical mood vacillations [e.g., pseudo-cyclothymia: see chapter 12]
Dissociation via distracting activities or mental processes
Hair-triggered fight/flight response
Oversensitivity to stressful situations
Suicidal Ideation

Suicidal Ideation

Suicidal ideation is a common phenomenon in Cptsd, particularly during intense or prolonged flashbacks. Suicidal ideation is depressed thinking or fantasizing about wanting to die. It can range from active suicidality to passive suicidality.

Passive suicidality is far more common with the Cptsd survivors who I have known, and it ranges from wishing you were dead to fantasizing about ways to end your life. When lost in suicidal ideation, the survivor may even pray to be delivered from this life, or fantasize about being taken by some calamitous act of fate. He may even think or obsess - without being serious - of stepping in front of a car or jumping off a building.

Fantasy typically ends, however, without a serious intent to kill yourself. This is as opposed to active suicidality where the person is actively proceeding in the direction of taking her life.

I am discussing passive suicidality because it does not merit the same kind of alarm as active suicidality. Passive suicidality is typically a flashback to early childhood when our abandonment was so profound, that it was natural for us to wish that God or somebody or something would just put an end to it all.

When the survivor catches himself in a suicidal reverie, he will benefit from seeing it both as an emblem of how much pain he is in, and as a sign of a particularly intense flashback. This then can direct him to use the flashback management steps in chapter 8.

If however, flashback management does not help, and suicidality becomes increasingly active, please call the national suicide hotline [1-800-273-8255] or visit www.suicidepreventionlifeline.org, because this is a flashback that you may need help managing, and you will get good help there.

Skilled therapists and caregivers learn to discriminate between active and passive suicidal ideation, and do not panic and catastrophize when encountering the latter. Instead, the counselor invites the survivor to explore his suicidal thoughts and feelings knowing that in most cases, verbal ventilation of the flashback pain underneath it will deconstruct the suicidality.

In the much less common scenario of active suicidality, encouraging verbal ventilation will also help the therapist or helper discern if there is indeed a real risk and if action needs to be taken to protect the survivor.

What You may have been Misdiagnosed with

I once heard renowned traumatologist, John Briere, quip that if Cptsd were ever given its due, the DSM [The Diagnostic and Statistical Manual of Mental Disorders] used by all mental health professionals would shrink from its dictionary like size to the size of a thin pamphlet. In other words, the role of traumatized childhoods in most adult psychological disorders is enormous.

I have witnessed many clients with Cptsd misdiagnosed with various anxiety and depressive disorders. Moreover, many are also unfairly and inaccurately labeled with bipolar, narcissistic, code-pendent, autistic spectrum and borderline disorders. [This is not to say that Cptsd does not sometimes co-occur with these disorders.]

Further confusion also arises in the case of ADHD [Attention Deficit Hyperactive Disorder], as well as obsessive/compulsive disorder, both of which are sometimes more accurately described as fixated flight responses to trauma [see the 4F's below]. This is also true of ADD [Attention Deficit Disorder] and some depressive and dissociative disorders which similarly can more accurately be described as fixated freeze responses to trauma.

Furthermore, this is not to say that those so misdiagnosed do not have issues that are similar and correlative with the disorders above. The key point is that these labels are incomplete and unnecessarily shaming descriptions of what the survivor is actually afflicted with.

Reducing Cptsd to "panic disorder" is like calling food allergies chronically itchy eyes. Over-focusing treatment on the symptoms of panic in the former case and eye health in the latter does little to get at root causes. Feelings of panic or itchiness in the eyes can be masked with medication, but all the associated problems that cause these symptoms will remain untreated.

Moreover, most of the diagnoses mentioned above are typically treated as innate characterological defects rather than as learned maladaptations to stress – adaptations that survivors were forced to learn as traumatized children. And, most importantly, because these adaptations were learned, they can often be extinguished or significantly diminished, and replaced with more functional adaptations to stress.

In this vein, I believe that many substance and process addictions also begin as misguided, maladaptations to parental abuse and abandonment. They are early adaptations that are attempts to soothe and distract from the mental, emotional and physical pain of Cptsd.

Origins of Cptsd

How do traumatically abused and/or abandoned children develop Cptsd?

While the origin of Cptsd is most often associated with extended periods of physical and/or sexual abuse in childhood, my observations convince me that ongoing verbal and emotional abuse also causes it.

Many dysfunctional parents react contemptuously to a baby or toddler's plaintive call for connection and attachment. Contempt is extremely traumatizing to a child, and at best, extremely noxious to an adult.

Contempt is a toxic cocktail of verbal and emotional abuse, a deadly amalgam of denigration, rage and disgust. Rage creates fear, and disgust creates shame in the child in a way that soon teaches her to refrain from crying out, from ever asking for attention. Before long, the child gives up on seeking any kind of help or connection at all. The child's bid for bonding and acceptance is thwarted, and she is left to suffer in the frightened despair of abandonment.

Particularly abusive parents deepen the abandonment trauma by linking corporal punishment with contempt. Slaveholders typically use contempt and scorn to destroy their victims' self-esteem. Slaves and children who are made to feel worthless and powerless devolve into learned helplessness and can be controlled with far less energy and attention. Cult leaders also use contempt to shrink their followers into absolute submission after luring them in with brief phases of fake unconditional love.

Furthermore, Cptsd can also be caused by emotional neglect alone. This key theme is explored at length in chapter 5. If you notice that you are berating yourself because your trauma seems insignificant compared to others, please skip ahead to this chapter and resume reading here upon completion.

Emotional neglect also typically underlies most traumatizations that are more glaringly evident. Parents who routinely ignore or turn their backs on a child's calls for attention, connection or help, abandon their child to unmanageable amounts of fear, and the child eventually gives up and succumbs to depressed, death-like feelings of helplessness and hopelessness.

These types of rejection simultaneously magnify the child's fear, and eventually add a coating of shame to it. Over time this fear and shame begets a toxic inner critic that holds the child, and later the adult, totally responsible for his parents' abandonment, until he becomes his own worst enemy and descends into the bowels of Cptsd.

More about Trauma

Trauma occurs when attack or abandonment triggers a fight/flight response so intensely that the person cannot turn it off once the threat is over. He becomes stuck in an adrenalized state. His sympathetic nervous system is locked "on" and he cannot toggle into the relaxation function of the parasympathetic nervous system.

One common instance of this occurs when a child is attacked and hurt by a bully after school. He may remain in a hypervigilant, fearful state until someone takes action to insure him that he will not be revictimized, and until someone helps him release the hyperactivation in his nervous system.

If the child has learned through experience that he can come to at least one of his parents when he is hurting, frightened or needing help, he will tell mom or dad about it. With them, he will grieve the temporary death of his sense of safety in the world by verbally ventilating, crying and angering about it [chapter 11 expands on these processes of grieving].

Moreover, his parent will report the bully and take steps to assure that it will not happen again, and the child will typically be released from the trauma. He will naturally relax back into the safety of parasympathetic nervous system functioning.

"Simple", one incident traumas can often be resolved relatively easily if Cptsd is not already present.

If however the bullying happens on numerous occasions and the child does not seek help, or if the child lives in an environment so dangerous that the parent is powerless to ensure a modicum of safety, it may take more than parental comforting to release the trauma. If the trauma is not too continuous over too long a time, a short course of therapy may be all that is needed to resolve the trauma, provided of course the danger in the environment can effectively be remediated.

When the trauma however is repetitive and ongoing and no help is available, the child may become so frozen in trauma that the symptoms of "simple" ptsd begin to set in. This can also occur during the prolonged trauma of combat or entrapment in a cult or domestic violence situation.

If however, a person is also afflicted by ongoing family abuse or profound emotional abandonment, the trauma will manifest as a particularly severe emotional flashback because he already has Cptsd. This is particularly true when his parent is also a bully.

The Four F's: Fight, Flight, Freeze and Fawn

Earlier, I mentioned the fight/flight response that is an innate automatic response to danger in all human beings. A more complete and accurate description of this instinct is the fight/flight/freeze/fawn response. The complex nervous system wiring of this response allows a person in danger to react in four different ways.

A fight response is triggered when a person suddenly responds aggressively to something threatening. A flight response is triggered when a person responds to a perceived threat by fleeing, or symbolically, by launching into hyperactivity. A freeze response is triggered when a person, realizing resistance is futile, gives up, numbs out into dissociation and/or collapses as if accepting the inevitability of being hurt. A fawn response is triggered when a person responds to threat by trying to be pleasing or helpful in order to appease and forestall an attacker. This fourfold response potential will heretofore be referred to as the 4Fs.

Traumatized children often over-gravitate to one of these response patterns to survive, and as time passes these four modes become elaborated into entrenched defensive structures that are similar to narcissistic [fight], obsessive/compulsive [flight], dissociative [freeze] or codependent [fawn] defenses.

These structures help children survive their horrific childhoods, but leave them very limited and narrow in how they respond to life. Even worse, they remain locked in these patterns in adulthood when they no longer need to rely so heavily on one primary response pattern.

It is important to understand that variances in the childhood abuse/neglect patterns, birth order, and genetic predispositions result in people polarizing to their particular 4F type.

In the next section we will explore examples of how children are driven into these defenses by traumatizing parents. The four children in the vignette below match the four basic types of trauma survivors:

Bob=Fight - Narcissistic
Carol=Flight - Obsessive/Compulsive
Maude=Freeze - Dissociative
Sean=Fawn - Codependent

The 4F's in a Cptsd-Inducing Family

Carol was the scapegoat of her family. Narcissistic and borderline parents typically choose at least one child to be the designated family scapegoat.

Scapegoating is the process by which a bully offloads and externalizes his pain, stress, and frustration by attacking a less powerful person. Typically scapegoating brings the bully some momentary relief. It does not however effectively metabolize or release his pain, and scapegoating soon resumes as the bully's internal discomfort resurfaces.

Wilhelm Reich, in his brilliant book *The Psychology of Fascism*, explains how scapegoating occurs on a continuum that stretches from the persecution of the targeted child by a bullying parent to the horrific scapegoating of the Jews by the Nazi's. In especially dysfunctional families like Carol's, the scapegoating parent often organizes the rest of the family to also gang up on the scapegoat.

Carol discovered a great deal about her early childhood from watching home videos. Her parents were so narcissistically oblivious, that they unabashedly recorded many incidents of Carol being verbally and emotionally abused by them. This was usually in the background of recordings of the performances of their favorite child, her older brother. Severely narcissistic parents are rarely embarrassed by their aggressive behavior. They feel entitled to punish a child for anything that displeases them, no matter how unreasonable it might appear to an impartial observer.

Carols' parents started in on her early by disdainfully blaming her for soiling her diaper before she was even one. By the time she was three, she had been so frequently punished for making noise while talking and playfully exploring her house, that her constant state of fear generated an ADHD-like condition in her.

Carol's large backyard was her refuge where she would play with great gusto - climbing, running, cavorting, and building and ransacking villages that she made with her toys and leaves, grass, sticks and stones. She would busy herself from breakfast until supper, often forgetting to come in for lunch, which she thought in retrospect made life even easier for her mother, who never called her in to eat.

One family video from this time was the straw that broke the camel's back of Carol's denial that her family was abusive. It showed her playing a game whereby she would repetitively smack herself hard on the hand and call herself a bad girl as she wobbled around the living room touching various knick-knacks. There was a considerable amount of footage that showed her parents and siblings roaring with mocking delight in the background.

When contempt replaces the milk of human kindness at an early age, the child feels humiliated and overwhelmed. Too helpless to protest or even understand the unfairness of being abused, the child eventually becomes convinced that she is defective and fatally flawed. Frequently she comes to believe that she deserves her parents' persecution.

When Carol was four, she "accidentally" fell out of a second story window. A few years later, she stepped out into the street in front of a car and was knocked to the ground. As an adult, she was convinced that both injuries contributed to her extremely painful, early onset scoliosis. She also believed that she was in so much pain, that she was unconsciously trying to end her life.

Fortunately for Carol, school eventually offered a glimmer of reprieve. A kindly third grade teacher perceived her intelligence, and praised her enough that she soon became an excellent student. Unfortunately, the terrible anxiety that she lived with 24/7 soon morphed into an obsessive/compulsive approach to school work. This, in turn, later manifested into a life-spoiling perfectionism and workaholism.

Carol's older brother, Bob, the favorite and hero of her parents was not molded with fear and rejection like Carol. Bob, the recipient of the parents' narcissistic expectations, was shaped into a multi-dimensional achiever by their withdrawal of approval for less than perfect performances. He was then given tidbits of praise for outstanding accomplishments that would reflect positively on his parents. He was also enlisted to further scapegoat Carol, and as time went on outdid his parents in tormenting her.

I believe there is an epidemic of sibling abuse that afflicts many dysfunctional families. Siblings in such families can traumatize the victim-scapegoat as severely as the parents. In families with checked out, disinterested parents, they can in fact be the chief sources of trauma. This is especially true in our culture where emotional neglect of children is rampant and where parents are routinely advised to let the kids "work it out themselves." But how does a child who has half the strength of his older sibling work it out, and stop him from tormenting her without the aid of a stronger ally?

Bob, himself, did not escape the pathological influence of his parents. Scapegoating became a habit for him, and he developed the narcissist's sixth sense for identifying others whose families had victimized and used them as targets. Bob, hurting from his parents using him and holding him to perfectionistic standards, grew up to become a full-fledged narcissist and "control-freak". He aggressively tried to mold his "loved" ones as he had been molded, and was working on whipping his fourth wife into shape at the time of Carol's therapy.

Let us return to Carol. As an adolescent, her trauma was painfully reinforced by her surrounding community who so admired her brother's accomplishments, that they joined the family in pathologizing Carol as a "bad seed".

Unfortunately things deteriorated further for Carol as an adult, even though she had seemingly escaped from the family. Carol remained symbolically enthralled to the family by getting ensnared with narcissistic people who were just as abusive and neglectful as her parents. This well known psychological phenomenon is called *repetition compulsion* or *reenactment,* and trauma survivors are extremely susceptible to it. We will explore this extensively throughout the book.

A third child, Maude, was born two years after Carol. By this time, her parents were worn out from incessantly molding Bob and Carol. Having whipped Bob and Carol into hero- and scapegoat-shape, they had little use for Maude. They did not have enough energy or interest left to whip her into anything.

Maude became the classic lost child and was left on her own to raise herself. She soon discovered food and daydreaming as her sole sources of comfort. However, because Bob also enjoyed using her for target practice, she stayed in her room as much as possible.

In retrospect, Carol also thought that Bob was molesting Maude. She hypothesized that these two factors contributed to the fact that Maude could not tolerate the various nurseries and pre-schools in which her mother tried to dump her. Over time, Maude numbed out into a low grade dissociative depression, and felt extremely anxious and avoidant whenever she was in a social situation.

At four, an eccentric aunt gave Maude a television for her room and she was soon entranced. She was forced to develop an attachment disorder in which she bonded with TV rather than with a human being. Sadly, she is still lost in that relationship living on disability in an apartment cluttered with an enormous amount of useless hoarded material.

Poor Parenting Creates Pathological Sibling Rivalry

Like many children in Cptsd-engendering families, Maude could not turn to her siblings for comfort because her parents unconsciously practiced the "divide and conquer" principle. Her parents modeled and encouraged sarcasm and constant fault finding among the children. Moreover, interactions of cooperation or warmth were routinely ridiculed.

Sibling rivalry is further reinforced in dysfunctional families by the fact that all the children are subsisting on minimal nurturance, and are therefore without resources to give to each other. Moreover, competition for the little their parents have to give creates even fiercer rivalries.

Two years later, Sean was born. At first, it seemed as if he was destined for the same lost, dissociated destiny as Maude, but as he matured he fell into the role of "gifted child" as described by Alice Miller in *The Drama of the Gifted Child*.

Sean's inborn gift coming into this life was his compassion and his sense that if he studied his mother enough and figured out what she needed, he could provide for her needs. This would sometimes calm her down and make her less dangerous, bitter and sarcastic.

Over the years Sean honed this skill and could almost clairvoyantly anticipate her sore spots, moods and preferences. Sometimes it seemed he knew what she needed before she did, and with practice he became adept at defusing her anger and sometimes even gaining morsels of her approval.

Synchronistically, his mother realized she was getting old and that her alcohol-ravaged husband would likely precede her. Not wanting to be alone, she exploited his compassionate nature and primed him for domestic service for as long as she would need it. Sean remained living at home until his mother's death released him from emotional captivity at the age of twenty-nine. This was the codependent enslavement we will explore more in chapter 7.

A friend of Sean's who knew all the siblings as adults, marveled that it seemed as if each had different parents.

Finally, it is also important to note that the scapegoat role does not fall exclusively on the flight type as it did with Carol. It can be bestowed on anyone of the 4F types depending on the given family. The scapegoating role can also shift over time from one person to another and each parent or sibling may choose a different scapegoat.

Chapters 6 and 7 explore each of the 4F's and their corresponding defensive structures in greater detail. These chapters will also help you determine your key 4F defense, and help you address issues that are more specific to your type of Cptsd.

CHAPTER 2

LEVELS OF RECOVERING

Healing from Complex PTSD is, above all, <u>complex</u>. This is important to emphasize because there are numerous one dimensional approaches to trauma that bill themselves as cure-alls. In my opinion, however, singular approaches are unable to address all the levels of wounding that combine to cause Cptsd.

Moreover, working with simplistic approaches can leave you stranded in toxic shame when you do not achieve the touted results. I was motivated to write this book in large part because of the many times I sank into new levels of self-contempt when the latest panacea therapy did not cure me.

I will use the word "key" repeatedly to describe the various tasks upon which recovering hinges. This book offers a keychain of perspectives and techniques to unlock yourself from being what Alice Miller called a "Prisoner of Childhood."

Abusive and abandoning parents can injure and abandon us on many levels: cognitive, emotional, spiritual, physical and relational.

To recover, you need to learn how to support yourself – to meet your unmet developmental needs on each level that is relevant to your experience of childhood trauma.

This chapter is a brief overview of the many tasks involved in Cptsd recovery. These tasks are explored at greater length in Part II. The comprehensive Table of Contents at the beginning of this book will direct you to further information on each of the topics covered in this chapter. Please allow yourself to also use the Table of Contents to explore sections of the book that peak your interest.

Key Developmental Arrests in Cptsd

What follows is a list of some of the most common developmental arrests that occur in Cptsd. You may find that you experience a diminishment or absence of these key features of healthy human being. Typically, survivors will vary on which and how many of these arrests relate to them. Factors affecting this are your 4F type, your childhood abuse/ neglect pattern, your innate nature and any recovery work that you have already accomplished.

Self-acceptance
Clear sense of identity
Self-Compassion
Self-Protection
Capacity to draw comfort from relationship
Ability to relax
Capacity for full self-expression
Willpower & Motivation
Peace of mind
Self-care
Belief that life is a gift
Self-esteem
Self-confidence

My efforts to nurture myself in these arrested areas of development were limited and spoiled in early recovery by a feeling of resentment. "Why do I have to do this?" was a common internal refrain. Resentment that should have been directed toward my parents often boomeranged onto me and spoiled or thwarted my efforts at self-nurturance.

Thankfully ongoing recovery work helped remedy this resentment. It taught me to practice self-care in a spirit of giving to a child who needed and really deserved to be helped.

—————

I find it helpful to approach developmental arrests from the viewpoint of novelist David Mitchell's quip that "...fire is the sun unwinding itself out of the wood". Similarly, effective recovery is unwinding the natural potential you were born with out of your unconscious. This is your innate potential which may be, as yet, unrealized because of your childhood trauma.

An especially tragic developmental arrest that afflicts many survivors is the loss of their will power and self-motivation. Many dysfunctional parents react destructively to their child's budding sense of initiative. If this occurs throughout his childhood, the survivor may feel lost and purposeless in his life. He may drift through his whole life rudderless and without a motor.

Moreover, even when he manages to identify a goal of his own choosing, he may struggle to follow through with extended and concentrated effort. Remedying this developmental arrest is essential because many new psychological studies now show that *persistence* – even more than intelligence or innate talent - is the key psychological characteristic necessary for finding fulfillment in life.

I have worked with many survivors stranded in this form of adult helplessness. Those who recover from it typically do so by engaging extensively in the angering work of grieving that is discussed throughout this book. The ability to invoke willpower seems to be allied to your ability to healthily express your anger. With sufficient recovering, you can learn to manufacture your volition. In the beginning you can fake it until you make it. This is what Stephen Johnson calls "the hard work miracle."

———·———

What follows is a concluding comment about development arrests. Some survivors have confidence but not self-esteem. In childhood, my own flight response got channeled into acquiring academic skills for which the outside world rewarded me. But the benefit of these rewards never penetrated my toxic shame enough to allow me to feel that I was a worthwhile person.

My critic, like my parents, always found something flawed in me to contradict the feedback that I was getting. Ninety-nine percent on a test was never a cause for pride. Rather, it was the impetus for a great deal of self-criticism about the missing one percent. Like many other survivors that I have worked with, I developed the *imposter's syndrome*. This syndrome contradicted the outside positive feedback that I was receiving. It insisted that if people really knew me, they would see what a loser I was. Eventually, however, I became confident in my intelligence even though my self-esteem was still abysmal.

COGNITIVE HEALING

The first level of recovery usually involves repairing the damage that Cptsd wreaks on our thoughts and beliefs about ourselves.

Cognitive recovery work aims to make your brain user friendly. It focuses on recognizing and eliminating the destructive thoughts and thinking processes you were indoctrinated with in childhood.

Cognitive healing also depends on learning to choose healthy and more accurate ways of talking to and thinking about yourself. On the broadest level, this involves upgrading the story you tell yourself about your pain.

We need to understand exactly how appalling parenting created the now self-perpetuating trauma that we live in. We can learn to do this in a way that takes the mountain of unfair self-blame off ourselves. We can redirect this blame to our parents' dreadful child-rearing practices. And we can also do this in a way that motivates us to reject their influence so that we can freely orchestrate our journey of recovering.

This work then requires us to build a fierce allegiance to ourselves. Such loyalty strengthens us for the cognitive work of freeing our brains from being conditioned to attack so many normal parts of our selves.

Cognitive work is fundamental to helping you disidentify from the self-hating critic with which your parents inculcated you. As I am writing this, my son's friend synchronistically tells him: "This Lego creature I made spreads brain attack and eats away at the person." I marvel at this synchronicity and think: "What a fitting image for the trauma-inducing parent".

Shrinking the Critic

Early abuse and abandonment forces the child to merge his identity with the superego, the part of the child's brain that learns the rules of his caretakers in order to get and maintain acceptance. However, because acceptance is impossible in the Cptsd-engendering family, the superego gets stuck working overtime to achieve the impossible. Perseverating on finding a formula to win over her parents, the child eventually embraces perfectionism as a strategy to make her parents less dangerous and more engaging. Her one hope is that if she becomes smart, helpful, pretty, and flawless enough, her parents will finally care for her.

Sadly, continued failure at winning their regard forces her to conclude that she is fatally flawed. She is loveless not because of her mistakes, but because she is a mistake. She can only see what is wrong with or missing in her.

Anything she does, says, thinks, imagines or feels has the potential to spiral her down into a depressed abyss of fear and toxic shame. Her superego fledges into a full-blown, trauma-inducing critic.

Self-criticism, then, runs non-stop in a desperate attempt to avoid rejection-inducing mistakes. Drasticizing becomes obsessive to help the child foresee and avoid punishment and worsening abandonment. At the same time, it continuously fills her psyche with stories and images of catastrophe.

The survivor becomes imprisoned by a jailer who will accept nothing but perfection. He is chauffeured by a hysterical driver who sees nothing but danger in every turn of the road. Chapters 9 and 10 focus extensively on practical tools for shrinking your critic.

The Developmentally Arrested Healthy Ego

Over time the critic becomes more and more synonymous with the survivor's identity. The superego morphs into a totalitarian critic that trumps the development of a healthy ego. [The ego develops later than the superego.]

"Ego", contrary to popular usage, is not a dirty word. In psychology, the term *ego* represents what we typically mean when we use terms like my "self" or my identity. The healthy ego is the user friendly manager of the psyche. Unfortunately, Cptsd-inducing parents thwart the growth of the ego by undermining the development of the crucial egoic processes of self-compassion and self-protection.

They do this by shaming or intimidating you whenever you have a natural impulse to have sympathy for yourself, or stand up for yourself. The instinct to care for yourself and to protect yourself against unfairness is then forced to become dormant.

Psychoeducation and Cognitive Healing

Becoming psychoeducated about Cptsd is the first level of addressing this poisonous indoctrination of your mind against your healthy ego. When you intricately understand how antagonistic your parents were to your healthy sense of self, you become more motivated to engage in the self-help processes of rectifying their damage. The more you identify their damage the more you know what to fix.

This is essential because without a properly functioning ego, you have no center for making healthy choices and decisions. All too often, your decisions are based on the fear of getting in trouble or getting abandoned, rather than on the principles of having meaningful and equitable interactions with the world.

You can learn to gradually replace the critic's toxic perspective with a viewpoint that supports you in your life, and that stops you from unnecessarily scaring yourself.

You are free now as an adult to develop peace of mind and a supportive relationship with yourself. A self-championing stance can transform your existence from struggling survival to a fulfilling sense of thriving.

You can begin right now by inviting your instincts of self-compassion and self-protection to awaken and bloom in your life.

———————

Cognitive healing may have begun or been reinforced by reading what has preceded this. Hopefully you are having some epiphanies about what is at the core of your suffering.

Some readers may have been searching for cognitive answers for years, and through their reading and therapy already created a sizable foundation for doing this work.

At the same time, those who have only tried a Cognitive-Behavioral Approach [CBT] to healing their trauma may feel great resistance to hearing that cognitive work is important. If you are like me, you may have been introduced to it in a way that promised more than could be delivered. Cognitive tools are irreplaceable in healing cognitive issues, but they do not address all the levels of our wounding. They are especially limited in addressing emotional issues, as we will see below.

———

In early recovery, the psychoeducation piece of cognitive work typically comes from the wisdom of others: teachers, writers, friends and therapists who are more informed on this subject than we are. When psychoeducation reaches its most powerful level of effectiveness, however, it begins to morph into mindfulness.

MINDFULNESS

Psychologically speaking, *mindfulness* is taking undistracted time to become fully aware of your thoughts and feelings so that you can have more choice in how you respond to them. Do I really agree with this thought, or have I been pressured into believing it? How do I want to respond to this feeling – distract myself from it, repress it, express it or just feel it until it changes into something else?

Mindfulness is a perspective that weds your capacity for self-observation with your instinct of self-compassion. It is therefore your ability to observe yourself from an objective and self-accepting viewpoint. It is a key function of a healthily developed ego and is sometimes described as the *observing ego* or the *witnessing self.*

Mindfulness is a perspective of benign curiosity about all of your inner experience. Recovery is enhanced immeasurably by developing this helpful process of introspection. As it becomes more developed, mindfulness can be used to recognize and dis-identify from beliefs and viewpoints that you acquired from your traumatizing family.

———————

I cannot overstate the importance of becoming aware of your inner self-commentary. With enough practice, mindfulness eventually awakens your fighting spirit to resist the abusive refrains from your childhood, and to replace them with thoughts that are self-supportive. Mindfulness also helps you to establish a perspective from which you can assess and guide your own efforts of recovering.

Chapter 12 contains detailed instruction for enhancing mindfulness, as do the writings of Steven Levine, Jack Kornfield and John Kabat-Zinn.

———————

Finally, it is important to note that mindfulness tends to develop and expand in a progressive manner to all levels of our experience, cognitive, emotional, physical and relational. Mindfulness is essential for guiding us at every level of recovering, and we will examine this principle more closely throughout the book.

EMOTIONAL HEALING

Traumatizing parents do as much damage to our emotional natures as they do to our thinking processes. Consequently, there is a great deal of recovery work that needs to be done on this level. This is especially true because of the damage our wider society also does to our emotional natures.

Recovering the Emotional Nature

This section is an updated version of an article I wrote in 1991. I originally wrote it as a prelude to my first book, *The Tao of Fully Feeling*, and it was written as an appeal to the general public to understand the consequences of trying to sanitize one's emotions. Thankfully, the response I received encouraged me to complete that book, which is a guide to overcoming the familial and societal damage meted out on children's emotional life.

The survivor, who is seeking a healthy relationship with his emotional being, will strive to accept the existential fact that the human feeling nature is often contradictory and frequently vacillates between opposite polarities of feeling experiences. It is quite normal for feelings to change unpredictably along continuums that stretch between a variety of emotional polarities. As such, it is especially human and healthy to have shifts of mood between such extremes as happy and sad, enthused and depressed, loving and angry, trusting and suspicious, brave and afraid, and forgiving and blaming.

Unfortunately, in this culture only the "positive" polarity of any emotional experience is approved or allowed. This can cause such an avoidance of the "negative" polarity, that at least two different painful conditions result.

In the first, the person injures and exhausts himself in compulsive attempts to avoid a disavowed feeling, and actually becomes more stuck in it. This is like the archetypal clown whose frantic efforts to free himself from a piece of fly paper, leave him more immobilized and entangled.

In the second, repression of one end of the emotional continuum often leads to a repression of the whole continuum, and the person becomes emotionally deadened. The baby of emotional vitality is thrown out with the bathwater of some unacceptable feeling.

A reluctance to participate in such a fundamental realm of the human experience results in much unnecessary loss. For just as without night there is no day, without work there is no play, without hunger there is no satiation, without fear there is no courage, without tears there is no joy, and without anger, there is no real love.

Most people, who choose or are coerced into only identifying with "positive" feelings, usually wind up in an emotionally lifeless middle ground – bland, deadened, and dissociated in an unemotional "no-man's-land."

Moreover, when a person tries to hold onto a preferred feeling for longer than its actual tenure, she often appears as unnatural and phony as ersatz grass or plastic flowers. If instead, she learns to surrender willingly to the normal human experience that good feelings always ebb and flow, she will eventually be graced with a growing ability to renew herself in the vital waters of emotional flexibility.

The repression of the so-called negative polarities of emotion causes much unnecessary pain, as well as the loss of many essential aspects of the feeling nature. In fact, much of the plethora of loneliness, alienation, and addictive distraction that plagues modern industrial societies is a result of people being taught and forced to reject, pathologize or punish so many of their own and others' normal feeling states.

Nowhere, not in the deepest recesses of the self, or in the presence of his closest friends, is the average person allowed to have and explore any number of normal emotional states. Anger, depression, envy, sadness, fear, distrust, etc., are all as normal a part of life as bread and flowers and streets. Yet, they have become ubiquitously avoided and shameful human experiences.

How tragic this is, for all of these emotions have enormously important and healthy functions in a wholly integrated psyche. One dimension where this is most true is in the arena of healthy self-protection. For without access to our uncomfortable or painful feelings, we are deprived of the most fundamental part of our ability to notice when something is unfair, abusive, or neglectful in our environments.

Those who cannot feel their sadness often do not know when they are being unfairly excluded, and those who cannot feel their normal angry or fearful responses to abuse, are often in danger of putting up with it without protest.

Perhaps never before has humankind been so alienated from so many of its normal feeling states, as it is in the twenty-first century. Never before have so many human beings been so emotionally deadened and impoverished.

The disease of emotional emaciation is epidemic. Its effects on health are often euphemistically labeled as stress, and like the emotions, stress is often treated like some unwanted waste that must be removed.

Until all of the emotions are accepted indiscriminately (and acceptance does not imply license to dump emotions irresponsibly or abusively), there can be no wholeness, no real sense of well being, and no solid sense of self esteem. Thus, while it may be fairly easy to like yourself when feelings of love or happiness or serenity are present, deeper psychological health is seen only when you can maintain a posture of self-love and self-respect in the times of emotional hurt that accompany life's inevitable contingencies of loss, loneliness, confusion, uncontrollable unfairness, and accidental mistake.

The human feeling experience, much like the weather, is often unpredictably changeable. No "positive" feeling can be induced to persist as a permanent experience, no matter what Cognitive-Behavioral Therapy tells us. As disappointing as this may be, as much as we might like to deny it, as much as it causes each of us ongoing life frustration, and as much as we were raised and continue to be reinforced for trying to control and pick our feelings, they are still by definition of the human condition, largely outside the province of our wills.

EMOTIONAL INTELLIGENCE

Daniel Goleman defines emotional intelligence as our ability to successfully recognize and manage our own feelings and to healthily respond to the feelings of others. As implied above, I believe the quality of our emotional intelligence is reflected in the degree to which we accept all of our feelings without automatically dissociating from them or expressing them in a way that hurts ourselves or others. When we are emotionally intelligent we also extend this acceptance to our intimates. One of my clients calls this the hallmark of "relationships."

Another way of saying this is that I have self-esteem to the degree that I keep my heart open to myself in all my emotional states. And, I have intimacy when my friend and I offer this type of emotional acceptance to each other. Once again, this does not condone destructive expressions of anger which are, of course, counterproductive to trust and intimacy.

Cptsd-engendering parents often hypocritically attack their children's emotional expression in a bi-modal way. This occurs when the child is both abused for emoting and is, at the same time, abused by her caretaker's toxic emotional expression.

Most traumatizing parents are especially contemptuous towards the child's expression of emotional pain. This contempt then forces the child's all-important capacity for healthy grieving into developmental arrest.

One archetypal example of this is seen in the parent who hurts his child to the point of tears, and then has the nerve to say: "Stop crying or I'll give you something to cry about!" A client once told me that he often fantasized about giving his father this angry reply: "What are you talking about, you already gave me something to cry about?!" He did not, however, because he had long since learned that getting angry back was a capital crime that would elicit the most savage retaliation. Typically it would be delivered with homicidal rage: "I'll knock you from here to Kingdom come!"

The above is of course a blatant example of the slaughtering of emotional expression. Just as common is the insidious, passive-aggressive assault on emoting which is seen in the parent who shuns her child for expressing his feelings. This is seen in the emotionally abandoning parent who sequesters the child in a timeout for crying, or routinely retreats from the crying child into her room.

The worst, most damaging example of this occurs when this is done to the pre-verbal toddler [or baby!] who only has emotions with which to express herself. Pre-verbal children are by definition far too young to learn the 2-3 year-olds' developmental task of using her words to communicate about her feelings.

An especially nasty form of emotional abuse occurs in the traumatizing family when the child is even attacked for displays of pleasant emotion. As I write this I flashback to scenes of my mother sneering at my little sister and snarling: "What are you so happy about!", and my father's frequent: "What are you laughing at – wipe that smile off your face!"

Emotional abuse is also almost always also accompanied by emotional abandonment, which can most simply be described as a relentless lack of parental warmth and love. Sometimes this is most poignantly described as not being liked by your parents, which belies the many Cptsd-inducing parents who say they love their children, but demonstrate in a thousand ways that they do not like them. "The sight of you makes me sick" was very popular with such parents when I was growing up.

It can still bring tears to my eyes to remember my emotionally abandoned young sister secreted in a corner of the house begging our family dog: "Like me, Ginger, Like me!"

Toxic Shame and Soul Murder

The rejecting responses of our parents to our emotional expression alienate us from our feelings. Emotional abuse/neglect scares us out of our own emotions while simultaneously making us terrified of other people's feelings.

John Bradshaw describes the devastation of the child's emotional nature as "soul murder". He explains this as involving a process where the child's emotional expression [his first language of self-expression] is so assaulted with disgust that any emotional experience immediately devolves into toxic shame.

I believe that toxic shame is the affect of the inner critic, and that inner critic thought-processes are the cognitions of shame – a terrible yin/yang process emanating from our original abandonment.

———

Because of the deadly one-two punch of familial and societal attacks on our emotional selves, we need to recover our innate emotional intelligence. This is also deeply important because, as Carl Jung emphasized, our emotions tell us what is really important to us. When our emotional intelligence is restricted, we often do not know what we really want, and can consequently struggle mightily with even the smallest decisions.

As emotional recovery progresses, the mindfulness described above begins to extend toward our emotional experience. This helps us to stop automatically dissociating from our feelings. We then learn to identify our feelings and choose healthy ways to respond to them and from them. Such emotional development illuminates our own natural preferences, and, in turn aids us in making easier and better choices.

Towards the end of a long term therapy, a male client told me: "Yesterday, I was contemplating what I have discovered in the years of our work together, and I'm amazed at how much my values have shifted away from those of the macho family and culture I grew up in. I feel now like I prefer the arts to science, novels to non-fiction, gardening to watching golf, and hanging out with my partner at home to partying at the bar."

Grieving as Emotional Intelligence

Grieving is the key process for reconnecting with our repressed emotional intelligence. Grieving reconnects us with our full complement of feelings. Grieving is necessary to help us release and work through our pain about the terrible losses of our childhoods. These losses are like deaths of parts of our selves, and grieving can often initiate their rebirth.

Grieving and Verbal Ventilation

Grieving restores our crucial, developmentally arrested capacity to verbally ventilate. *Verbal ventilation* is the penultimate grieving practice. It is speaking from your feelings in a way that releases and resolves your emotional distress.

I believe the following description of a six panel cartoon visually conveys the powerful transformative power of verbal ventilation. In the first panel of the wordless cartoon, a woman with a dark cloud over her head is talking to a friend who has a shining sun over hers. In panel two, as the first woman gestures in a way that indicates complaining, the cloud covers her friend's sun. In panel three, the cloud emits a bolt of lightning, as she angrily purges, and her friend glowers along with her. In panel four, the cloud rains on them as they embrace, commiserating in the rain of their shared tears. In panel 5, relief spreads over their faces as the cloud moves away from the sun. In panel 6 the sun shines over both of them, as they smile and slip into pleasant conversation.

This cartoon reflects the fully realized power of verbal ventilation, which is the key bonding process in intimacy. It is also the key healing process of effective therapy, and here is an example of what verbally ventilating looks like in a therapy session.

A client arrives flashbacked and in pain. He verbally ventilates about it. He is the regressed hurt child, feeling bad, and part of him is sad and part of him is mad. He is once again lost in the painful feelings of his original abandonment, and this state is like a death that responds well to grieving.

As he lets his feelings come into his voice, he talks, cries and angers out his pain. Through this processing of his pain, he then gradually moves out of his flashback. He is restored to his normal everyday sense that he is no longer trapped in his traumatic childhood. Relief about this returns him to his normal ability to cope. If his grieving is deep enough, he customarily feels more hopeful and lighthearted. Not infrequently, his sense of humor resurfaces, and laughter punctuates his continuing verbal ventilation. This laughter is usually much different than the sarcastic, self-bullying humor of his critic that he might have begun the session with.

The inner critic is sometimes so hostile to grieving that shrinking the critic may need to be your first recovery priority. Until the critic is sufficiently tamed, grieving can actually make flashbacks worse, rather than perform the restorative processes it alone can initiate.

I have worked with numerous clients who were so traumatized around grieving that we needed to spend many months working on the cognitive level before grieving was released from the spoiling effects of the toxic critic. Chapter 11 provides a great deal of practical guidance for restoring your ability to grieve.

SPIRITUAL HEALING

Soothing Abandonment Losses via a Higher Sense of Belonging

Spiritual beliefs are of course a subject of personal and sometimes private concern, and I believe and hope what I write here is not proselytizing. My aim, instead, is to point out psychological concepts that have a non-sectarian spiritual aspect. I am aware, however, that some survivors have suffered terrible spiritual abuse in childhood, and if the term "spiritual" is offensive or triggering in any way, please feel free to bypass this section. There are many other useful tools in this toolbox.

———•·•———

A key aspect of the abandonment depression in Cptsd is the lack of a sense of belonging to humanity, life, anyone or anything. I have met many survivors whose first glimmer of "belonging" came to them on a quest that began as a spiritual pursuit. Finding nothing but betrayal in the realm of humans, they turned to the spiritual for help.

Spiritual pursuits are sometimes fueled by an unconscious hope of finding a sense of belonging. The worst thing that can happen to a child is to be unwelcomed in his family of origin - to never feel included. Moreover, many survivors have little or no experience of any social arena that feels safe and welcoming.

Many survivors also do not find a sense of belonging in traditional or organized religions. Finding conventional religion too reminiscent of their dysfunctional families, some survivors look to more solitary spiritual approaches. They find a sense of belonging to something larger and more comforting by reading spiritual books or engaging in meditative practices. This also allows them to bypass the danger of direct human contact.

Other survivors have spiritual experiences of belonging to something greater and worthwhile by being in nature, by listening to music or by appreciating the arts. I once marveled at a book, whose title now eludes me, that was a compendium of quotes from many renowned people who had numinous experiences through the direct perception of nature's beauty.

A *numinous* experience is a powerful moving feeling of well being accompanied by a sense that there is a positive, benign force behind the universe, as well as within yourself. This in turn sometimes brings enough grace with it, that you have a profound feeling that you are essentially worthwhile, that you belong in this life, and that life is a gift.

———•·•———

One of my website respondents sent me her personal account of therapeutic gratitude. Her name is Mary Quinn [of Ireland]. In answer to my request to reprint her writing, she replied: "Yes, and in honor of my little one and for all the times her voice went unheard, you may use my name."
"I went to the beach a couple of days ago in the morning and sat watching the sun coming up. I had an incredible moment of the purest clarity. I was watching birds flying low over the water, the moon was still visible and the sun was rising. I realized I was looking at three planets and there was not another person in sight.

"It was a moment of breathtaking beauty and the tears slid down my face at how deep it is possible to feel. I have been numb for so long. I wrapped my arms around myself and felt the presence of the little one so strongly it was almost painful but in a healing way if that makes sense. I realized that all the life experiences I have had to date brought me to that exact moment and gave me the depth to appreciate it at that level. A sense of peace washed through me like a gentle wave and for a few moments I felt a connection to a feeling of everything being part of life. It was breathtakingly beautiful. I felt like I was experiencing this moment with all of my senses and I never knew it was possible to be so much in my body.

"The gratitude feeling is deep and profound when it occurs. It feels like a moment of connection to life itself on the deepest level and all life circumstances and what I deem as problems pale to insignificance in those moments and there is only love in its purest form. It truly feels like a blessing albeit fleeting but gives enough sustenance and hope to continue the journey."

Whatever the source, spiritual or numinous occurrences sometimes provide the survivor with her first sense of belonging to something bigger and essentially good. Such experiences can lead a survivor to an author or speaker or fellow traveler with similar sensibilities, and sometimes a door opens for finding comfort with a fellow human. Eventually, this may even grow into a sense that there are some humans out there who are good and safe enough to engage with.

Gratitude and Good Enough Parenting

When developing children receive "good enough parenting", they feel that life is a gift even though it typically comes with difficult and painful experiences.

The term *good enough parenting* derives from the work of renowned adult and child psychologist, D.W. Winnicott, who coined the term "good enough mothering" to describe his observation that children do not need parents to be perfect. He noticed through his long career that children grew up with their self-esteem and capacity for intimacy intact when their parents were reasonably consistent with their love and support.

Nowadays, many therapists attach the phrase "good enough" to concepts like friend, partner, therapist or person. This is usually done to deconstruct perfectionistic expectations of relationships

- expectations that are so unrealistic that they are destructive to essentially worthwhile relationships.

When I apply the concept of "good enough" to people, I generally mean that a person is essentially good hearted, tries to be fair, and meets his or her commitments a large portion of the time.

I also like to apply "good enough" to other concepts such as a good enough job, a good enough try, a good enough outing, a good enough day or a good enough life. I apply this concept liberally to contradict the black-and-white, all-or none thinking of the critic which reflexively judges people and things as defective unless they are perfect.

———

Good enough parents provide generous amounts of support, protection and comforting. They also guide their children to deal constructively with recurring existential difficulties such as loss, real villains, painful world events and normal disappointments with friends and family.

Most importantly, they model how disappointments with intimates can be repaired. A key way they do this is to easily forgive their children for normal mistakes and shortcomings.

Children who receive good enough parenting easily recognize and protect themselves from bullying and exploitive people because they do not have to become accustomed to being treated unfairly.

Growing up in a safe and loving enough family naturally enhances the child's capacity to notice and enjoy the many gifts that life also brings. He learns that there is enough good in life to significantly outweigh its necessary losses and travails.

In the traumatizing family however, there is little or nothing that is good enough and hence little for which to be grateful. The child instead is forced to over-develop a critic that hyper-focuses on what is dangerously imperfect in her as well as others. This sometimes helps her to hide aspects of herself that might be punished. It may further assist her to avoid people who might be punishing.

Unfortunately, years of this habituates the child into *only* seeing herself, life and others in a negative light. Consequently, when she grows up and becomes free of her truly harmful family, she cannot see that life offers her many new possibilities. Her ability to see the good in herself and certain safe enough others remains developmentally arrested.

The cultivation of gratitude requires a balanced perspective. You can learn to see and appreciate the good in life without giving up your ability to discern what is truly negative and unacceptable in the present.

SOMATIC HEALING

Trauma takes its toll on the body in many ways. We need to comprehend the physical damage that Cptsd wreaks on our bodies to motivate us to adopt practices that help us to heal on this level.

Most of the physiological damage of extended trauma occurs because we are forced to spend so much time in hyper-arousal – stuck in fight, flight, freeze or fawn mode.

When we are chronically stressed out [stuck in sympathetic nervous system activation], detrimental somatic changes become ingrained in our bodies. Here are some of the most common examples of body-harming reactions to Cptsd stress:

Hypervigilance
Shallow and Incomplete Breathing
Constant Adrenalization
Armoring, i.e., Chronic muscle tightness
Wear and tear from rushing and armoring
Inability to be fully present, relaxed and grounded in our bodies
Sleep problems from being over-activated

Digestive disorders from a tightened digestive tract

Physiological damage from excessive self-medication with alcohol, food or drugs

Moreover, in cases of physical and sexual abuse, our capacities to be physically comforted by touch are eliminated or compromised; and, in cases of verbal and emotional abuse, our capacities to be comforted by eye- and voice-contact are undeveloped or seriously diminished.

Somatic Self-Help

The good news is that some somatic repair happens automatically when we reduce our physiological stress by more efficient flashback management. Particularly potent help also comes from the grieving work of reclaiming the ability to cry self-compassionately and to express anger self-protectively. Both processes can release armoring, promote embodiment, improve sleep, decrease hyperarousal and encourage deeper and more rhythmic breathing.

Without further expressly somatic work, however, a full relaxed inhabitancy of your body may not be achieved. Fortunately, there are other modes of self-help for healing the physiological wounds of Cptsd. The "Somatic Mindfulness" and "Introspective Somatic Work" sections of chapter 12 describe techniques that can help you to decrease adrenalization, to relax more deeply and to improve your digestion. Moreover, Step 7 of the flashback management steps at the beginning of chapter 8 contains six somatic, self-help techniques for relaxing out of the physiological hyperarousal of a flashback.

Another especially helpful somatic practice is stretching. Regular systematic stretching of the body's major muscle groups can help you to reduce the armoring that occurs when your 4F response is chronically triggered. This results from the fact that 4F activation tightens and contracts your body in anticipation of the need to fight back, flee, get small to escape notice, or rev up to launch into people-pleasing activity.

Learning to stretch was a major ordeal for me because of my extreme body armoring. As noted above, it was a task of self-nurturing that I resented intensely, and it took me a long time to adopt stretching as a regular practice.

The fact that I had to weather many toxic shame attacks because I was always the least flexible person in the group did not help matters. Moreover, when various people commented about how good it felt to stretch, I felt both puzzled and further shamed, because it was anything but pleasant for me.

Thankfully however, reading the literature about it convinced me about its great importance, and persistent practice eventually gave me results that I could not discount. I was rewarded by the resolution of decades old back problems. And although I still rarely enjoy the practice, I am absolutely convinced that it explains why I am still able to run, swim and play basketball in my mid sixties. Stretching has become for me a true labor of love and self-nurturance.

———•·•———

Yoga, massage, meditation and relaxation training are formalized disciplines to aid in letting go of unnecessary body tension. Reasonably priced classes in these modalities are usually available in most communities.

———•·•———

Finally, freeze types and freeze subtypes also typically benefit from various types of movement therapy and aerobic exercise regimes. Moreover, assertiveness training and anger release work are especially helpful for survivors who have difficulty accessing their assertiveness or instincts of self-protection.

Cptsd and Somatic Therapy

There are also various somatic therapies that can help our bodies heal. As with my earlier comments about CBT, I encourage you to be wary of somatic approaches that claim to heal Cptsd without working on the cognitive and emotional levels described above. Some approaches, in fact, blanketly dismiss cognitive work in a way that sidesteps the crucial work of shrinking the inner critic. Some approaches also believe that their techniques eliminate the fundamental necessity of grieving the losses of childhood, and understanding how abusive and negligent parenting is at the root of our problems.

Nonetheless, some somatic therapists can ease the physiological traumas that are locked in our bodies, as long as the practitioner is not actively dismissing or impeding the client's cognitive and emotional work.

In this vein, it is my opinion that techniques like EMDR [Eye Movement Desensitization Reprocessing] and Somatic Experiencing are very powerful tools for stress-reduction. They are especially helpful in resolving simple ptsd. However, they are not complete Cptsd therapies, unless the practitioner is eclectic enough to be incorporating inner critic and grieving-the-losses-of-childhood work.

Other helpful somatic techniques include Rosen Work, Rolfing, Rebirthing and Reichian work. These techniques can also be very helpful in aiding the recovery of the ability to therapeutically emote both tears and anger.

For survivors of physical and/or sexual abuse, I believe Rosen Work is especially helpful. I found that Rosen Work's emphasis on soft touch helped heal my Cptsd startle response to physical touch. A *startle response* is the sudden full body-flinching that survivors experience at loud noises or unanticipated physical contact. This is usually a somatic flashback to previous abuses. In my case, the startle response was installed in me by my parents through frequent face-slapping. As a lap-swimmer in public pools, it has taken me ages to significantly reduce being triggered by the hand and arm movements of people who swim alongside me.

I also had to shop around to find a Rosen worker who welcomed my use of the verbal ventilation process. Some practitioners prefer to work in silence, and this limits or eliminates the therapeutic benefit to most survivors.

It is also important to emphasize here that somatic therapies can be especially helpful in healing the anxiety reaction to touch and physical closeness that many survivors of physical or sexual abuse experience. Exceptions to this are the survivors that I have met who have experienced remediation of this symptom through the help of an especially kind and safe partner.

The Role of Medication

As a psychotherapist, I am not authorized to give pharmaceutical advice, but I have frequently noticed that survivors who need pharmaceutical help seem to benefit most from SSRI anti-depressants. Taken at the right dosage SSRI's do not usually blunt your affect in a way that makes grieving impossible. Moreover, if your critic does not budge with extended critic-shrinking work, SSRI's can usually reduce its volume and vitriol enough so that you can effectively shrink it. Once it is diminished enough, you can dispense with medication. One caveat here is that unless you do extensive critic shrinking work, the critic will be as strong as ever when the medications wear off.

Self-Medication

For those who have been repeatedly unsuccessful at stopping or reducing the use of non-therapeutic medications and substances, Gabor Mate's work on harm reduction may be helpful. Drug and alcohol recovery is beyond the scope of this book, but if you are stuck in habits of self-medication that are not allowing you to progress in your Cptsd recovery, I encourage you to get help from a substance abuse recovery program or from Twelve Step programs like Alcoholics or Narcotics Anonymous.

Working with Food Issues

Let us explore one last arena of physical healing, and that is dietary self-help. I agree with John Bradshaw who says that almost everyone who grows up in a dysfunctional family has an eating disorder. This is a key factor in the digestive track problems that are a common symptom of Cptsd.

Changing your eating habits is extremely difficult. A client left this quote on my waiting room bulletin board: "Alcohol and other drug recovery is like dealing with a tiger in a cage. Recovery from eating disorders is like taking that tiger out of the cage three times a day and then taking it for a walk."

Deconstructing food addictions, then, is daunting work that needs to be approached gradually and with a sense of compassion. This is because children who are traumatically abandoned naturally turn to food for comfort. Food offers us our first outside source of self-soothing, and when a child is starving for love, he frequently makes food his love object. Over the years he commonly "elevates" it to the status of a drug. Moreover, increasing scientific evidence is showing that processed food products combining high levels of sugar, salt and fat are especially addictive.

Food addictions begin pre-verbally. They are functional and useful at the time and help us to survive the unbearable feelings of the abandonment mélange. Unfortunately, we are typically forced to rely on food-soothing for so long that this over-dependence is extremely difficult to overcome, and I do not recommend that anyone in early recovery make this their primary focus unless they have a life-threatening food issue. Instead, I prefer to recommend Mate's harm reduction approach. Additionally, Geneen Roth's book, *Breaking Free from Compulsive Eating*, also offers a moderate and sensible approach to dietary improvement.

While many survivors can be unconscious of their damaging eating habits, I have met various survivors who take it to the opposite extreme. I was once in the ranks of those who obsessively over-focus on dietary self-help hoping and expecting that all their suffering will be resolved if they can just find the perfect diet. Many also chase after every new highly touted supplement in this pursuit. Some of us also approach exercise in this manner.

These are understandable but simplistic versions of the salvation fantasy, and are typically pursued at the exclusion of working on more core issues of recovering. Nonetheless, almost everyone has some ideas about how they can eat [and exercise] more healthily. My recommendation is to try dietary adjustments when you can on a moderate, doable level.

CHAPTER

IMPROVING RELATIONSHIPS

Forewarning:

There are instances of parental betrayal so extreme, that it is not fair or reasonable to expect the survivor to try to trust human beings again. If the recommendation in this chapter to open to the help of others feels too upsetting or overwhelming, please feel free to skip this chapter. There is a great deal of other material in this book that can help alleviate the many symptoms of Cptsd, and since recovery is relative and never complete, you do not need to implement everything in this book. As they say in the Twelve Step Movement: "Take the best and leave the rest."

Moreover, as I have experienced personally, and as numerous of my clients and website respondents have demonstrated to me, real relational healing can and does come from non-human sources. This is especially true of mammalian pets whose attachment needs and wiring are similar enough to ours that mutually healing connections can evolve between us. Dogs and cats can be a tremendous source of what Carl Rogers describes as the "unconditional positive regard" that young children must have in order to thrive.

Other therapeutic relational sources include nature, music and the arts. Moreover, for some survivors, authors of helpful books can be kept at safe distances while they contribute to your healing.

Finally, even with the most heinous betrayals, miracles sometime happen in terms of discovering a healing human connection, particularly in the later stages of recovery.

Cptsd as an Attachment Disorder

Many therapists see Cptsd as an *attachment disorder*. This means that as a child the survivor grew up without a safe adult to healthily bond with. As bears repeating, Cptsd almost always has emotional neglect at its core. A key outcome of this is that the child has no one in his formative years who models the relational skills that are necessary to create intimacy.

When the developmental need to practice healthy relating with a caretaker is unmet, survivors typically struggle to find and maintain healthy supportive relationships in their adult lives.

The Origin of Social Anxiety

A child who grows up with no reliable human source of love, support and protection typically falls into a great deal of social unease. He "naturally" becomes reluctant to seek support from anyone, and he is forced to adopt self-sufficiency as a survival strategy.

Needing anything from others can feel especially dangerous. The survivor's innate capacity to experience comfort and support in relationship becomes very limited or non-existent. This is despite the fact that many high functioning survivors learn to socially function quite adequately.

This is particularly the case in structured situations where expectations are clear and common goals take the focus off conversing and put it on task accomplishments. Unstructured social situations however, like attending parties or just hanging out can be considerably more triggering. Spontaneous self-expression feels like the same setup for disaster that it was in childhood.

Either way, structured or spontaneous, relating often involves hiding a great deal of anxiety and discomfort. One very successful businessman client of mine told me: "I'm so cool, calm and collected in meetings. A veritable wordsmith with the composure of Michael Caine. I'm a king on the outside, but on the inside I'm a drama queen anguishing in doubt and shame about everything I say or do."

In worst case scenarios, social anxiety can devolve into social phobia, especially during prolonged flashbacks. Extensive childhood abuse installs a powerful people-are-dangerous program.

When I was at my least recovered, I couldn't take out the garbage when I was in flashback. I feared that my neighbor – my sweet, always affirming neighbor – would look out the window and see how wretched and pitiful I was. Even worse, I dreaded the prospect that she might come out and want to interact with me.

Nonetheless, I socialized for decades when necessary, and seemed to be doing it with a considerable amount of success, no matter how dreadful the reviews were from my critic. I even eventually came to see, when not in flashback, that a lot of people really liked me.

Unfortunately, however, I rarely derived any satisfaction or comfort from this perception, because underneath my smooth persona, I was writhing in discomfort, and typically measuring the time until I could least obtrusively make my escape.

A Journey of Relational Healing

The incident I am about to describe marked a huge step in my long, gradual journey of opening to real intimacy. I was sitting on my porch with my dog George, the only being I could truly relax with, when he broke his lead and sprinted across the street in pursuit of a cat. Before he could get to the cat, he was run over by a car – both axels-run over. It was the worst thing that ever happened in my adult life, and when the shock [dissociation] wore off, I was drowning in the abandonment mélange.

Beyond devastated, I felt panicky and catatonic at the same time. As I had to in childhood when feeling overwhelmed, I hid in my room for thirty-six hours - dreading contact with my fair weather friend-roommates. I was 28 and still thoroughly phobic about showing any vulnerability. All my relationships had been developed under the guise of my people-pleasing, funny guy persona, and in my current state there was not a joke anywhere to be found. There was no way I would let myself be seen in what felt like a repulsive condition.

I could not sleep, and as sleep deprivation deteriorated into a fear that I was truly going crazy, out of nowhere came this amazing grace. Grace disguised in a form I usually abhorred. It was the grace of a deep surrender into weeping - a long sobbing release more soothing than anything I had ever experienced before.

It was the release I describe in chapter 11 and extensively throughout my first book. When the tears were cried out I knew I would be okay and I knew I was not going to go crazy. I could face my roommates with the realest, perhaps the first sense of self-esteem I had ever known. And from that point on, I knew I wanted more of these incredibly healing tears.

Healing the Shame that Binds Us in Loneliness

I soon discovered however, that my tears were as stuck as they had ever been, or at least since I was six – the last time I could remember crying. Further reading and researching then lead me to seek help, and so ensued my baptism into therapy, blessed by the great fortune of finding a good enough therapist on the first try.

This was a milestone achievement for me, and it evolved into a long meandering journey of finding more relational help with an array of healers, therapists, therapeutic groups and deeper friendships. These experiences ranged from extremely helpful to counter-therapeutic, but as time went on they became increasingly helpful.

A central aspect of the truly helpful relational work was what John Bradshaw called "healing the shame that binds." I believe toxic shame cannot be healed without some relational help. Several therapists and groups aided me greatly to unbind from the shame that made me hide whenever I could not invoke my perfect persona. Concurrently, I learned that real intimacy correlated with the amount I shared my vulnerabilities. As I increasingly practiced emotional authenticity, the glacier of my lifelong loneliness began to melt.

It is important to note here that groups can be even more powerful for the healing of shame than individual work. This is because there is typically more *mutual* vulnerability in a group than in individual work. Moreover, feeling compassion for someone who has suffered similarly to us sometimes naturally expands into feeling the same for ourselves.

Therapeutic relational experiences enhanced my self-compassion considerably further than what I was able to accomplish on my own. Moreover, I believe that insufficient self-compassion is the worst developmental arrest of all, and restored self-compassion is the keystone of all effective recovery.

In retrospect I can clearly see that as my self-compassion increased, my toxic shame decreased. Modern advances in neuroscience [see: *A General Theory of Love*] suggest that we are intrinsically limited in our ability to emotionally regulate and soothe ourselves. More and more research suggests that our ability to metabolize painful emotional states is enhanced by communicating with a safe enough other person.

Finding Good Enough Relational Help

In chapter 13, I provide guidance about how to shop for a good enough therapist. I also explore more deeply the principles of *therapeutic relational healing* to help you know what is reasonable to expect from your therapist.

———

I have also met a number of survivors who have been lucky enough to get this kind of relational healing from a partner or a friend, typically one who had good enough parents or who "has a lot of recovery".

Finally, attachment theorists have developed the concept of *earned secure attachment* to describe the *recovered enough state* where the attachment disorder of Cptsd becomes sufficiently healed. This is typically evidenced by the survivor forming at least one supportive and reliable enough relationship.

Many of the successful therapies I have guided come to an end when the client gains an earned secure relationship outside of our therapy. This is typically a partner or best friend with whom the person can truly be themselves.

Another potential source of relational healing is the co-counseling relationship. Guidelines for creating a co-counseling relationship are also contained in chapter 13.

———

Many respondents to my website have reported glowingly about the help they get from others through online recovery groups and forums. These groups can be particularly helpful for those who still find it difficult to be vulnerable in person. Sometimes the distance and relative anonymity of these forums can decrease the fear of self-disclosure, and this in turn can enhance therapeutic relating. An increasing number of therapists also' seem to be offering telephone sessions for this same reason.

The section "Finding an online group" in chapter 13, lists recommended online groups.

Parentdectomy and Relational Healing

I have worked with many clients who began therapy with me while they were still over-controlled by their traumatizing parents – both externally, as well as internally. Sometimes the control was enforced by as little as one phone call a week.

Not infrequently, these clients were also being overpowered and /or abandoned in relationships as abusive and neglectful as the ones they had with their parents. This is repetition compulsion at its most destructive, and it strands survivors in experiencing the worst of both worlds.

Through in depth exploration of their childhood trauma, many of my still-trapped clients achieved psychological freedom from their parents for the first time in their lives. Once again, this was a freedom that they had not actually achieved even though they had been living on their own for decades.

These clients gradually learned to live more successfully on their own without their parents over-controlling spoiling influence. Their ability to build self-nurturing relationships with themselves almost always correlated with a major reduction or complete severing of their relationships with their parents.

My client, Joe, who was variously misdiagnosed as Schizoid, Asperger's, and Paranoid, was living alone when he began therapy with me. He was extremely shut down and self-contained but recognized himself as a freeze type from reading articles on my website.

Getting him to talk at first was like pulling teeth, but over time I discovered that he was engaged in daily phone contact with his narcissistic, emasculating mother. Through our work and tremendous courage on his part, he gradually reduced the phone contact with his mother: at first to once a week, then once a month, then only major holidays, and after a few years to almost never.

When a parent is unrelentingly toxic, hearing even a few words from them can trigger the survivor into an intense emotional flashback. I have worked with numerous clients who made very little progress in their recovery while they maintained contact with the toxic parent[s]. For this reason, such clients usually require a parentdectomy to progress. There is a classic book by Bob Hoffman on this topic entitled *Getting Divorced from Mother & Dad*.

As external freedom from "smother-mothering" continued, Joe gradually achieved more and more internal freedom from her. During this time he began to experience the first meaningful relating of his life in an ACA group that for many years provided him with a great deal of positive companionship and relational healing. Joe finally concluded therapy with me when a healthy primary relationship that he formed with a group member reached the two year mark.

Learning to Handle Conflict in Relationship

One caveat for recovering the ability to authentically be yourself is that it is unreasonable and unfair to expect anyone to accept you if you are being abusively angry or contemptuous. Some trauma survivors flashback into this type of behavior by acting out from their Outer Critic. If this is an issue for you, chapter 10 provides guidance for deconstructing this intimacy-destroying habit.

In this vein, it is important to note that intimacy does not mean unconditional love. As John Gottman's scholarly research shows, a certain amount of disagreement, disaffection and disappointment is normal in relationship. The hallmark of successful couples is their ability to handle feelings of anger and hurt in a constructive and civil way. Gottman's studies have identified this as a key char-acteristic of couples who still really like each other after ten years.

"Tools for Lovingly Resolving Conflict" [Toolbox 4 in chapter 16] is a pragmatic list of techniques and perspectives to help couples resolve disruptions in their mutual attunement. Moreover, books by the Gottmans and Sue Johnson provide a great deal of practical help. I also find that *Beyond The Marriage Fantasy*, by Dan Beaver is especially helpful for men.

Reparenting

Reparenting is a key aspect of relational healing. It is primarily a pro-cess of addressing the many developmentally arrested needs of the traumatized child that we were. In this book we repeatedly address the two most fundamental of these needs: love and protection.

"Suggested Intentions for Recovery" [Toolbox 1 in chapter 16] renders yet another picture of the diverse developmental arrests that may as yet be unaddressed in the Cptsd survivor. The toolbox presents these needs as tangible goals that we can use to direct our recovery efforts.

Self-Mothering and Self-Fathering

An important, yin/yang dynamic of reparenting involves balancing self-mothering and self-fathering. When a child's mothering needs are adequately met, self-compassion is installed at the core of her being. When the same is true of her fathering needs, self-protection also becomes deeply imbedded.

Self-compassion is the domicile of recovery, and self-protection is its foundation. When self-compassion is sufficiently established as a "home base" to return to in difficult times, an urge to be self-protective naturally arises from it. Living in the world without access to these primal instincts of survival is truly terrifying.

We advance our recovery process immeasurably when we commit to re-mothering and re-fathering ourselves. I encourage you now to commit to becoming an unshakeable source of compassion and protection for yourself.

Self-Mothering Grows Self-Compassion

The most essential task of self-mothering is building a deeply felt sense that we are lovable and deserve to be loved. Self-mothering is the practice of loving and accepting the inner child in all phases of his mental, emotional, and physical experience. [If "inner child" is a problematic concept for any reason, you can imagine nurturing the developmentally arrested part of yourself.]

Self-mothering is based on the precept that unconditional love is every child's birthright. Recovering from the loss of unconditional love is problematic. Not getting enough of it as children was the greatest loss we had. Sadly, this loss can never be completely remediated, because unconditional love is only appropriate and developmentally helpful during the first two years or so of life.

After this time, the toddler has to begin to learn that human love comes with some conditions. Although love still needs to be copious at this time, the child must be gently shown that behaviors like hitting, biting and breaking things are not acceptable. The period of conditional love has begun and is successfully guided via a very gradual increase in learning about necessary and healthy limits and rules.

The toddler who receives good enough parenting learns relatively easily to survive the very gradually diminishing supply of unconditional love. During this time she learns little by little that other people also have rights and needs. Her absolute entitlement to gratification is coming to an end, and the needs of her parents will not always be forfeited to accommodate her.

Once again, psychological health is based on having about two years of this no questions asked entitlement to unconditional love. It is the normal healthy narcissism that Freud described as "His Majesty the Baby".

Serious problems accrue however when the toddler does not begin to learn that there are limits to his original entitlement. If there are no limits for too long, then the journey toward adult narcissism begins. On the other hand, if there are too many limits too soon, the matrix of trauma begins to form.

Enlightened parents introduce limits slowly but surely. They do it at such a rate that by the time the child reaches adolescence he can balance satisfying his needs with helping his intimates to satisfy theirs. He learns to be sharing and reciprocal, a developmental task that is essential to keeping intimacy alive in his life.

Cptsd is a syndrome of the dearth of unconditional love, or what the great therapist, Carl Rogers, called "unconditional positive regard". Cptsd can also occur when unconditional love is shut off in an all-or-nothing way in early childhood.

Some parents can shower love on babies. But as soon as the child begins toddling around and expressing a will of her own, they become severely punishing and rejecting.

The Limits of Unconditional Love

The terrible absence of love - or its abrupt premature termination - is extremely painful and its loss is very difficult to address. We cannot help desperately wanting the unconditional love we were so unfairly deprived of, but we cannot, as adults, expect others to supply our unmet early entitlement needs.

The one exception to this is therapy, but that of course is usually only one or two hours a week. Miraculously, I have seen the unconditional positive regard of the therapist be enough on numerous occasions to significantly repair the damage of not being parentally loved. And when it is enough, the therapist's consistent caring facilitates the awakening of the developmentally arrested need to hold yourself with enough unconditional love.

———•———

We survivors often struggle with managing our understandable but unrealistic yearnings to receive permanent unconditional love from a friend or partner. Like the toddler, we eventually have to accept the limits of adult love. This is especially true in romance where the intoxication of unconditional love rarely lasts for more than year. Around this time, partners inevitably begin to feel some frustration with each other because of differences in their individual needs.

Nonetheless, romantic love can be a significant source of therapeutic unconditional-like love, especially when it survives the inevitability of some disappointment. Susan Campbell's *A Couples' Journey* is a pragmatic, research-based book on how to reap more intimacy out of normal relationship disappointments

Inner Child Work

Let us return to the concept of self-mothering. As mother to ourselves, we commit to increasing our self-compassion and unconditional positive regard. Self-mothering is a resolute refusal to indulge in self-hatred and self-abandonment. It proceeds from the realization that self-punishment is counterproductive. It is enhanced by the understanding that patience and self-encouragement are more effective than self-judgment and self-rejection in achieving recovery.

You can enhance your self-mothering skills by imaginatively creating a safe place in your heart where your inner child and your present time self are always welcome. Consistent tenderness towards yourself welcomes the child into the adult body you now inhabit, and shows him that it is now a nurturing place protected by a warm and powerful adult.

Self-mothering can be enhanced by thought-correcting the critic's negative messages with healing words that the child in all likelihood never heard from his parents. A client of mine once shared this pearl of wisdom with me: "Thoughts - just mere thoughts - are as powerful as electric batteries - as good for you as sunlight is, or as bad for you as poison."

Here then are some useful messages for nurturing the growth of your self-compassion and self-esteem. I recommend that you imagine speaking them to your inner child, especially when you are suffering with a flashback.

Reparenting Affirmations

I am so glad you were born.
You are a good person.
I love who you are and am doing my best to always be on your side.
You can come to me whenever you're feeling hurt or bad.
You do not have to be perfect to get my love and protection.
All of your feelings are okay with me.
I am always glad to see you.
It is okay for you to be angry and I won't let you hurt yourself or others when you are.
You can make mistakes - they are your teachers.
You can know what you need and ask for help.
You can have your own preferences and tastes.
You are a delight to my eyes.
You can choose your own values.
You can pick your own friends, and you don't have to like everyone.
You can sometimes feel confused and ambivalent, and not know all the answers.
I am very proud of you.

Self-Fathering and Time Machine Rescue Operation

Many abandoned children enter adulthood feeling that the world is a dangerous place where they are ill-equipped to defend themselves. While self-mothering focuses primarily on healing the wounds of neglect, self-fathering heals the wounds of being helpless to protect yourself from parental abuse, and by extension from other abusive authority figures.

Self-fathering aims at building assertiveness and self-protection. It includes learning to effectively confront external and/or internal abuse, as well as standing up for the adult child's rights, as described in Tool Box 2 of chapter 16. Many survivors benefit greatly from classes and books on assertiveness training.

One of my favorite self-fathering exercises is the *time machine rescue operation*. I have used it to help myself and to help clients. With clients I use it to model a process for fighting off the overwhelming sense of helplessness that often accompanies emotional flashbacks.

This is a version of the time machine rescue operation that I use with myself as well as with my clients. I tell my inner child that, if time travel is ever possible, I will travel back into the past and put a stop to my parents' abusiveness. In the course of this I say things like: "I'll call 911. I'll call CPS [Child Protective Services] on them. I will grab their arms and pin them behind their backs the second they try to strike you. I will muffle them with a gag so they can't scream at you or even mumble their criticisms. I'll put bags over their heads so they can't frown or glare at you. I'll send them to bed without dessert. I'll do anything you want me to do to protect you."

Such imagery often provides me an exit out of fear and shame, and sometimes even makes my inner child laugh in delight. I sometimes finish this exercise by telling my inner child I would also report my parents to the authorities so they would be sent to counseling to learn how to be a better parent.

Or, I say that, if I could, I would take him back to live with me in the future before all those horrible things could happen to him. I remind him that he in fact lives in the present with me now, where I will always do my best to protect him. We now have a powerful body, greater skills of self-protection and access to allies and a legal system that will protect us.

When the recoveree consistently welcomes his inner child in every aspect of his being, the child feels increasingly safe and becomes more and more alive and self-expressive. As he experiences his adult self consistently rising to his defense, he will feel safe enough to begin accessing his innate vitality, playfulness, curiosity, and spontaneity.

Reparenting by Committee

Reparenting at its best is a yin/yang dynamic that balances the mutually enhancing processes of *reparenting by others* and *self-reparenting.* Reparenting sometimes needs to be initiated and modeled by someone else, such as a therapist, a sponsor, a kind friend or supportive group to show us how to self-reparent ourselves.

Alternatively, many survivors instinctively initiate *reparenting by others,* via entering what one of my clients describes as "the community of books". They receive reparenting from authors who encourage them to value and support themselves.

Alice was such a survivor. Her family traumatized her during childhood so thoroughly that she quickly learned that being vulnerable around others was dangerous, foolish and totally out of the question. Yet the urge to get the support and the help she was so unfairly deprived of worked its way back into her awareness via a strong attraction to self-help books. By reading a great deal of psychology, she eventually found enough help that she began to think that there might be a kind, safe and helpful person out there in the flesh and entered into some very helpful therapy. [Chapter 15,

Bibliotherapy, contains my favorite recommendations for therapeutic self-help books].

I too went through a long gradual process of reading and attending lectures before I was able to take the frightening and embarrassing plunge into therapy, where, as stated earlier, I was fortunate enough to find a good enough therapist to take my relational healing to the next level.

Therapy allowed me to internalize and mimic my therapists' consistent and reliable stance of being on my side. This in turn led me to gravitate toward safer and more truly intimate friendships. I have seen this same result with numerous clients and friends.

Eventually, I achieved my first earned secure attachment outside of therapy and was subsequently ready to let go of therapy as the only place where I could have deep and meaningful connection.

I believe the need to have mothering- and fathering-type support from others is a lifelong need and not just limited to childhood. Fortunately I am now blessed many years later to experience a multileveled form of reparenting by others which I call reparenting by committee. I conceptualize *reparenting by committee* as a circle of friends that has varying layers and levels of intimacy. The inner circle of my reparenting committee includes my five closest friends.

I think of this inner circle as friends with whom nothing is too vulnerable or taboo to talk about. My wife, a therapist friend, my exercise buddy and two members of a long term men's group that I was in are in this circle. This circle also has an outer layer of people who would be inner if circumstances allowed me to see them more.

Outside this orb are levels of succeeding less intimate, yet still meaningful circles of relationship. The next circle out is intimates who I rarely see anymore but who have shared enough intimacy with me in the past that I now draw comfort from imagining them caring for me in the present. My deceased grandmother is in this circle as are three of my former therapists, a couple of army buddies, old high school and college friends, and my four best friends from the ten years I lived in Australia.

The next circle out from this consists of my nurse practitioner, the body worker I occasionally see, some therapist colleagues and the wise old school librarian who helps me pick books for my son to read.

The next circle out from this are friends I play sports with, parents of my son's friends and people in my neighborhood with whom my contact is not especially vulnerable, but with whom there is an easy chemistry that adds to my general overall sense of belonging.

And the final circle is occasional strangers, who from time to time, I am graced to have easy and comforting interactions with.

I also know various survivors whose effective recovery practices have similarly rewarded them with enough portions of love from a variety of others that their childhood starvation for help and support is significantly assuaged. And like me, their committees, started with the first person they had good enough intimacy with. Counting yourself, this then is a committee of two, which with grace can then build slowly, one friendship at a time.

The Tao of Self-Relating and Relating to Others

Recovering is therefore enhanced on every level by safe human help. Once again however, survivors with especially harsh betrayal histories may need to do a great deal of work on other levels before they are ready to risk the vulnerability of opening to relational help.

Nonetheless, deep level recovering, as well as healthy "human-being" is typically a vacillating blend of self-help and help from others. Relational work helps heal the initial wound of family abandonment, and self work decreases the self-abandonment that occurs because the child was forced to imitate his parents' abandonment of him. The more time you practice the various techniques of self-care described throughout this book, the less time you spend in self-abandonment. With enough persistence, self-care becomes an invaluable, irreplaceable habit.

In advanced recovery, self-help and relational-help blend in an all important Tao. A Tao is a yin/yang combination of opposite and complementary forces. *The Tao of relational recovery* involves balancing healthy independence with healthy dependence on others.

For the survivor, this therapeutic synthesis can come into being when an improved supportive relationship with yourself allows you to choose and open to a helpful relationship. Sometimes simultaneously, the attainment of a safe, supportive relationship with another person promotes the growth of your ability to be self-supportive. This then rewards you with a decrease in your automatic tendency toward self-abandonment. Complementarily, this then fosters the gradual development of community – the vital life resource that you were so unfairly deprived of in childhood.

The more self-supportive we become the more we attract supportive others. The more we are supported by others, the more we can support ourselves. Sometimes we get initiated into this dynamic Tao by our own efforts - sometimes by the grace of finding a supportive friend or professional helper.

For many of us survivors a considerable amount of self-help work has to take place before we are able to open to relational support – before we become discerning enough to choose truly safe and helpful support.

CHAPTER 4

THE PROGRESSION
OF RECOVERING

Signs of Recovering

Effective recovery work leads to an ongoing reduction of emotional flashbacks. Over time, with enough practice, you become more proficient at managing triggered states. This in turn results in flashbacks occurring less often, less intensely and less enduringly.

Another key sign of recovering is that your critic begins to shrink and lose its dominance over your psyche. As it shrinks, your user-friendly ego has room to grow and to develop the kind of mindfulness that recognizes when the critic has taken over. This in turn allows you to progressively reject the critic's perfectionistic and drasticizing processes. More and more, you stop persecuting yourself for normal foibles. Additionally, you perseverate less in disappointment about other people's minor miscues.

A further sign of recovering is a gradual increase in your ability to relax. With this comes an increasing ability to resist overreacting from a triggered position. This further allows you to use your fight, flight, freeze and fawn instincts in healthy and non-self-destructive ways. This means you only fight back when under real attack, only flee when odds are insurmountable, only freeze when you need to go into acute observation mode, and only fawn when it is appropriate to be self-sacrificing.

An alternative way of describing this decrease in overreacting is that you have a good balance between the polar opposites of fight and fawn. As this becomes increasingly realized, you vacillate healthily between asserting your own needs and compromising with the needs of others.

A further example of decreased reactivity is seen in a more balanced movement between the polar opposites of flight and freeze. This manifests as an improving equilibrium between doing and being, between sympathetic and parasympathetic nervous system arousal, and between left and right-brain processing. The importance of balancing the fight-fawn and flight-freeze polarities within yourself is explored in greater detail at the end of chapter 6.

Deep-level recovery is also evidenced by you becoming gradually more relaxed in safe enough company. This in turn leads to an increasing capacity to be more authentic and vulnerable in trustworthy relationships. With enough grace, this may then culminate in you acquiring an intimate, mutually supportive relationship where each of you can be there for the other through thick and thin.

Advanced recovery also correlates with letting go of the salvation fantasy that you will never have another flashback. Giving up the salvation fantasy is another one of those two steps forward, one step backward processes. We typically have to wrestle with denial a great deal to increasingly accept the unfair reality that we will never be totally flashback-free. Unless we do however, we impair our ability to easily recognize and quickly respond to flashbacks from a position of self-compassion, self-soothing and self-protection.

The Stages of Recovering

Although we often work on many levels of recovering at the same time, recovering is to some degree progressive. It begins on the cognitive level when psychoeducation and mindfulness helps us understand that we have Cptsd. This awakening then allows us to learn how to approach the journey of deconstructing the various life-spoiling dynamics of Cptsd.

Still on the cognitive level, we take our next steps into the long work of shrinking the critic. Some survivors will need to do a great deal of work on this level before they can move down to the emotional layer of work which is learning how to grieve effectively.

The phase of intensely grieving our childhood losses can last for a couple of years. When sufficient progress is made in grieving, the survivor naturally drops down into the next level of recovery work. This involves working through fear by grieving our loss of safety in the world. At this level, we also learn to work through our toxic shame by grieving the loss of our self-esteem.

As we become more adept in this type of deep level grieving, we are then ready to address the core issue of our trauma – the abandonment depression itself. Work here involves releasing the armoring and physiological reactivity in our body to the abandonment depression via the somatic work discussed in chapter 12. This work culminates with learning to compassionately support ourselves through our experiences of depression.

Finally, as we will learn more about in chapter 13, many survivors need some relational help in achieving the complex tasks involved in deconstructing each layer of our old pain-exacerbating defenses.

Cultivating Patience with the Gradual Progression of Recovery

As stated earlier, recovery from Cptsd is complex. Sometimes, it can feel so hopelessly complex that we totally give up and get stuck in inertia for considerable lengths of time. This is why it is so important to understand that recovery is gradual and frequently a backwards and forwards process.

Effective recovery is often limited to only progressing in one or two areas at a time. Biting off more than we can chew and trying to accomplish too much too soon is often counterproductive. As a flight type, I spent years in mid-range recovery workaholically spinning my wheels trying to fix and change everything at once. I describe this at greater length in the "When Recovery becomes Obsessive-Compulsive" section of my first book [p140-141].

We often need to simplify our self-help efforts in early recovery. Accordingly, I recommend making shrinking the critic [chapter 9] your "go to" response if you feel unsure of how to proceed.

Once the critic is reduced enough that you can notice increasing periods of your brain being user-friendly, impulses to help and care for yourself naturally begin to arise. As this happens it becomes easier to tell whether you are guiding yourself with love or a whip. When you realize it's the whip, please try to disarm your critic and treat yourself with the kindness you would extend to any young child who is struggling and having a hard time.

———·•·———

Nowhere is patience with ourselves more important than with the inner critic work. Typically the inner critic is too omnipresent to confront on every occasion. To do so would often leave no time for anything else.

But when we practice critic-shrinking in a gradually increasing way over time, we can more consistently disidentify from its negative focus and switch to a more self-supportive perspective. Eventually a new positive habit of rescuing ourselves from shame and self-hate takes on its own life. I still have my unfair share of flashbacks, but rarely do I ever side with my toxic critic.

Any self-help practices that we are trying to make second nature often work in this way. When we practice enough, self-help starts to become a matter of common sense. It reverberates as *right action* and gradually takes on its own life as we attune to the true nature of our spirits and souls which are inherently self-supportive.

We also aid our recovery greatly by challenging the all-or-none thinking of the critic whenever it judges us for not being perfect in our efforts. "Progress not perfection" is a powerful mantra for guiding our self-help recovery efforts.

Moreover as recovering progresses, and especially as the critic shrinks, the desire to help yourself- to care for yourself - becomes more spontaneous. This is especially true when we mindfully do things for ourselves in a spirit of loving-kindness. As such, we can do it for the child we were – the child who was deprived through no fault of her own. And, we can do it because we believe every child, without exception, deserves loving care.

Finally, if the reader is like I was in the past and has no overall perspective on his suffering, he may feel like he is spinning his wheels on one icy patch of road after another. I had decades of trying everything under the sun with what felt like a deepening sense of futility and defectiveness. Gratefully, I eventually reached an invisible critical mass, and realized I had actually come a long way. I had acquired quite a few pieces in this puzzle of recovery, and only needed to organize them into a map to move along further. As such,

I have designed a ground plan that has helped me, my clients and website respondents to make sense of their suffering and to see how to effectively reduce it. I hope and pray that the cartography in this book will also offer you relief.

Surviving vs. Thriving

Recovery involves learning to handle unpredictable shifts in our inner emotional weather.

Perhaps the ultimate dimension of this is what I call the Surviving ◄───►Thriving continuum.

Before we enter into recovery, it may feel like life is nothing but a struggle to survive. However, when recovery progresses enough, we begin to have some experiences of feeling like we are thriving. These may start out as feelings of optimism, hopefulness and certainty that we are indeed recovering.

And then, the bottom inevitably drops out because recovery is never all forward progress. Oh so unfairly, we are back to feeling that we can barely survive. To make matters worse, we are amnesiac that we even had a respite from surviving. Another flashback has hit and we polarize back onto the surviving end of the continuum. We are stuck in the anxious and deadened feelings of the abandonment mélange.

In survival mode, even the most trivial and normally easy task can feel excruciatingly difficult. As in childhood, it is all feels just too hard. And if the flashback is especially intense, Thanatos may start knocking down the door. *Thanatos* is the death urge described by Freud and in a flashback it corresponds with the suicidal ideation we looked at in chapter 1.

Once again, it is important to repeat that this feeling-state is a flashback to the worst times in childhood when our will to live was so compromised. As mindfulness improves we can recognize suicidal ideation as evidence of a flashback and begin to rescue ourselves with the chapter 8 flashback management steps.

As recovery progresses, polarizations back into survival mode do not take us to the utter despair end of the continuum so often. Nonetheless survival mode can still feel pretty awful, especially when it is characterized by high anxiety or immobilizing depression.

Being in survival is especially difficult during those times when flashback management is less effective, and feelings that life is a struggle can hang on for days and even weeks. This is the territory where flashbacks morph into extended regressions.

I believe regressions are sometimes a call from our psyche to address important developmental arrests. In this case, it is the need to learn unrelenting self-acceptance during a period of extended difficulty. It is also the need to develop a staunch and unyielding sense of self-protection. This fundamental instinct of fiery willingness to defend ourselves from unfairness needs to strengthen progressively so that we can withstand inner critic attacks.

Moreover we can grow in our ability to survive "survival" by using the chapter 13 mindfulness techniques to practice and build enduring self-compassion. Moreover, if we are far enough along in recovery to have a safe ally, we can enlist their support to help us verbally ventilate out our pain at being stuck in survival.

Temptations can be great at such times to revert to the less functional ways of self-soothing that we learned when we younger. Depending on your 4F type this commonly manifests as increased eating, substance abuse, working, sleeping and/or sexually acting out.

Sometimes we are triggered into self-medicating in this way because we are desperately trying to keep ourselves on the thriving end of the continuum. Desperately clinging to thriving is a hard impulse to resist, even when we are in reality way past its expiration date.

Yet as recovery and mindfulness increase we begin to notice that this type of self-medicating indicates that we are in a survival-flashback. We are no longer authentically on the thriving end of the continuum. We have compounded our regression, by regressing further - by self-medicating to unnaturally prolong a preferred experience. At such times, we benefit most by reinvoking our intention to practice self-acceptance – by recommitting to being there for ourselves no matter where we are on the continuum.

As bears repeating, all human beings are existentially challenged to handle disappointing shifts out of thriving into surviving. We survivors however have greater difficulties handling these transitions because we were abandoned for so long at the surviving end of the continuum. Yet as our recovery progresses, we can learn to become increasingly self-supportive in times of being stuck in survival.

Difficulties in Identifying the Signs of Recovering

Some readers may work on their recovery for a long time, and erroneously and shamefully feel they are not making any progress. Because of the all-or-none thinking that typically accompanies Cptsd, survivors in the early stages of recovery often fail to notice or validate their own actual progress.

If we do not notice the degrees of our own improvement in our recovery work, we are in great danger of giving up on recovering. Because of black-and-white thinking, we can regularly fall into the trap of not acknowledging and valuing what we are actually accomplishing. Perfectionistic dismissal of improvement that is not 100% is common in early recovery.

Here are some common areas where I see that recovering survivors fail to notice and self-validate their progressive degrees of improvement.

1. Less intense launching into a 4F response
2. Increasing resistance to the critic
3. Increased Mindfulness about flashbacks or inner critic attacks

4. Increased time feeling good enough about yourself
5. Progress in meeting arrested developments listed in chapter 2
6. Decreased overeating or use of self-medicating substances
7. Increased experiences of good enough relating with others
8. Decrease in the painfulness and intensity of flashback feelings

In terms of number 3 above, it is important to note that even when mindfulness does not immediately terminate a flashback or critic attack, noticing and identifying these Cptsd phenomena is more progressive than just being blindly lost in them. Moreover, ongoing recognition makes effective ameliorative action more accessible. It makes us increasingly likely to remember to use the flashback management steps listed in chapter 8.

Furthermore, it is important that we notice the gradually decreasing intensity of the flashback feelings of anxiety, shame and depression. In this regard, social anxiety can gradually reduce along a continuum that stretches from panicky withdrawal... to a more tolerable social discomfort... to periods of social ease. Additionally, depression can gradually diminish along a continuum that stretches from paralyzing despair... to anhedonia – an inability to enjoy normal life pleasures... to a state of tired, and relatively unmotivated peacefulness. Of course both these processes typically improve at a vacillating, back-and-forth rate.

As I write this I feel some old sadness about the many decades that I judged my emotional tone and mood as either good or bad in a very all-or-nothing way. If I was not feeling very good than I felt as if everything was really bad. And since feeling very good is something most human beings only get to experience a relatively small proportion of the time, my perception of feeling bad became a much more dominant experience than was necessary. In fact, mildly unpleasant feeling typically morphed me quickly into feeling terrible via shame-tinged, all-or-none thinking.

I am so grateful for the life-changing epiphany that lead me to trade in my old primary aspiration of "Celebration" for my new one of "Serenity."

Inner critic thought processes refute signs of progress whenever a new flashback occurs, no matter how much less intense it is than before. Every recurrence of feeling shame, fear or depression is interpreted as proof that nothing has changed, even when there are increasing periods of not being triggered.

The critic's black-and-white assessment is: "Either I'm cured or I'm still hopelessly defective." And once you identify with your critic's pronouncement of defectiveness, you are off and spiraling downward into a full-fledged flashback - captured once again in the ice veneer of toxic shame that freezes one in the Cptsd stranglehold of helplessness and hopelessness.

Accepting Recovery as a Lifelong Process

It is exceedingly difficult to accept the proposition – the fact – that recovery is never complete. And although we can expect our flashbacks to markedly decrease over time, it is tremendously difficult, and sometimes impossible, to let go of the salvation fantasy that we will one day be forever free of them.

Yet when we do not loosen our grip on the salvation fantasy, we remain extremely susceptible to blaming ourselves every time we have a flashback. Understanding this is so crucial because recovery typically progresses in a process that has many temporary regressions. Moreover, most recoverees often have the unfortunate subjective experience that the temporary regression feels as permanent as concrete. This is especially true because of the *interminability* feeling of flashbacks. When we flashback, we regress to our child-mind which was incapable of imagining a future any different than the everlasting present of being so abandoned.

So how can we come to bear the knowledge that our awful childhoods have created some permanent damage? It helps me to see my Cptsd as somewhat analogous to diabetes, i.e., a condition that will need management throughout my life. This is a piece of bad news that naturally feels offensively unpalatable, but the good news, as with diabetes, is that as we become more skilled at flashback management, Cptsd can gradually become infrequently bothersome. And even more importantly, we can evolve towards leading increasingly rich and rewarding lives.

Even better news is that Cptsd, when efficiently managed, eventually bestows gifts. It comes with significant silver linings - unavailable to those less traumatized - as we will see at the end of the chapter.

Therapeutic Flashbacks and Growing Pains

Healing from childhood trauma is also a long gradual process because recovering your full self-expression requires a great deal of practice. Being yourself can be intimidating and flashback-inducing. Healthy self-assertion was punished like a capital crime in many dysfunctional families. Expressing yourself in ways that your parents forbade typically triggers intense flashbacks at first. This can cause you to lose sight of how this practice gradually reduces the chronic pain of remaining invisible.

We can encourage ourselves to face these growing pains by conceptualizing them as therapeutic flashbacks. We then choose to weather these flashbacks to stop the past from holding us back, to reclaim the fundamental human rights that our parents denied us, and to finally own what is rightfully ours for the taking.

We can further bolster ourselves for such necessary flashbacks by comparing "speaking up" to going to the dentist for a toothache. Unless we accept the acute pain of the dentist's therapeutic procedure, we will suffer chronic dental discomfit indefinitely. Unless we speak up, the loneliness of our silence will imprison us forever.

Recovering from overwhelmingly painful childhoods is also so difficult because we understandably want to avoid any further pain at all. We may even believe that we need to risk a flashback and practice speaking up. But at the moment of facing the triggering that silence can so easily avoid, we cannot sometimes help giving up and remaining mute.

However, if we are ever to recover our real voice, we must sometimes invoke the energy of bravery. Bravery is, in my opinion, defined by fear. It is taking right action despite being afraid. It is not brave to do things that are not scary.

The anger work described in chapter 11 can help you with this enormously. With a strong enough intention you can begin by occasionally invoking the kind of courage that involves *feeling the fear and doing it anyway*. You can nudge yourself to do it to rescue your inner child from the loneliness of never being seen or heard.

Moreover, when we embrace this practice we will eventually learn that fear does not have to disabling. We can be afraid and still act powerfully. We can refuse to tolerate never speaking up, never having our say, never stating a preference, and never saying "no" to set a boundary.

With enough practice, therapeutic flashbacks not only diminish, but begin to be replaced by a healthy sense of pride in ourselves for our courageous self-championing. More and more we are rewarded with feelings of safe belonging in the world.

———•·—

It is crucial for deeper level recovery that we learn that feelings of fear, shame and guilt are sometimes signs that we have said or done the right thing. They are emotional flashbacks to how we were traumatized for trying to claim normal human privileges.

As our recovery progresses, we need to learn to endure these feelings. Reinterpreting the deeper meaning of these feelings is key to accomplishing this. Typically this involves epiphanies like the following. "I feel afraid now, but I am not in danger like I was as a child." "I feel guilty not because I am guilty, but because I was intimidated into feeling guilty for expressing my opinions, my needs and my preferences." "I feel shame because my parents rained disgust on me for being me. I say no to these toxic parental curses, and I am proud and right to see how they tried to murder my soul. I give them their shame back as disgust – the disgust any healthy adult feels when he sees a parent bullying a child with contempt, or when he sees a parent heartlessly ignoring a suffering child."

Optimal Stress

The quest to ongoingly grow and evolve out of my childhood trauma sometimes becomes more embraceable to me when I remember the poet's words: "He not busy being born is busy dying." In fact, some of the latest research in neuroscience suggests that we actually need a modicum of stress in our life. This type of stress is called optimal stress.

Optimal stress is the balanced, moderate amount of stress that appears to be necessary to grow the new neurons and neuronal connections that correlate with keeping the brain healthy. Research shows that just as too much stress creates a biochemical condition that damages neurons in the brain, too little stress leads to the atrophy, death and lack of replacement of old neurons. This is why lifelong learning is widely recognized as one of the key practices necessary to avoid Alzheimer's disease.

In my opinion, lifelong recovering is an exalted subset of lifelong learning. I believe that optimal stress is frequently attained when we practice the behaviors that remedy our developmental arrests. Examples of this include reading self-help books, attending self-improvement workshops, working at deeper self-discovery through journaling, or struggling to be more vulnerable and authentic in a therapy session or an evolving relationship. Moreover, it might be that minor flashbacks sometimes function as optimal stress. I certainly know a number of long term recoverees who seem to be evolving and becoming sharper in their old age.

SILVER LININGS

We live in an emotionally impoverished culture, and those who stick with a long term recovery process are often rewarded with emotional intelligence far beyond the norm. This is somewhat paradoxical, as survivors of childhood trauma are initially injured more grievously in their emotional natures than those in the general population.

The silver lining in this, however, is that many of us were forced to consciously address our suffering because our wounding was so much more severe. Those who work an effective recovery program not only recover significantly from emotional damage, but also evolve out of the emotional impoverishment of the general society. One of my clients described this as becoming "way more emotionally intelligent than the 'normies'."

Perhaps the greatest reward of improved emotional intelligence is seen in a greater capacity for deeper intimacy. Emotional intelligence is a foundational ingredient of relational intelligence – a type of intelligence that is also frequently diminished in the general populace.

As stated earlier, intimacy is greatly enhanced when two people dialogue about all aspects of their experience. This is especially true when they transcend taboos against full emotional communication. Feelings of love, appreciation and gratitude are naturally enhanced when we reciprocally show our full selves - confident or afraid, loving or alienated, proud or embarrassed. What an incredible achievement it is when any two of us create such an authentic and supportive relationship! Many of the most intimate relationships that I have seen are between people who have done a great deal of freeing themselves from the negative legacies of their upbringings.

"The Unexamined Life is not Worth Living"

A further silver lining in recovery is the attainment of a much richer internal life. The introspective process, so fundamental to effective recovery work, eventually deepens and enriches survivors' psyches. Ongoing mindful exploration of all aspects of our experience helps us see firsthand what Socrates meant when he said: "The unexamined life is not worth living".

The survivor who follows the introspective "road less travelled" becomes increasingly free of compulsive and unconscious allegiance to unhelpful familial, religious and societal values that were instilled at an impressionable age.

The recoveree now gets to choose her own values and reject those that are not in her own best interest. She develops a deeper more grounded self-respect that is not contingent upon going with the herd and shifting center with every new popular trend. In psychological parlance, she becomes free and brave enough to individuate and develop more of her full potential.

In Joseph Campbell's words, the survivor learns to "follows his own bliss". He is freer to pursue activities and interests that naturally appeal to him. He evolves into his own sense of style. He may even feel emboldened to coif and dress himself without adherence to the standards of fashion. He may extend this freedom into his home décor. In this vein, I have seen many survivors discover their own aesthetic, as well as an increased appreciation of beauty in general. How this contrasts with many of the homes of my "normal" sports-buddies, whose homes are often sparsely decorated, as if they are too afraid to put something out or up lest it not be cool enough.

As the survivor recovers the right of free choice, she becomes more open to trying new things – healthy things that mainstream society might consider uncool or even taboo. Here are some examples of this that I believe are conducive to both recovery and healthy everyday living: voluntary simplicity, improved diet, meditation, alternative medicine, broad scale compassion, environmentalism, deeper emotional communication and a broader use of the grieving process.

The survivor who pursues long-term development on his journey of recovering generally achieves greater overall evolution than the average citizen. For many untraumatized people, the pursuit of ongoing learning often stops after their last formal learning experience – whether that is high school or college.

Introspective development also rewards the recoveree with more perspective and wisdom in making important life choices. It also improves his everyday instinctual choices, such as whether to fight, flee, freeze or fawn in times of real danger.

———·—·———

Finally, another silver lining, often achieved in later stage recovery, is a greater ability to handle normal pain in the most healthy and least retraumatizing way. By normal pain, I mean the recurring existential pain all human beings experience from time to time via encounters with loss, illness, money troubles, time pressures, etc. Such painful encounters can produce emotional reactions like anger, sadness, fear and depression. The average person has not learned how to verbally ventilate and metabolize their feelings about such events. This results in them getting stuck in painful emotional places, especially depression, for inordinate amounts of time.

The Emotional Imperialism of "Don't Worry, Be Happy"

One reason that recovering survivors attain greater emotional intelligence is that they eventually see through the mainstream media's indoctrination that people should be happy all the time.

Much of the general populace, however, becomes increasingly dissociated from their full emotional experience by anxiously pushing to pump up their mood. Many "normal" people strive to fulfill the pursuit of happiness as if it were a patriotic duty. More and more they employ socially acceptable addictions to accomplish this. Snacking, spending, self-medicating, and online puttering are widespread addictions that seem to be ever on the rise.

A particularly rampant example of unhealthy mood-altering behavior is porn addiction. Addiction to pornography creates a terrible narrowing of consciousness in the many men who are afflicted with it. It commonly destroys their capacity for real intimacy. Tragically, the use of porn is more and more "normalized", even in many psychological circles.

Here are two enlightening references on this latter subject: http://www.interchangecounseling.com/blog/why-men-are-so-obsessed-with-sex/ and http://www.youtube.com/watch?v=wSF82AwSDiU.

───·•·───

As we become more emotionally intelligent, we free ourselves from the hysteria-inducing pressure to continuously pump up the joy in our life.

Please do not read this as an "Ode against Joy". It is a blessing to have our natural fair share of laughter and feeling good. But I believe it is also a blessing to resist the growing emotional imperialism that demands we become fountains of joy. We are assaulted daily with messages from advertisements, from laugh track-saturated TV shows, and from new age enlightenment gurus who shame us into believing that we are "less than", if we are not constantly bub-bling over with ecstatic Disneyland-like enthusiasm.

The pressure to be always up was an enormous shame trig-ger for me for decades. Sadly, I increasingly see clients and friends struggling with self-contempt for not being happy enough.

Once again, I am certainly not knocking joy, but when it is inauthentic, it is disconcertingly sad and sometimes alienating. In worst case scenarios, a controlling narcissist can emotionally blackmail us to join him in falsely emoting joy. Just as painful is when we codependents force ourselves to laugh to cover up our fear or shame.

This is also not to say that authentic joy cannot be contagious. Contagious joy is the wonderful experience of being positively triggered into vicariously sharing someone else's authentic delight. [For an experience of this, go to www.youtube.com and search for "Quadruplets Laughing"].

In my experience, it seems that authentic joy is much more common in the lives of well parented children. I also do not think that joy is typically as dominant an emotional theme in adult life unless it is synthetically induced with drugs or alcohol. On the other hand, experiences of joy for survivors can gradually become more frequent as a person's recovery efforts promote increasing feelings of safety in the world.

As our emotional intelligence increases, I see considerable evidence that our expectations of joy become more reasonable. This allows us to let go of permanent happiness as the unrealistic goal of recovery. Until this happens, we remain at the mercy of the critic's contemptuous diatribes that we are not being joyful enough. One of my clients recently became mindful enough to see how he was shaming himself for not being as jubilant as those in the beer commercials.

———·—

As a concluding comment to this overview, it is important to emphasize that, like most things in life, there are degrees of Cptsd. The continuum of Cptsd ranges from mild neurosis to psychosis, and from highly functioning to non-functioning. Its severity ranges from having extended periods without flashbacks to being in full flashback horror much of the time. This range also varies from a condition of increased experiences of thriving to a condition of barely surviving disability.

Progress in recovery is seen, then, in flashbacks becoming more manageable and life satisfaction becoming continuously more frequent. A friend of mine once joked with me: "I've got so much recovery, I'm beyond normal – I'm supernormal. I make the normies look like they're the ones with Cptsd."

As we end the overview, we are ready to move to the next chapter, which explains how varying childhood trauma histories can cause Cptsd. Here we will also see how verbal and emotional abuse alone can cause Cptsd, and how profound emotional abandonment is typically at the core of most Cptsd.

PART II

THE FINE POINTS OF RECOVERING

CHAPTER 5

WHAT IF I WAS NEVER HIT?

Physical and sexual abuse are the most obvious traumas that a child can experience, especially when they are ongoing. However, much that is also traumatic goes unnoticed in Cptsd-engendering families. This often occurs because parental acts of physical abuse are more blatant than acts of verbal and emotional abuse and neglect. It appears to me that just as many children acquire Cptsd from emotionally traumatizing families as from physically traumatizing ones.

Denial about the traumatic effects of childhood abandonment can seriously hamper your ability to recover. In childhood, ongoing emotional neglect typically creates overwhelming feelings of fear, shame and emptiness. As an adult survivor, you may continuously flashback into this abandonment mélange. Recovering depends on realizing that fear, shame and depression are the lingering effects of a loveless childhood. Without such understanding, your crucial, unmet needs for comforting human connection can strand you in a great deal of unnecessary suffering.

Denial and Minimization

Confronting denial is no small task. Children so need to believe that their parents love and care for them, that they will deny and minimize away evidence of the most egregious neglect and abuse.

De-minimization is a crucial aspect of confronting denial. It is the process by which a person deconstructs the defense of "making light" of his childhood trauma. The lifelong process of de-minimizing the impact of childhood trauma is like peeling a very slippery and caustic onion. The outer layer for some is the stark physical evidence of abuse, e.g., sexual abuse or excessive corporal punishment. Subsequent layers involve verbal, spiritual and emotional abuse. *Core* layers have to do with verbal, spiritual and emotional neglect.

In a perversely ironic way, my parents' physical abuse of me was a blessing, for it was so blatant that my attempts to suppress, rationalize, make light of and laugh it off lost their power in adolescence, and I was able to see my father for the bully that he was. [Seeing my idealized mother's abusiveness came much later].

Identifying my father's behavior as abusive eventually helped me become aware of less blatant aspects of my parents' oppression, and I subsequently discovered the verbal and emotional abuse layer of the onion of my childhood abandonment.

Verbal and Emotional Abuse.

The fact that verbal and emotional abuse can be traumatic is lost on many childhood trauma victims, though it is rarely lost on recovering victims of cult brainwashing who also are prone to developing Cptsd.

Many survivors of verbal and emotional abuse never learn to validate its soul-damaging effects. They never accurately assign current time suffering to it. Attempts to acknowledge it are typically blindsided with thoughts that it was nothing compared to kids who were repeatedly beaten – who "had it so much worse." As a child, I minimized my father's frequent face-slapping by comparing it to my friend's father who used to punch him.

Much later, however, I finally realized that for me, and many of my clients, verbal and emotional abuse damaged us much more than our physical abuse.

Ongoing assault with critical words systematically destroys our self-esteem and replaces it with a toxic inner critic that incessantly judges us as defective. Even worse, words that are emotionally poisoned with contempt infuse the child with fear and toxic shame. Fear and shame condition him to refrain from asking for attention, from expressing himself in ways that draw attention. Before long, he learns to refrain from seeking any kind of help or connection at all.

Theoretical Neurobiology of the Critic

Unrelenting criticism, especially when it is ground in with parental rage and scorn, is so injurious that it changes the structure of the child's brain.

Repeated messages of disdain are internalized and adopted by the child, who eventually repeats them over and over to himself. Incessant repetitions result in the construction of thick neural pathways of self-hate and self-disgust. Over time a self-hate response attaches to more and more of the child's thoughts, feelings and behaviors.

Eventually, any inclination toward authentic or vulnerable self-expression activates internal neural networks of self-loathing. The child is forced to exist in a crippling state of self-attack, which eventually becomes the equivalent of full-fledged self-abandonment. The ability to support himself or take his own side in any way is decimated.

With ongoing parental reinforcement, these neural pathways expand into a large complex network that becomes an Inner Critic that dominates mental activity. The inner critic's negative perspective creates many programs of self-rejecting perfectionism. At the same time, it obsesses about danger and catastrophizes incessantly. Chapters 9 and 10 expand on shrinking and deconstructing these life-ruining programs. Until this is accomplished, the survivor typically lives in varying degrees of emotional flashback much of the time.

The verbal and emotional layer of the abuse onion has many sub-layers of minimization. I have heard clients jokingly repeat numerous versions of this over and over: "I know I'm hard on myself, but if I don't constantly kick my own ass, I'll be more of a loser than I already am. In fact, I really need you to come down on me if I try to get away with anything!" A childhood rife with verbal and emotional abuse forces the child to so thoroughly identify with the critic, that it is as if the critic is his whole identity.

Disidentification from the critic is the fight of a lifetime. To liberate your identity from the toxic critic, you will have to repetitively confront it for a long time. You will have greater success if you are prepared to forgive yourself for repeatedly collapsing back into the old habit of self-blame. Progress is always a gradual back and forth process. Ironically, a pernicious type of self-hate can constellate around the self-judgment that one is especially defective because she cannot simply banish the critic. This is the typical toxic, all-or-none thinking of the critic.

Sadly, many survivors give up on fighting the critic before recognizing the myriad subtle ways it tortures them. Yet, there is no more noble recovery battle than that which gradually frees the psyche from critic dominance. Until this happens to a significant degree, there is minimal development of the healthy, user-friendly ego.

Let us look now at how emotional neglect alone can create a psyche-dominating critic.

Emotional Neglect: The Core Wound in Complex PTSD

Minimization about the damage caused by extensive emotional neglect is at the core of the Cptsd denial onion. Our journey of recovering takes a quantum leap when we really feel and understand how devastating it was to be emotionally abandoned. An absence of parental loving interest and engagement, especially in the first few years, creates an overwhelming emptiness. Life feels harrowingly frightening to the infant or toddler who is left for long periods without comfort and care. Children are helpless and powerless for a long time, and when they sense that no one has their back, they feel scared, miserable and disheartened. Much of the constant anxiety that adult survivors live in is this still aching fear that comes from having been so frighteningly abandoned.

Many survivors never discover and work through the wounds that correlate with this level. This happens because they over-assign their suffering to overt abuse and never get to the core issue of their emotional abandonment. As stated above, this is especially likely to occur with survivors who dismissively compare their trauma to those who were abused more noticeably and more dramatically. I find this painfully ironic because some people suffer significant active abuse without developing Cptsd. Typically, they are "spared" because there is one caretaker who does not emotionally neglect them.

Traumatic emotional neglect occurs when a child does not have a single caretaker to whom she can turn in times of need or danger. Cptsd then sets in to the degree that there is no alternative adult [relative, older sibling, neighbor, or teacher] to turn to for comfort and protection. This is especially true when the abandonment occurs 24/7, 365 days a year for the first few years.

Growing up emotionally neglected is like nearly dying of thirst outside the fenced off fountain of a parent's warmth and interest. Emotional neglect makes children feel worthless, unlovable and excruciatingly empty. It leaves them with a hunger that gnaws deeply at the center of their being. They starve for human warmth and comfort.

The Failure to Thrive Syndrome

When a child is continuously deprived of a nurturing caretaker, love-starvation steadily increases and sometimes devolves into the Failure to Thrive Syndrome.

Failure to thrive is a term coined in the mid twentieth century to describe the epidemic of baby deaths that occurred when new germ-phobic practices were introduced into hospitals. The new standard was that nurses were prohibited from holding babies for fear of contaminating them. Infant mortality immediately began to climb.

Modern medical practice has abandoned this heartless approach because of the *Failure to thrive* research. This research has since been corroborated by data from Eastern European orphanages where there are insufficient staff to meet the *contact-comfort needs* of babies. Modern medicine now accepts as scientific fact the principle that babies need a great deal of physical touch and nurturing in order to thrive.

In my experience, failure to thrive is not an all-or-none phenomenon, but rather a continuum that stretches from the abandonment depression to death. Many Cptsd survivors never thrived as babies. I believe that many suffered painful bouts of lingering near the end of the continuum that feels death-like. Several of my clients commonly have quipped that they "feel like death warmed over" when they are in a flashback.

Moreover, I suspect that some traumatized children do die from their abandonment. Perhaps, their immune systems weaken and make them more susceptible to diseases. Perhaps, as David Kalshed hints, they unconsciously gravitate toward lethal "accidents" to terminate their misery.

One of my clients reported this painful memory when we were processing a flashback that she was trapped in. She was ten, in a daze, and walked out between two parked cars into traffic. She was hit by a truck and it took months of hospitalization to save her leg. Her most tearful re-experiencing of this event was remembering how she woke up in the hospital and felt tremendous disappointment that she was still alive.

Emotional Hunger and Addiction

The emotional hunger that comes from parental abandonment often morphs over time into an insatiable appetite for substances and/ or addictive processes. Minimization of early abandonment often transforms later in life into the minimizing that some survivors use to rationalize their substance and process addictions. Fortunately, many survivors eventually come to see their substance or process addictions as problematic. But many also minimize the deleterious effects of their addiction and jokingly dismiss their need to end or reduce their reliance on them.

When the survivor has no understanding of the effects of trauma or no memory of being traumatized, addictions are often understandable, misplaced attempts to regulate painful emotional flashbacks. However many survivors are now in a position to see how self-destructive their addictions are. They are now old enough to learn healthier ways of self-soothing.

Accordingly, substance and process addictions can be seen as misguided attempts to distract from inner pain. The desire to reduce such habits can therefore be used as motivation to learn the more sophisticated forms of self-soothing that Cptsd recovery work has to offer.

As we will see in chapter 11, grieving work offers us irreplaceable tools for working through inner pain. This then helps obviate the need to harmfully distract ourselves from our pain.

The Evolutionary Basis of Attachment Needs

The human brain evolved during the Hunter-Gatherer era that represents 99.8% of our time on this planet. For a child, safety from predators during these times depended on being in very close proximity to an adult. Even the briefest loss of contact with a parental figure could trigger panicky feelings as beasts of prey only needed seconds to snatch away an unprotected child.

Fear hard-wired in the child as a healthy response to separation from a protective adult. Fear also linked automatically with the fight response so that the infant and toddler would automatically cry angrily for attention, help, and cessation of abandonment.

Cptsd-inducing families however loathe angry crying, and many can find professionals to back them up for routinely leaving babies and very young children to "cry it out" on their own.

In most dysfunctional families, parents disdain children for needing any kind of help or attention at all. Moreover, even the most well-intentioned parent can seriously neglect their children by subscribing to the egregious 20th century "wisdom" that "Kids need quality time - quantity does not matter."

When children experience long periods of being powerless to obtain needed connection with a parent, they become increasingly anxious, upset and depressed. In Cptsd-engendering families, the absence of care and concern is extreme. A caretaker is rarely or never available for support, comfort or protection.

If this is what you suffered, you then grew up feeling that no one likes you. No one ever listened to you or seemed to want you around. No one had empathy for you, showed you warmth, or invited closeness. No one cared about what you thought, felt, did, wanted or dreamed of. You learned early that, no matter how hurt, alienated, or terrified you were, turning to a parent would do nothing more than exacerbate your experience of rejection.

When caretakers turn their backs on a child's need for help and support, her inner world becomes an increasingly nightmarish amalgam of fear, shame and depression. The child who is abandoned in this way experiences the world as a terrifying place.

Over time the child's dominant experience of herself is so replete with emotional pain and so unmanageable that that she has to dissociate, self-medicate, act out [aggression against others] or act in [aggression against the self] to distract from it.

The situation of the abandoned child further deteriorates as an extended absence of warmth and protection gives rise to the cancerous growth of the inner critic as described above. The child projects his hope for being accepted onto self-perfection. By the time the child is becoming self-reflective, cognitions start to arise that sound like this: "I'm so despicable, worthless, unlovable, and ugly; maybe my parents would love me if I could make myself like those perfect kids I see on TV."

In this way, the child becomes hyperaware of imperfections and strives to become flawless. Eventually she roots out the ultimate flaw – the mortal sin of wanting or asking for her parents' time or energy. Intrinsic to this process is noticing – more and more hypervigilantly - how her parents turn their back or become angry or disgusted whenever she needs anything, whether it be attention, listening, interest, or affection.

Emotional neglect, alone, causes children to abandon themselves, and to give up on the formation of a self. They do so to preserve an illusion of connection with the parent and to protect themselves from the danger of losing that tenuous connection. This typically requires a great deal of self-abdication, e.g., the forfeiture of self-esteem, self-confidence, self-care, self-interest, and self-protection.

Moreover, endangerment programs proliferate in the critic as the child learns that he cannot ask his parent to protect him from dangers and injustices in the outside world, never mind in the home.

His only recourse is to become hypervigilant about things that can go wrong. His critic compiles lists of possible calamities, especially those that are graphically portrayed in the media.

The media gives the critic of the abandoned child much fodder to play with. She may be exposed daily to hours of programs that glorify sarcasm, backbiting and bullying. Moreover news programs, with a ninety percent content of bad news, fill her head with impressions that the world is predominantly hostile and dangerous. Even worse, emotionally neglectful parents commonly abandon their children to their favorite babysitter – the TV.

Through such neglect the child's consciousness eventually becomes overwhelmed with the processes of *drasticizing* and *catastrophizing*. Drasticizing and catastrophizing are critic processes that lead the child to constantly rehearse fearful scenarios in a vain attempt to prepare himself for the worst. This is the process by which Cptsd with its overdeveloped stress and toxic shame programs sets in and becomes triggerable by a plethora of normally innocuous stimuli.

Most notable of these stimuli are other people, especially unknown people or people even vaguely reminiscent of the parents. Over time, the critic comes to assume that all other people are dangerous and automatically triggers the fight, flight, freeze or fawn response whenever a stranger or unproven other comes into view.

This people-are-dangerous process typically devolves into the social anxiety that is frequently a symptom of Cptsd. In worst case scenarios it manifests as social phobia and agoraphobia. In my opinion, agoraphobia is rarely the fear of open spaces. It is instead a disguised form of social phobia. It is the fear of going out lest you run into someone or anyone.

Abandonment Stultifies Emotional and Relational Intelligence

As stated above, emotionally abandoned children often devolve into experiencing all people as dangerous, no matter how benign or generous they may in fact be. Even love, coming their way, reverberates threateningly on a subliminal level. Unconsciously, they fear that if they momentarily "trick" someone into liking them, the forbidden prize will vanish once their social perfectionism inevitably fails and exposes their unworthiness. Moreover, when this occurs, they will be triggered even more deeply into the abandonment mélange.

Emotional intelligence and its cohort, relational intelligence, are forced into developmental arrest by abandoning parents. Children never learn that a relationship with a healthy person can be comforting and enriching. The ability to open to and benefit from love and caring from others often lays dormant and undeveloped.

Moreover, the appropriate management of the normal emotions that recurrently arise in significant relationships is never modeled for them. Emotional intelligence about the healthy and functional aspects of anger, sadness, and fear lies fallow.

De-Minimizing Emotional Abandonment

As with physical abuse, effective work on the wounds of verbal and emotional abuse can sometimes open the door to de-minimizing the awful impact of emotional neglect. I sometimes feel the most for my clients who were "only" neglected, because it is so difficult to see neglect as hard core evidence. Most people remember little before they were four years old. And by that time, much of this kind of damage is done. It typically takes some very deep introspective work, to realize that current time flashback pain is a re-creation of how bad it felt to be emotionally abandoned.

The remembering and de-minimizing of the impact of emotional neglect can take a long time. It is typically an intuitive piecing together of a lot of clues. The puzzle is often solved when a critical mass of childhood reconstruction is reached. Sometimes this fosters an epiphany that neglect is indeed at the core of present time suffering. Sometimes this epiphany brings a great relieving certainty that fragile self-esteem, frequent flashbacks, and recurring reenactments of unsupportive relationships were caused by the closed hearts of your parents.

I sometimes regret that I did not know what I now know about this kind of neglect when I wrote my first book. I wish I had not over-focused on the role of abuse in my childhood trauma. It is so hard to convey this to a client whose critic minimizes and shames them for their plight by comparing them unfavorably to me: "I didn't have it anywhere near as bad as you. My mother never hit me!"

How ironic that this typically invokes a feeling-sense in me that the worst thing that happened to me, by far, was growing up so emotionally abandoned. In fact, it was not until I learned to assign the pain of numerous current time emotional flashbacks to the abject loneliness of my childhood, that I was able to work effectively on the repetition compulsion that lead me into so many neglectful relationships.

And once again this is not to deny or minimize the C-ptsd-inducing traumatization that does come from each and every type of abuse; physical, sexual, verbal and emotional.

Practicing Vulnerability

Emotional abandonment is healed by the type of real intimacy that we have been discussing. And once again real intimacy depends on us showing up in times of vulnerability. Deep-level recovering occurs when we successfully connect with a safe enough other during the flashbacked-times of feeling trapped in the fear, shame and depression of the abandonment mélange.

———·•·——

In this vein, I had to painstakingly practice showing up in my pain for years. At first I could only do this infrequently. I was too habituated to my childhood default positions of hiding or camou-flaging with substances whenever I was in the grip of the abandon-ment mélange. Yet I drew strength to increase my practice from a growing distaste for the social perfectionism of my people-pleas-ing codependence. I somehow knew my loneliness would never decrease unless I took the risk to see if certain well chosen others would accept me in all aspects of my experience, not just the shiny ones.

And of course, like most survivors, I was ignorant at first that I was even experiencing the emotional pain of the abandonment mélange. How could I help but conceal it?

Moreover, even after considerable de-minimization of my child-hood abuse/neglect picture, I was still convinced that everyone but my therapist would find me abhorrent if I shared about my flash-back feelings. Furthermore, my trust of my therapist also wavered quite a bit at first, especially during my deepest flashbacks.

Gratefully, sufficient positive experiences with my therapist eventually emboldened me to bring my authentic vulnerability to other select and gradually proven relationships, where I found the acceptance, safety and support that, previously, I would not have known to wish for.

———·—·———

There are limitations of the analogy of the onion. Later recovery does typically involve working at various levels at the same time. De-minimization is a lifetime process. Revisiting a central issue of our abandonment picture sometimes impacts us even more deeply than it did at first.

One such occasion left me reeling with the certain knowledge that getting hit felt preferable to being abandoned for long hours outside my depressed mother's locked bedroom door. I would pound on the door even though I knew she would explode because

I just could not bear the isolation. I have known about the latter for quite some time now and yet writing about it brings up some new bitter-sweet tears.

Bitter-sweet tears are not uncommon in the ongoing work of peeling the layers of the denial onion. The tears are bitter because we realize the abandonment was even more devastating than we previously realized. And then the tears are sweet because they validate the truth of the recollection and put the blame where it truly belongs. And then they may be bitter again because the horrible abandonments happened over and over again when we were so young and legitimately needed so much help. And then they can turn sweet again, as in tears of gratitude, because a person often comes through this kind of depth work with an enhanced compassion for what she suffered and a healthy pride about having survived.

In my latest experience of this type of grieving my sweet tears came from realizing that I do regularly experience good enough love and safety in relationship. And then my tears were bitter again because I can still emotionally flashback to that bereft state of feeling stranded from the comfort of others, even occasionally from my wife and son. And then my tears were sweet again because my flashbacks are so much easier to handle these days, especially as I increasingly master the use of the tools I describe in chapter 8.

The Power of Narrative

There is also growing evidence that recovery from Complex PTSD is reflected in the narrative a person tells about her life. The degree of recovery matches the degree to which a survivor's story is complete, coherent, and emotionally congruent and told from a self-sympathetic perspective.

In my experience, deep level recovery is often reflected in a narrative that highlights the role of emotional neglect in describing what one has suffered and what one continues to deal with.

My client, Matt, peeled a large layer off his onion of denial and minimization two days before Mother's Day. He came into his session in a terrible flashback. "Life sucks and I suck even more. I couldn't even do something as simple as pick out a Mother's Day card."

Fortunately, Matt had achieved a great deal of de-minimization since the previous Mother's Day when he thought his mother was a good mother because she had never hit him. Now however, he was heavily triggered by spending an hour in a card shop unable to find a card that he could send to his mother. As we explored this further, we discovered that the sentiments written in every card made him feel like he would be betraying his inner child if he sent it.

"I tell you, Pete, not one of those cards describes something that I could be grateful for. I don't have one memory of anything nice she ever said or did for me!" Before long, he was deep into grieving about how little mothering he had received from his mother.

He cried and angered about the scornful look and the sarcastic tone of voice that so characterized his interactions with her. "Why did I have to get such a bad deal from the mothering deck?!"

Towards the end of the session, as often happens with healthy grieving, he felt his flashback resolve and was restored to feeling like he was once again on his own side. The relief of being out of the flashback also allowed his healthy sense of humor to return.

He started riffing: "I'm going to start a greeting card business for people like me. I'm going to make a line of cards for people with dysfunctional mothers. How about this? 'Thanks Mom for never knowing what grade I was in'; or 'Thanks Mom for all the memories of you walking away whenever I was hurting'; or 'Thanks Mom for teaching me how to only notice what was wrong me'; or 'Thanks Mom for teaching me how to frown at myself in self-disgust.'"

Understanding how profoundly derelict your parents were in their duty to nurture and protect you is a master key to your recovery. You will benefit greatly from seeing emotional flashbacks as direct messages from your child-self about how much your parents rejected you. When denial is significantly deconstructed, you will typically feel genuine compassion for the child that you were. This self-compassion assuages emotional neglect by providing you with the missed childhood experience of receiving empathy in painful emotional states instead of contempt or abandonment. This, then, helps you to reverse the childhood-survival habit of automatic self-abandonment. In turn, this can further motivate you to identify and address the many ways you were abused and/or neglected. Chapter 8 of my book, *The Tao of Fully Feeling,* provides detailed guidelines for assessing and remediating your abuse/neglect picture.

Finally, it is an empowering accomplishment to really get the profound significance of childhood emotional neglect. It is often flashback-resolving to realize in the moment that a flashback into bewilderment and hopelessness is an emotional reliving of your childhood trauma. Like nothing else, this can generate a self-protective impulse toward your child-self and your present-time self, kick-starting the process of resolving any given flashback.

CHAPTER

WHAT IS MY TRAUMA TYPE?

This chapter describes a trauma typology for recognizing and recovering from the different types of Cptsd. We human beings respond with some variability to childhood trauma. This model elaborates four basic survival strategies and defensive styles that develop out of our instinctive Fight, Flight, Freeze and Fawn responses.

Variances in your childhood abuse/neglect pattern, birth order and genetics result in you gravitating toward a specific 4F survival strategy. You do this as a child to prevent, escape or ameliorate further traumatization. Fight types develop a narcissistic-like defense. Flight types develop an obsessive/compulsive-like defense. Freeze types develop a dissociative-like defense. Fawn types develop a codependent-like defense.

Healthy Employment of the 4 F's

People who experience "good enough parenting" in childhood arrive in adulthood with a healthy and flexible response repertoire to danger. In the face of real danger, they have appropriate access to all of their 4F choices.

Easy access to the *fight* response insures good boundaries, healthy assertiveness and aggressive self-protectiveness if necessary.

Untraumatized people also easily and appropriately access their *flight* instinct and disengage and retreat when confrontation would exacerbate their danger.

Untraumatized people also *freeze* appropriately and give up and quit struggling when further activity or resistance is futile or counterproductive. Additionally, the freeze response is sometimes our first response to danger, as when we become still, quiet and camouflaged to buy time, to assess the danger and decide whether fight, flight, continued freeze or fawn is our best option.

And finally, untraumatized people also *fawn* in a non-groveling manner and are able to listen, help, and compromise as readily as they assert and express themselves and their needs, rights and points of view. A deeper elaboration of the origins of these four defenses is found below and in the next chapter.

POSITIVE CHARACTERISTICS OF THE FOUR F'S

Fight	Flight	Freeze	Fawn
Assertiveness	Disengagement	Acute awareness	Love & Service
Boundaries	Healthy Retreat	Mindfulness	Compromise
Courage	Industriousness	Poised Readiness	Listening
Moxie	Know-How	Peace	Fairness
Leadership	Perseverance	Presence	Peacemaking

Those who are repetitively traumatized in childhood often learn to survive by over-using one or two of the 4F Reponses. Fixation in any one 4F response not only limits our ability to access all the others, but also severely impairs our ability to relax into an undefended state. Additionally, it strands us in a narrow, impoverished experience of life.

Over time a habitual 4F defense also "serves" to distract us from the nagging voice of the critic and the painful feelings that underlie it. Preoccupation with 4F behaviors dulls our awareness of our unresolved past trauma and the pain of our current alienation.

This chart compares the harmful behaviors of each defensive structure. Real or imagined danger typically triggers us into these roles and behaviors when we are in an emotional flashback.

DETRIMENTAL CHARACTERISTICS OF THE 4F DEFENSES

Fight	Flight	Freeze	Fawn
Narcissistic	Obsessive/Compulsive Dissociative	Codependent	
Explosive	Panicky	Contracting	Obsequious
Controlling	Rushing or worrying	Hiding	Servitude
[Enslaving]	[Outrunning pain]	[Camouflaging]	[Groveling]
Entitlement	Driven-ness	Isolation	Loss of self
Type-A	Adrenaline junkie	Couch Potato	People-pleaser
Bully	Busyholic	Space case	Doormat
Autocrat	Micromanager	Hermit	Slave
Demands	Compelled by	Achievement-	Social
perfection	perfectionism	phobic	perfectionism
Sociopath	Mood disorder[Bipolar] Schizophrenic	D.V. victim	
Conduct disorder	ADHD	ADD	Parentified child

CPTSD AS AN ATTACHMENT DISORDER

Excessive reliance on a fight, flight, freeze or fawn response is the traumatized child's unconscious attempt to cope with constant danger. It is also a strategy to strengthen the illusion that her parents really care about her.

In adult life, all 4F types are commonly ambivalent about real intimacy. This is because closeness often triggers us into painful emotional flashbacks. It reminds us of how we had to survive without comforting connection in childhood. Our 4F defenses therefore offer protection against further re-abandonment by precluding the type of vulnerable relating that leads to deeper bonding.

A survivor also avoids vulnerable relating because his past makes him believe that he will be attacked or abandoned as he was in childhood. This is why showing vulnerability often triggers painful emotional flashbacks.

Many *fight types* avoid real intimacy by alienating others with their angry and controlling demands for unconditional love. This unrealistic demand to have their unmet childhood needs met destroys the possibility of intimacy. Moreover, some fight types delude themselves into believing that they are perfect. They see the other as the one who needs to be perfected. This defensive belief then *entitles* them to totally blame their partners for relationship problems.

Many *flight types* stay perpetually busy and industrious to avoid being triggered by deeper relating. Others also work obsessively to perfect themselves hoping to someday become worthy enough of love. Such flight types have great difficulty showing anything but their perfect persona.

Many *freeze types* hide away in their rooms and reveries fully convinced that the world of relating holds nothing for them. Freeze type who have not been totally turned off relationships by horrible childhood neglect or abuse, gravitate to online relationships.

Online relating can be pursued safely at home with as little contact as desired.

Many *fawn types* avoid emotional investment and potential disappointment by barely showing themselves. They hide behind their helpful personas and over-listen, over-elicit and/or overdo for the other. By over-focusing on their partners, they then do not have to risk real self-exposure and the possibility of deeper level rejection.

This chart compares and contrasts the differences between the four types.

4F DISTORTIONS OF ATTACHMENT AND SAFETY INSTINCTS

Fight	Flight	Freeze	Fawn
Control to connect	Perfect to connect	No way I'll connect	Merge to connect
Rage to be safe	Perfect to be safe	Hide to be safe	Grovel to be safe

Now let us examine each of the 4F defenses more closely with a view toward decreasing our overreliance on them.

THE FIGHT TYPE AND THE NARCISSISTIC DEFENSE

Fight types are unconsciously driven by the belief that power and control can create safety, assuage abandonment and secure love. Children who are spoiled and given insufficient limits [a uniquely painful type of abandonment] can become fight types. Children who are allowed to imitate the bullying of a narcissistic parent may also develop a habitual fight response. Numerous fight types start out as older siblings who over-power their younger siblings just as their parent over-powers them.

Fight types learn to respond to their feelings of abandonment with anger. Many use contempt, a poisonous blend of narcissistic rage and disgust, to intimidate and shame others into mirroring them. Narcissists treat others as if they are as extensions of themselves.

The entitled fight type commonly uses others as an audience for his incessant monologing. He may treat a "captured" freeze or fawn type as a slave in a dominance-submission relationship. The price of admission to a relationship with an extreme narcissist is self-annihilation. One of my clients quipped: "Narcissists don't have relationships; they take prisoners."

The Charming Bully

Especially devolved fight types can become sociopathic. Sociopathy can range along a continuum that stretches from corrupt politician to vicious criminal. A particularly nasty sociopath, who I call the charming bully, probably falls somewhere around the middle of this continuum. The charming bully behaves in a friendly manner some of the time. He can even occasionally listen and be helpful in small amounts, but he still uses his contempt to overpower and control others.

This type typically relies on scapegoats for the dumping of his vitriol. These unfortunate scapegoats are typically weaker than him. They may be members of a disenfranchised group: the "ethnic" employees, the gays, women, his "problem" child or wife, etc. He generally spares his favorites from this behavior, unless they get out of line.

If the charming bully is charismatic enough, those close to him will often fail to register the unconscionable meanness of his scapegoating. The bully's favorites often slip into denial, relieved that they are not the target. Especially charismatic bullies may even be admired and seen as great. Being the scapegoated child or spouse of such a bully is especially problematic because it is so difficult to get anyone to validate that you were or are being abused by them.

———————

I remember how perplexed I used to be at photos of Hitler ostensibly acting kindly to his children. And I think as I write this of how many billionaires are venerated, and how most of them stand up very poorly to closer scrutiny. So many billionaires use sociopathic tactics to accrue their fortunes. Examples of this are hostile takeovers, exploitive labor policies, health destroying work conditions, devastating environmental practices and various other forms of cheating, lying and back-stabbing.

The "great" icon, Henry Ford, would regularly place new young workers at the front of his "innovative" assembly lines. The tired, used-up workers further down the line who could not then keep up were unceremoniously ushered out the back door. Labor unions eventually curtailed that practice in this country, but many jobs have since been exported to unregulated third world countries where workers labor in the same atrocious soul- and body-destroying conditions.

And then, on a much less grand level, I remember a best friend I had in my twenties. I thought he was a great guy for almost two years until one day, shopping in the supermarket with him, I witnessed his demeaning lambasting of an innocent checker just out of sheer spite.

Other Types of Narcissists

Rageaholic narcissists are infamous for using other people as dumping grounds for their anger. They are addicted to the emotional release of catharting in this way. The relief often does not last long before they are looking for another fix of venting their spleen.

This type of narcissism is pure bullying, and bullying alone can cause ptsd. If it goes on long enough as it does with bullying parents in a dysfunctional family, it can cause Cptsd. If this rings a bell with you, please check out www.nobully.com .

Furthermore, and closer to a key theme of this book, I report the evidence of more than a few clients who were horribly abused by their pillar-of-the-community, narcissistic parents. Among them is my suave silent-type father, who regularly raged at and backhanded me and my sisters. He was much admired in our neighborhood.

A final example of narcissism is the charming narcissist who is not necessarily a bully. I call this type *the narcissist in codependent clothing*. My friend's father is this type of charming narcissist. When you meet him, he lures you in with questions and elicitation that make you feel like he is interested in you. But, within a few minutes [once you have taken the bait], he suddenly shifts into monologing like a filibusterer. This particular type often masters the run-on sentence and there is nary a pause to interject or even offer an excuse for escaping. You have become a captive audience and your release will not be procured easily.

Recovering from a Polarized Fight Response

I agree with the widely held notion that extreme narcissists and sociopaths are untreatable. Typically they are convinced that they themselves are perfect and that everyone else the problem.

Fight types who are not true narcissists, however, benefit from understanding the costly price they pay for controlling others with intimidation, criticism and sarcasm. Some who I worked with eventually saw how their aggressive behavior scared away their potential intimates. One survivor also realized that although her partner stayed, he was so afraid and resentful of her demandingness and irritability, that he could not manifest the warmth or real liking that she so desperately desired.

I have also helped a number of fight types understand the downward spiral of power and alienation that comes from being over-controlling. It looks like this: excessive use of power triggers a fearful emotional withdrawal in the other, which makes the fight type feel even more abandoned. In turn, he becomes more outraged and contemptuous, which then further distances his "intimate". This once again increases the fight type's rage and disgust, which then creates increasing distance and the withholding of warmth, ad infinitum.

Fight types benefit from learning to redirect their rage toward the awful childhood circumstances that caused them to adopt such an intimacy-destroying defense. This can help them to deconstruct their habits of instantly morphing abandonment feelings into rage and disgust.

As the recovering fight type becomes more conscious of his abandonment feelings, he can learn to release his fear and shame with tears. I have helped several fight types by guiding them to cry to release their hurt, rather than always polarizing to angering it out. When we are hurt, part of us is sad and part of us is mad, and no amount of angering can ever metabolize our sadness.

———·———

Fight types need to see how their condescending, moral high-ground position alienates others and perpetuates their present time abandonment. They must renounce the illusion of their own perfection and the habit of projecting perfectionistic inner critic processes onto others. This is the work of shrinking the Outer Critic as we will see in chapter 10.

Fight types also benefit from learning to take self-initiated time-outs whenever they notice that they are triggered and feeling over-critical. Timeouts can then be used to redirect the lion's share of their hurt feelings into grieving and working through their original abandonment, rather than displacing it destructively onto current intimates.

Furthermore, like all 4F fixations, fight types need to become more flexible and adaptable in using the other 4F responses. If you are a recovering fight type, it will especially benefit you to learn the empathy response of the fawn position. Begin by trying to imagine how it feels to be the person you are interacting with. Do it as much as you can. Moreover, you can expand on this by developing mindfulness about the needs, rights and feelings of those with whom you would like to have real intimacy.

In early recovery you can "fake it until you make it." For without practicing consideration for the other, and without reciprocity and dialogicality [as opposed to monologing], the intimacy you crave will allude you.

THE FLIGHT TYPE AND THE OBSESSIVE-COMPULSIVE DEFENSE

Extreme flight types are like machines with the switch stuck in the "on" position. They are obsessively and compulsively driven by the unconscious belief that perfection will make them safe and loveable. They rush to achieve. They rush as much in thought [obsession] as they do in action [compulsion].

As children, flight types variably respond to their family trauma on a hyperactive continuum. The flight defense continuum stretches between the extremes of the driven "A" student and the ADHD [Attention Deficit Hyperactive Disorder] dropout running amok. Flight types relentlessly flee the inner pain of their abandonment with the symbolic flight of constant busyness.

Left-Brain Dissociation

When the obsessive/compulsive flight type is not doing, she is worrying and planning about doing. She becomes what John Bradshaw calls a Human Doing [as opposed to a Human Being.] Obsessiveness is left-brain dissociation, as opposed to the classic right-brain dissociation of the freeze type described below.

Left-brain dissociation is using constant thinking to distract yourself from underlying abandonment pain. When thinking is worrying, it is as if underlying fear wafts up and taints the thinking process. Moreover, if compulsivity is hurrying to stay one step ahead of your repressed pain, obsessing is worrying to stay one level above underlying pain.

As a flight type myself, I sometimes find myself obsessively worrying through my outline just before a lecture. I do it, in part, to stay buoyant above my performance anxiety [a subset of my abandonment fear]. In my early days of teaching I would also employ a compulsive defense and pace as I anxiously searched my brain for a missing word. Sometimes I would even scramble frantically through the dictionary or thesaurus to find it. Unconsciously it was like I was searching for a safe place beyond the gravity of my anxiety.

Flight types are also prone to becoming addicted to their own adrenalin. Some recklessly and regularly pursue risky and dangerous activities to jumpstart an adrenalin-high. Flight types are also susceptible to the process addictions of workaholism and busyholism. To keep these processes humming, they can deteriorate into stimulating substance addictions.

Severely traumatized flight types may devolve into obsessive-compulsive disorder [OCD].

Recovering from a Polarized Flight Response

The flight types that I have worked with are so busy trying to stay one step ahead of their pain that introspecting out loud in the therapy hour is the only time they find for self-examination. Learning about the 4F model often helps them to renounce the perfectionistic demands of the inner critic.

I gently and repetitively focus on confronting their denial and minimization about the costs of perfectionism. This is especially important with workaholics who often admit their addiction but secretly hold onto it as a badge of pride and superiority.

Flight types can get "stuck in their head" by being over-analytical. Once a critical mass of understanding Cptsd is achieved, it is crucial for them to start moving into their feelings. Sooner or later, they must deepen their work by grieving about their childhood losses.

Self-compassionate crying is an unparalleled tool for shrinking the obsessive perseverations of the critic, and for ameliorating the habit of compulsive rushing. As her recovery progresses, the flight type can acquire a "gearbox" that allows her to engage life at a variety of speeds, including neutral. Neutral is especially important for flight types to cultivate.

If you are a flight type, there are a plethora of self-help books, CD's and classes that can help you learn to relax and decrease the habit of habitual doing. This is so essential because you can get so lost in busyness, that you have difficulty seeing the forest from the trees. This makes you prone to prioritizing the wrong tasks and getting lost in inessential activities. When I am triggered, I often feel pulled to busy myself with the simplest and easiest tasks, sometimes losing sight of my key responsibilities.

In flashback, flight types can deteriorate into *chicken-with-its-head-cut-off* mode, as fear and anxiety propel them into scattered activity. Spinning their wheels, they can rush about aimlessly, as if motion itself is the only thing important.

At such times the flight type can rescue himself from panicky flight by inverting an old cliché into: "Don't just do something, stand there." And, by stand there I mean stop and take some time to become centered - and to re-prioritize. To accomplish this I recommend three minute, mini-chair meditations. If you are a flight type, you can enhance your recovery greatly by giving yourself a few of these each day. You can start a chair meditation by closing your eyes. Gently ask your body to relax. Feel each of your major muscle groups and softly encourage them to relax. Breathe deeply and slowly.

When you have relaxed your muscles and deepened and slowed your breathing, ask yourself: "What is my most important priority right now? What is the most beneficial thing I can do next?"

As you get more proficient at this and can manage sitting for a longer time, try the question: "What hurt am I running from right now? Can I open my heart to the idea and image of soothing myself in my pain?"

Finally, there are numerous flight types who exhibit symptoms that may be misdiagnosed as Cyclothymia, a minor bipolar disorder. This issue is addressed at length in chapter 12.

THE FREEZE TYPE AND THE DISSOCIATIVE DEFENSE

The freeze response, also known as the camouflage response, often triggers a survivor into hiding, isolating and avoiding human contact. The freeze type can be so frozen in the retreat mode that it seems as if their starter button is stuck in the "off" position.

Of all the 4F's, freeze types seem to have the deepest unconscious belief that people and danger are synonymous. While all 4F types commonly suffer from social anxiety as well, freeze types typically take a great deal more refuge in solitude. Some freeze types completely give up on relating to others and become extremely isolated. Outside of fantasy, many also give up entirely on the possibility of love.

Right-Brain Dissociation

It is often the scapegoat or the most profoundly abandoned child, "the lost child", who is forced to habituate to the freeze response. Not allowed to successfully employ fight, flight or fawn responses, the freeze type's defenses develop around classical or right-brain dissociation. Dissociation allows the freeze type to disconnect from experiencing his abandonment pain, and protects him from risky social interactions - any of which might trigger feelings of being retraumatized.

If you are a freeze type, you may seek refuge and comfort by dissociating in prolonged bouts of sleep, daydreaming, wishing and right-brain-dominant activities like TV, online browsing and video games.

Freeze types sometimes have or appear to have Attention Deficit Disorder [ADD]. They often master the art of changing the internal channel whenever inner experience becomes uncomfortable. When they are especially traumatized or triggered, they may exhibit a schizoid-like detachment from ordinary reality. And in worst case scenarios, they can decompensate into a schizophrenic experience like the main character in the book, *I Never Promised You a Rose Garden*.

Recovering from a Polarized Freeze Response

Recovery for freeze types involves three key challenges.

First, their positive relational experiences are few if any. They are therefore extremely reluctant to enter into the type of intimate relationship that can be transformative. They are even less likely to seek the aid of therapy. Moreover, those who manage to overcome this reluctance often spook easily and quickly terminate.

Second, freeze types have two commonalities with fight types. They are less motivated to try to understand the effects of their childhood traumatization. Many are unaware that they have a troublesome inner critic or that they are in emotional pain. Furthermore, they tend to project the perfectionistic demands of the critic onto others rather than onto themselves. This survival mechanism helped them as children to use the imperfections of others as justification for isolation. In the past, isolation was smart, safety-seeking behavior.

Third, even more than workaholic flight types, freeze types are in denial about the life narrowing consequences of their singular adaptation. Some freeze types that I have worked with seem to have significant periods of contentment with their isolation. I think they may be able to self-medicate by releasing the internal opioids that the animal brain is programmed to release when danger is so great that death seems imminent.

Internal opioid release is more accessible to freeze types because the freeze response has its own continuum that culminates with the collapse response. *The collapse response* is an extreme abandonment of consciousness. It appears to be an out-of-body experience that is the ultimate dissociation. It can sometimes be seen in prey animals that are about to be killed. I have seen nature films of small animals in the jaws of a predator that show it letting go so thoroughly that its death appears to be painless.

However, the opioid production that some freeze types have access to, only takes the survivor so far before its analgesic properties no longer function. Numbed out contentment then morphs into serious depression. This in turn can lead to addictive self-medicating with substances like alcohol, marijuana and narcotics. Alternatively, the freeze type can gravitate toward ever escalating regimens of anti-depressants and anxiolytics. I also suspect that some schizophrenics are extremely traumatized freeze types who dissociate so thoroughly that they cannot find their way back to reality.

Several of my freeze type respondents highly recommend a self-help book by Suzette Boon, entitled *Coping with Trauma-related Dissociation*. This book is filled with very helpful work sheets that are powerful tools for recovering.

More than any other type, the freeze type usually requires a therapeutic relationship, because their isolation prevents them from discovering relational healing through a friendship. That said, I know of some instances where good enough relational healing has come through pets and the safer distant type of human healing that can be found in books and online internet groups.

Phyllis, a self-proclaimed couch potato, began therapy with me with a great deal of ambivalence. Her third brand of anti-depressants no longer worked and her daily pot use was making her increasingly paranoid. Fantasies of dying were becoming more frequent and morbid. She told me: "I know therapy won't help, but I'm afraid my husband is going to leave me. He says I'm starting to scare him."

Phyllis managed being married because her husband paid the bills and left her alone with her TV shows, science fiction books and online browsing. Additionally he was a workaholic, rarely around and gone in the computer when he was home.

In our therapy, trust building was a long gradual back and forth process. This is not un common with many survivors, regardless of their 4F type.

Phyllis's dark sense of humor was a saving grace, and helped her weather my psychoeducation. She frequently met my attempts to link her current suffering and her awful childhood with sarcastic rebuttal. Fortunately, growing up in New York gave me some resilience to sarcasm. I was willing to weather her sardonic sense of humor because there was no mean spiritedness in it.

Eventually I was able to help her direct the angry part of her sarcasm at her bullying family. With that, my psychoeducation finally began to seep in with a ring of truth. She gradually began to angrily vent about her father's sexual abuse, her mother's silent collusion, and all of the family using her for target practice. This in time morphed into crying which rewarded her with her first ever experience of self-compassion.

It was not until we reached this stage, some years into the therapy, that Phyllis got a glimpse of the vicious inner critic that persecuted her. Prior to this she rebuffed my "critic ravings" as absurd. When we progressed sufficiently with the inner critic, the same process occurred with my hypotheses that she had a great deal of underlying fear and anxiety that was keeping her housebound. She laughed with a great deal of ironic amusement: "Look at me, Pete! Nothing scares me. I am so relaxed that I can hardly hold my body up in this chair. Jeez! You know I'm always nodding out. My husband calls me 'Mellow Yellow.'"[Phyllis is blonde].

A breakthrough eventually happened here when she passed a man on the sidewalk outside my office that was a doppelganger for her father. She came into the session on the verge of hyperventilating. As I helped her slow and deepen her breathing, she had a therapeutic flashback in the office. She had a horrifying memory of her father sneaking into her bedroom at night. Much grieving then resolved this particular flashback to her sexual abuse.

Phyllis's denial shrunk significantly in this session. She really "got" that social anxiety was imprisoning her on her couch. Deep level recovery work then ensued from this point in time, and culminated with Phyllis feeling emboldened enough to go back to school. She went on to become a medical assistant. This in turn opened the door to her finding a meaningful place in the outside world. A key part of the meaningfulness was the healthy friendship that she developed with a fellow worker who was also in recovery.

The progression of recovery for a freeze type is often as follows. Gradual trust building allows the recoveree to open to psychoeducation about the role of dreadful parenting in his suffering. This then paves the way for the work of shrinking his critic, which in turn promotes the work of grieving the losses of childhood. The anger work of grieving is especially therapeutic for freeze types as is an aerobic exercise regime. Both help resuscitate the survivor's dormant will and drive.

THE FAWN TYPE AND THE CODEPENDENT DEFENSE

Fawn types seek safety by merging with the wishes, needs and demands of others. They act as if they believe that the price of admission to any relationship is the forfeiture of all their needs, rights, preferences and boundaries.

The disenfranchisement of the fawn type begins in childhood. She learns early that a modicum of safety and attachment can be gained by becoming the helpful and compliant servant of her exploitive parents.

A fawn type/codependent is usually the child of at least one narcissistic parent. The narcissist reverses the parent-child relationship. The child is *parentified* and takes care of the needs of the parent, who acts like a needy and sometimes tantruming child.

When this occurs, the child may be turned into the parent's confidant, substitute spouse, coach, or housekeeper. Or, she may be pressed into service to mother the younger siblings. In worst case scenarios, she may be exploited sexually.

Some codependent children adapt by becoming entertaining. Accordingly, the child learns to be the court jester and is unofficially put in charge of keeping his parent happy.

Pressing a child into codependent service usually involves scaring and shaming him out of developing a sense of self. Of all the 4F types, fawn types are the most developmentally arrested in their healthy sense of self.

Recovering from a Polarized Fawn Response

Fawn types typically respond to psychoeducation about the 4F's with great relief. This eventually helps them to recognize the repetition compulsion that draws them to narcissistic types who exploit them.

The codependent needs to understand how she gives herself away by over-listening to others. Recovery involves shrinking her characteristic listening defense, as well as practicing and broadening her verbal and emotional self-expression.

I have seen numerous inveterate codependents become motivated to work on their assertiveness when they realize that even the thought of saying "no" triggers them into an emotional flashback. After a great deal of work, one client was shocked by how intensely he dissociated when he contemplated confronting his boss's awful behavior. This shock then morphed into an epiphany of outrage about how dangerous it had been to protest anything in his family. This in turn aided him greatly in overcoming his resistance to role-playing assertiveness in our future work together.

With considerable practice, this client learned to overcome the critic voices that immediately short-circuited him from ever asserting himself. In the process, he remembered how he was repeatedly forced to stifle his individuality in childhood. Grieving these losses then helped him to work at reclaiming his developmentally arrested self-expression. Recovering from the fawn position will be explored more extensively in the next chapter.

TRAUMA HYBRIDS

There are, of course, few pure types. Moreover each type is on a continuum that runs from mild to extreme. Most trauma survivors are also hybrids of the 4F's. Most of us have a backup response that we go to when our primary one is not effective enough. When neither of these work, we generally then have a third or fourth "go to" position. Here are some common hybrid types.

The Fight-Fawn Hybrid

The Fight-Fawn type corresponds with the charming bully described earlier. This type combines two opposite polarities of relational style – narcissism and codependence. Narcissistic entitlement, however, is typically at the core of the fight-fawn type. This type, in the extreme, can also be Borderline Personality Disorder [BPD]. She can frequently and dramatically vacillate [split] between a fight and fawn defense. When a fight-fawn type is upset with someone, she can fluctuate over and over between attacking diatribes and fervent declarations of caring in a single interaction.

The fight-fawn is more deeply understood by contrasting him with the *fawn-fight*, described in the next chapter. This fawn-fight type is also subject to vacillating during an emotional flashback, but typically does so with less vitriol and entitlement.

The fight-fawn also differs from the fawn-fight in that his "caretaking" often feels coercive or manipulative. It is frequently aimed at achieving personal agendas which range from blatant to covert. Moreover, the fight-fawn rarely takes any real responsibility for contributing to an interpersonal problem. He typically ends up in the classic fight position of projecting imperfection onto the other. This essentially narcissistic type is also different than the fawn-fight in that entitlement is typically much more ascendant in the fight-fawn. His fawn behavior is typically devoid of real empathy or compassion.

————·•·————

I have worked with several clients who were unfairly labeled borderline by themselves or others. I could however tell by the quality of their hearts, that they were not. This was evidenced by their essential kindness and goodwill to others, which they always return to when the flashback resolves. They also exhibit this in their ability to feel and show true remorse when they hurt another, as we are all destined to do from time to time. Unlike the true borderline who has a narcissistic core, they can sincerely apologize and make amends when appropriate.

Another variant of the fight/fawn is seen in the person who acts like a fight type in one relationship while fawning in another. An example of this is the archetypal henpecked husband who is a tyrant at work, and who also stays at work to all hours because he so prefers the fight stance. This type also occurs in reverse: monster at home and lovely lady at the office.

The Flight-Freeze Hybrid

The Flight-Freeze type is the least relational and most schizoid hybrid. He prefers the safety of do-it-yourself isolationism. Sometimes this type may also be misdiagnosed as Asperger's Syndrome.

The flight-freeze type avoids potential relationship-retraumatization with an obsessive compulsive/dissociative "two-step." Step one is working to complete exhaustion. Step two is collapsing into extreme "veging out", and waiting until his energy reaccumulates enough to relaunch into step one. The price for this type of no-longer-necessary safety is a severely narrowed existence.

The flight-freeze cul-de-sac is more common among men, especially those traumatized for being vulnerable in childhood. This then drives them to seek safety in isolation or "intimacy-lite" relationships.

Some non-alpha type male survivors combine their flight and freeze defenses to become stereotypical technology nerds. Telecommuting is, of course, their preferred mode. Flight-freeze types are the computer addicts who focus on work for long periods of time and then drift off dissociatively into computer games, substance abuse or sleep-bingeing.

Flight-freeze types are prone to becoming porn addicts. When in flight mode, they obsessively surf the net for phantom partners and engage in compulsive masturbation. When in freeze mode, they drift off into a right-brain sexual fantasy world if pornography is unavailable. Moreover, if they are in intimacy-lite relationship, they typically engage more with their idealized fantasy partners than with their actual partner during real time sexual interactions.

The Fight-Freeze Hybrid

These types rarely seek recovery on their own initiative. A colleague of mine told me about a fight-freeze type who was dragged into therapy by his wife. She complained that she was lucky to get ten words out of him in a week. She was at the end of her rope and if therapy did not fix him, she was filing for divorce.

The husband was a computer engineer who telecommuted and only left his home office for bathroom breaks and meals which were eaten separately from his wife. He bullied his wife into providing these meals according to a written schedule that he e-mailed to her.

My colleague's initial "Hello" to the husband was met with a scowl and a grunt. Intuitively, she kept the focus off him as much as possible, but each delicate attempt to make connection with him was rebuffed with sarcastic scorn. "You expect me to fall for that phony smile?"; "You're not gonna shrink me with your psychobabble!"

My colleague, who is the most compassionate, non-intrusive person I know, was not able to crack the prickly fight shell that guarded this poor man's extreme social withdrawal. No miracle was performed, and my colleague said she was amazed in retrospect that he even lasted twenty minutes before he left in a wake of hostility and resentment.

I have met with fight-freeze types a few times in similar circumstances, i.e., they were dragged into therapy under the threat of divorce. Each was like the character in the famous poem: "The Autocrat at the Breakfast Table."

The fight-freeze is a yin or passive narcissist. He demands that things go his way, but he is not much interested in having any human interaction. No one gets to talk at the table, not even him – unless of course someone needs to be put in their place.

The fight-freeze type is a John Wayne couch potato, dominating family life with foul moods and monosyllabic grunts and curses. He is typically as untreatable as the extreme fight types mentioned earlier.

SELF-ASSESSMENT

I recommend that you self-assess your own hierarchical use of the 4F responses. Try to determine your dominant type and hybrid, and think about what percentage of your time is spent in each of the 4F responses.

You can also assess where you lie on the relevant continuums that stretch between the two extremes in each line of the chart below.

Continuums of Positive and Negative 4F Responses

Fight: Assertiveness ◄──► Bullying
Flight: Efficiency ◄──► Driven-ness
Freeze: Peacefulness ◄──► Catatonia
Fawn: Helpfulness ◄──► Servitude

Recovery & Self-Assessment

As stated earlier, a key goal of recovery is to have easy and appropriate access to all of the 4F's. There are also two more continuums that can be used to assess this. The degree to which we are balanced along each of them reflects the degree of our healing.

The Fight ←→ Fawn Continuum of Healthy Relating to Others

Healthy relating occurs when two people move easily and reciprocally between assertiveness and receptivity. Common and important examples of this are an easy back and forth [1] between talking and listening, [2] between helping and being helped, and [3] between leading and following.

Normal healthy narcissism and codependence happen at the midpoint of the continuum. To the degree that I polarize to the narcissistic/fight end of the continuum, I monologue and dominate the conversation. To the degree that I polarize to the codependent/fawn end, I get stuck in a listening defense, hiding from the vulnerability of showing what I think and feel.

Conversations, of course, will not always be exactly in the middle or it would be a Ping-Pong-like exchange of monosyllables. The real balance occurs more over time. For instance, in an hour's conversation, we each generally talk about half the time.

The Flight ←→ Freeze Continuum of Healthy Relating to Self

A healthy relationship with yourself is seen in your ability to move in a balanced way[1] between doing and being, [2] between persistence and letting go, [3] between sympathetic and parasympathetic nervous system activation, and [4] between intense focus and relaxed, daydreamy reverie.

CHAPTER 7

RECOVERING FROM TRAUMA-BASED CODEPENDENCY

If you assessed yourself in the last chapter as a fawn subtype or as being on the right side of the fight ⟵⟶ fawn spectrum, you may find this chapter relevant even if the fawn response is not your primary position. Moreover the first section below contains important information about the origins of all types.

I have dedicated a whole chapter to codependency because it is the 4F trauma response that I know the most about. This knowledge comes from my own personal recovery journey, and from specializing in treating codependency for over two decades.

———

I wrote the gist of this chapter one satori-blessed night when I noticed that I anxiously apologized to a chair that I had bumped into. I think I probably apologized to inanimate objects many times before in my life, but this was the first time I noticed it.

Realizing that I had just apologized to a chair suddenly made me feel enraged. I felt furious that something had happened to me to give me a Pavlovian "I'm sorry" response.

I had been pursuing family of origin exploration for quite some time, and the accumulated evidence quickly convinced me that my parents deeply imprinted me with a fawn response. I was brainwashed with a default program to ingratiatingly apologize when anything in the natural order of things changed around me.

Sudden anxiety responses to apparently innocuous circumstances like my example are often emotional flashbacks to earlier traumatic events. Sometimes a current event can have only the vaguest resemblance to a past traumatic situation, and this can be enough to trigger the psyche's hard-wiring for a fight, flight, freeze or fawn response.

In this case I fawned to the chair, subliminally experiencing it as a dangerous parent and codependently apologizing to it like a toddler anticipating punishment for touching something forbidden. As I free-associated on this I also realized that I was addicted to apologizing. I had apologized for long traffic lights, for changes in the weather, and most especially for other people's mistakes and bad moods.

COMPARING FAWN ORIGINS WITH FIGHT, FLIGHT AND FREEZE ORIGINS

I chose the name fawn for the fourth 'F' in the fight/flight/ freeze/ fawn typology, because according to Webster, it means: "to act servilely; to cringe and flatter". I believe it is this response that is at the core of many codependents' behavior.

As a toddler, the codependent learns quickly that protesting abuse leads to even more frightening parental retaliation. Thus she responds by relinquishing her fight response, deleting "no" from her vocabulary and never developing the language skills of healthy assertiveness.

Moreover, many abusive parents reserve their most harsh punishments for "talking back", and hence ruthlessly extinguish the fight response in their children. Unfortunately, this typically happens at such an early age that they later have little or no memory of it.

The future codependent also learns early on that her natural flight response intensifies her danger if she tries to flee. "I'll teach you to run away from me!" is a common response that precedes the spanking typically awarded to such behavior.

Later, when the child is older she may also learn that the ultimate flight response, running away from home, is hopelessly impractical and even more danger-laden. Traumatizing families, however, seem to be on the rise, as there is an epidemic of children [as young as pre-teens] becoming runaways and ending up in dire circumstances.

Many toddlers, at some point, transmute the flight urge into the running around in circles of hyperactivity. This adaptation "works" on some level to help them escape from the uncontainable feelings of the abandonment mélange. Many of these unfortunates later symbolically run away from their pain. They deteriorate into the obsessive-compulsive adaptations of workaholism, busyholism, spend-aholism, and sex and love addiction that are common in flight types.

The toddler who bypasses the adaptation of the flight defense may drift into developing the freeze response and become the "lost child." This child escapes his fear by slipping more and more deeply into dissociation. He learns to let his parents' verbal and emotional abuse "go in one ear and out the other." It is not uncommon for this type to devolve in adolescence into the numbing substance addictions of pot, alcohol, opiates and other "downers".

The future codependent toddler, however, wisely gives up on the fight, flight and freeze responses. Instead she learns to fawn her way into the occasional safety of being perceived as helpful. It bears repeating that the fawn type is often one of the gifted children that Alice Miller writes about in *The Drama Of The Gifted Child*. She is the precocious one who discovers that a modicum of safety can be purchased by becoming variously useful to her parent.

Servitude, ingratiation, and obsequiousness become important survival strategies. She cleverly forfeits all needs that might inconvenience her parents. She stops having preferences and opinions that might anger them. Boundaries of every kind are surrendered to mollify her parents, who repudiate their duty of caring for her. As we saw in the last chapter, she is often parentified and becomes as thoroughly helpful to the parent as she can.

I wonder how many therapists besides me were prepared for their careers in this way.

All this loss of self begins before the child has many words, and certainly no insight. For the budding codependent, all hints of danger soon immediately trigger servile behaviors and abdication of rights and needs.

These response patterns are so deeply set in the psyche, that as adults, many codependents automatically respond to threat like dogs, symbolically rolling over on their backs, wagging their tails, hoping for a little mercy and an occasional scrap. Webster's second entry for fawn is: "to show friendliness by licking hands, wagging its tail, etc.: said of a dog." I find it tragic that some codependents are as loyal as dogs to even the worst "masters".

Finally, I have noticed that extreme emotional abandonment, as described in chapter 5, also creates this kind of codependency. The severely neglected child experiences extreme lack of connection as traumatic, and sometimes responds to this fearful condition by overdeveloping the fawn response. Once a child realizes that being useful and not requiring anything for herself gets her some positive attention from her parents, codependency begins to grow. It becomes an increasingly automatic habit over the years.

A DEFINITON OF TRAUMA-BASED CODEPENDENCY

More than a few of my clients were initially put off by the term codependent. They found it confusing or irrelevant because the descriptions they read or heard were presented derogatorily. Moreover, some felt that the descriptions did not pertain to their condition. If that is true for you, the section below on codependent subtypes explains how the fawn response can manifest in a variety of different behaviors.

I define trauma-induced codependency as a syndrome of self-abandonment and self-abnegation. Codependency is a fear-based inability to express rights, needs and boundaries in relationship. It is a disorder of assertiveness, characterized by a dormant fight response and a susceptibility to being exploited, abused and/or neglected.

In conversations, codependents seek safety and acceptance in relationship through listening and eliciting. They invite the other to talk rather than risk exposing their thoughts, views, and feelings. They ask questions to keep the attention off themselves, because their parents taught them that talking was dangerous and that their words were indictments that would inevitably prove them guilty of being unworthy.

The implicit code of the fawn type is that it is safer [1] to listen than to talk, [2] to agree than to dissent, [3] to offer care than to ask for help, [4] to elicit the other than to express yourself and [5] to leave choices to the other rather than to express preferences. Sadly, the closest that the unrecovered fawn type comes to getting his needs met is vicariously through helping others. Fawn types generally enhance their recovery by memorizing the list of Human Rights in Toolbox 2, chapter 16.

I have this sardonic fantasy about two codependents going on their first date. Somehow they have agreed that they want to go to a movie, but how will they ever choose which one? "What do you want to see?" "Oh, I'm easy what do you want to see?" "It really doesn't matter to me, I like everything." 'Me too why don't you choose?" "Oh I think it would be much better if you pick." "Oh I couldn't, I never pick the right one." "Me too, but I'm sure my pick would definitely be the worst." And so it goes, ad infinitum, until it is too late to see any show, and relieved at not having to put themselves out there, they call it a night.

CODEPENDENT SUBTYPES

I think a certain amount of the confusion about codependency can be clarified through understanding the significant differences found in the three codependent subtypes that follow: fawn-freeze, fawn-flight and fawn-fight.

Fawn-Freeze: The Scapegoat

The fawn-freeze is typically the most codependently entrenched subtype. Not all scapegoats are fawn-freeze, but since fawn and freeze types are both prone to extreme self-denial, many end up in a scapegoat position.

This is also because these are the two most passive of the four F's. They have both typically suffered the most punishment or rejection for asserting themselves in the toddler stage.

When the fawn-freeze is not able to escape the scapegoat role in childhood, she is then set up to be similarly victimized in adulthood.

In worst case scenarios fawn-freezes are easily recognized by fight types who take them captive. They may then turn them into doormats and subject them to domestic violence [DV]. Sometimes, the fawn-freeze does not even recognize that she is being abused. Other times she blames herself [as she had to in childhood].

Moreover, as we know from studying the DV cycle, many narcissistic abusers know when and how to shower romantic tidbits on their victims just when they are at the point of leaving. These narcissists are often the charming bullies described in the last chapter. Their infrequent tidbits have more warmth in them than anything the codependent received at home, so she quickly becomes rehooked, and just as quickly the cycle of abuse begins again.

It is important to note that many charming bullies also offer copious tidbits briefly in the courtship stage, but these peter out to near starvation rations once the entrapment is complete.

Many fawn-freeze types only make token efforts at recovery, if they do not avoid it altogether. Often fawn-freezes were forced to so thoroughly abandon their protective instincts that they become trapped in what psychologists call *learned helplessness*.

Finally, there is growing evidence that a significant number of men also silently suffer domestic violence. A male client once told me that no matter how much his wife assaulted him, he couldn't stop himself from saying "I'm sorry" to her. This only made her madder, but not as mad as when he flashbacked into saying: "I'm sorry for saying 'I'm sorry' ", even though his wife would slap him in the face every time he did.

Not surprisingly, further investigation revealed a borderline mother who still slaps him in the face when she is displeased with him. As a child he was required to keep his hands down whenever she slapped him. He then had to apologize for making her "have to" punish him. Unfortunately, he left therapy after only a few sessions because his wife looked in his checkbook, and then hit him repeatedly for "wasting his time and her money."

I have worked a great deal with these fawn-freeze types in my years of doing telephone crisis counseling. Hope for them lies in understanding how their childhood abuse set them up for their current abuse. This is often difficult, because scapegoated fawn-freezes were often punished extra intensely for complaining.

Numerous times I have heard DV victims say: "But, I don't want to act like a victim!" Usually, I then try to help them see how much they truly were victims in childhood. However, if I cannot get them to see this they usually are not able to rescue themselves from their current victimization.

Fawn-Flight: Super Nurse

The fawn-flight type is most typically seen in the busyholic parent, nurse or administrative assistant who works from dawn until bed-time providing for the needs of the household, hospital or company. He compulsively takes care of everyone else's needs with hardly a gesture toward his own.

The fawn-flight is sometimes a misguided Mother Teresa type, who escapes the pain of her self-abandonment by seeing herself as the perfect, selfless caregiver. She further distances herself from her own pain by obsessive-compulsively rushing from one person in need to another.

Some fawn-flight clients also become OCD-like clean-aholics. One of my interns told me that her fawn-flight client had a dozen color-coded tooth brushes for various micro-cleaning tasks in her family's bathroom and kitchen.

Some fawn-flights project their perfectionism on others. They can appoint themselves as honorary advisers, and overburden oth-ers with their advice. However, it behooves fawn-flights to learn that caring is not always about fixing. This is especially true when the person we are trying to help is in emotional pain. Many times all that person needs is empathy, acceptance and an opportunity to verbally ventilate. Moreover some mood states also need time to resolve. Loving people when they are feeling bad is a powerful kind of caring.

The above also relates to allowing others to be imperfect. We all have minor limitations and foibles that may not be transformable. Loved ones need to be spared from being pressured to fix what is unfixable. My way of approaching this is to always frame my advice as take-it or leave-it. To prove this is so, I refrain from then going on about it repetitively. Additionally, I typically check in first to see if the other person actually wants some feedback.

Fawn-Fight: Smother Mother

The recommendations in the last two paragraphs also apply to many of those survivors who are fawn-fight types. Some can be quite aggressive in their attempts to help others. Typically they equate helping with changing, and can alienate others by persistently pressuring them to take their advice.

The fawn-fight type is the smother-love caretaker. Her caretaking approach of being over-focused on the other is sometimes a repetition of her childhood servant role. Moreover, her helpfulness is usually less self-serving than the fight-fawn that we discussed in the last chapter. Nonetheless, the zealousness of her caretaking sometimes makes the recipient believe it when she says "I just love you to death."

In flashback, the fawn-fight can deteriorate into manipulative or even coercive care-taking. He can smother love the other into conforming to his view of who she should be.

Fawn-fight types may periodically reach a critical mass of frustration that erupts when the "patient" refuses his advice or balks at his unwanted caretaking. Sometimes the fawn-fight feels an entitlement to punish the other "for their own good", especially in a primary relationship.

The fawn-fight is sometimes misdiagnosed as borderline personality disorder [BPD]. This is because the fawn-fight can be emotionally intense during flashbacks. When triggered into a panicky sense of abandonment, he feels desperate for love and can vacillate dramatically between clawing for it or flatteringly groveling for it. He does not however have the core narcissism of the true borderline that we looked at in the previous chapter.

Another distinction between these two types is that fawn-fight type seeks real intimacy. She is the most relational hybrid and most susceptible to love addiction. She stands in contradistinction to the fight-fawn who is more addicted to physical release, and hence more susceptible to sex addiction.

MORE ON RECOVERING FROM A POLARIZED FAWN RESPONSE

Psychoeducation about their parents' role in creating their fawn response has helped many of my clients. Many instantly grasped that their codependence comes from having been continuously attacked and shamed as selfish for even the most basic level of healthy self-interest.

One fortyish client estimated that she had scorned herself as "selfish" countless times, until one night she had the epiphany that she was by far not selfish enough. This occurred while she was reading the comments of respondents to a website for adult children of narcissistic mothers [www.narcissisticmothers.org]. Suddenly she realized that her mother was the one with a monopoly on self-interest in her family. My client then realized that every time she thought of doing something for herself, she not only felt very anxious, but also ashamed that she was acting as ghastly as her mother.

Fawns need to understand that fear of being attacked for lapses in ingratiation causes them to forfeit their boundaries, rights and needs. Understanding this dynamic is a necessary but not sufficient step in recovery. There are many codependents who realize their penchant for forfeiting themselves, but who instantly forget everything they know when self-assertion is appropriate in their relationships.

In early recovery, I became increasingly aware in new dating situations of how much I was over-eliciting my date. Eventually, I was struck by how little I had to say for myself, but I found it very difficult to break the pattern.

Over time, I realized that my intention to be more forthcoming was frightening me into a flashback. This made me dissociate and forget everything I had planned to say. All I could think to do, when an amygdala hijacking took my left-brain off line, was to get my date talking. I then regressed to the tried and true safety position of listening and eliciting.

It wasn't until my therapist recommended that I write down some key words on my palm that I began to master the situation. Looking at the words brought my left-brain back online, and I gradually got better at holding up my end of the getting-to-know-you conversation.

Much later, I had the realization: "No wonder I wind up with one narcissist after another. Narcissists love me because I am so enabling of their monologing. I probably met lots of nice balanced people who did not want another date with me because it seemed like I was hiding and hard to get to know."

Around this time I also had a fawn type friend who had the same problem. She liked to joke that her listening and eliciting defenses where so perfected that she could turn anyone, even a blank-screen therapist, into a monologing narcissist.

To break free of their codependence, survivors must learn to stay present to the fear that triggers the self-abdication of the fawn response. In the face of their fear, they must try on and practice an expanding repertoire of more functional responses to fear. [See the flashback management steps in the next chapter]

Facing the Fear of Self-Disclosure

Real motivation for surmounting this challenge usually comes from family of origin work. We need to intuit and puzzle together a detailed picture of the trauma that first frightened us out of our instincts of healthy self-expression.

When we emotionally remember how overpowered we were as children, we can begin to realize that it was because we were too small and powerless to assert ourselves. But now in our adult bodies, we are in a much more powerful situation.

And even though we might still momentarily feel small and helpless when we are triggered, we can learn to remind ourselves that we are now in an adult body. We have an adult status that now offers us many more resources to champion ourselves and to effectively protest unfairness in relationships.

Grieving through Codependence

I usually find that deconstructing codependence involves a considerable amount of grieving. Typically this entails many tears about the loss and pain of being so long without healthy self-interest and self-protection. Grieving also unlocks healthy anger about a life lived with such a diminished sense of self.

This anger can then be used to build a healthy fight response. Once again, the fight response is the basis of the instinct of self-protection, of balanced assertiveness, and of the courage that is needed to make relationships equal and reciprocal.

Later Stage Recovery

To facilitate the reclaiming of assertiveness, I encourage the survivor to imagine herself confronting a current or past unfairness. This type of role-playing is often delicate work, as it can invoke a therapeutic flashback that brings up old fear.

As the survivor learns to stay present in assertiveness role-plays, she becomes more aware of how fear triggers her into fawning. She can then practice staying present to her fear and acting assertively anyway.

With enough practice she then heals the developmental arrest of not having learned "to feel the fear and do it anyway." This in turn sets the stage for deconstructing self-harmful reactions to fear like giving or compromising too much. Moreover, it makes the survivor more adept at flashback management.

As later stage recovery progresses, the survivor increasingly "knows her own mind". She slowly dissolves the habit of reflexively agreeing with other people's preferences and opinions. She more easily expresses her own point of view and makes her own choices. And most importantly, she learns to stay inside herself.

Many fawns survived by *constantly* focusing their awareness on their parents to figure out what was needed to appease them. Some became almost psychic in their ability to read their parents moods and expectations. This then helped them to figure out the best response to neutralize parental danger. For some, it even occasionally won them some approval.

Survivors now need to deconstruct this habit by working to stay more inside their own experience without constantly projecting their attention outward to read others. Fawn-types who are still habituated to people-pleasing, must work on reducing their ingratiating behaviors. I have noticed over the years that the degree to which a survivor strains to please me reflects the degree to which his parents were dangerous.

Recovering requires us to become increasingly mindful of our automatic matching and mirroring behaviors. This helps us decrease the habit of reflexively agreeing with everything that anyone says.

It is a great accomplishment to significantly reduce verbal matching. It is an even more powerful achievement to reduce inauthentic emotional mirroring.

Dysfunctional emotional matching is seen in behaviors such as acting amused at destructive sarcasm, acting loving when someone is punishing, and acting forgiving when someone is repetitively hurtful.

I call this emotional individuation work. As such, recovery involves setting the kind of boundaries that help us to stay true to our own actual emotional experience.

In advanced recovery, this occurs when we reduce the habit of automatically shifting our mood to match someone else's emotional state. By this, I do not mean suppressing empathic attunement when it is genuine. Crying and laughing along with an intimate is a truly wonderful experience.

Rather, what I am recommending here is resisting the pressure to pretend you are always feeling the same as someone else. You do not have to laugh when something is not funny. When a friend is feeling bad, you do not have to act like you feel bad. When you are feeling bad, you do not have to act like you feel happy.

Thankfully, I learned a great deal about this from being a therapist. When my client is depressed, it does not help him if I adjust my mood and act depressed.

Yet I am always genuinely empathic toward my client's depression, because I can put myself in his shoes via my own experiences of depression. I can be there caringly for him without abandoning my own feeling of contentment in the moment.

Similarly I can be feeling depressed while you are enthused about something and genuinely appreciate your happiness without shamefully abandoning my temporarily depressed self.

Here is another example of this. You are in a great mood and tell me that you loved this old musical that you just saw. I, however, am feeling down and dislike old musicals. If I were a fight type, the table would be set for a great deal of mutual alienation.

If I were an unrecovered fawn type, however, I might strangle my bad mood and my musical taste, and anxiously squeeze out a high-pitched, forced frivolity about how wonderful Fred Astaire is. Instead, I can reach for a deeper more authentic truth. I can let you know that I am pleased you had such a nice time. After all, I really believe in different strokes for different folks.

As I write this, I flash on Bruno, a dear old hospice client of mine. During a visit, with him, he told me: "I can't stand talking to that new volunteer. She acts so morose whenever she visits me. I mean, who the hell's dying here... me or her? I tell ya I don't know who is worse – her or that other smiley volunteer, the one who always acts like she just walked into Disneyland."

"Disapproval is Okay with Me"

Early in recovery, an esteemed mentor gave me the affirmation "Disapproval is okay with me." Codependently, I enthusiastically welcomed his advice that I should practice it until it was true. Privately I thought "Surely you jest!" I had survived the previous thirty years with a Will Rogers-like mission to prove that "I never met a man I didn't like."

I did not yet know that I had unconsciously gravitated to this all-or-none nonsense because I was somewhat desperately trying to seduce everyone I met into liking me in the hope that I could finally feel safe.

As I thought further about this affirmation, I judged it as patently absurd and eminently unachievable. Yet within a week something ignited in me that really wanted it to become true.

Since it was still a long time before I knew anything about code-pendence, it took almost two decades to make any progress at all. The importance of learning to handle and accept disapproval faded in and out of my awareness myriad times.

But now as I write thirty years later, I feel it is one of the most important things I have ever learned. I rest most of the time in receiving so much approval from my friends and intimates that I can usually let in their constructive feedback fairly easily. As a corollary to this, I rarely care what people think about me who I do not know or who do not know me.

And, of course, this is not a perfect accomplishment. Disapproval can still on occasion trigger me into a flashback. But it delights me to report that I now experience most disapproval with considerable equanimity. I even occasionally experience some people's disapproval as a good thing. Sometimes it is a validation that I am doing the right thing and evolving in the right direction. Nowhere is this truer than with the disapproval of the narcissistic parents or partners of clients whom I am working to rescue from their enslavement. Their disapproval of me is actually an affirmation that I have indeed been involved in right action.

Most of the time, disapproval *is* okay with me.

CHAPTER 8

MANAGING EMOTIONAL FLASHBACKS

Emotional flashbacks are intensely disturbing regressions ["amygdala hijackings"] to the overwhelming feeling-states of your childhood abandonment. When you are stuck in a flashback, fear, shame and/or depression can dominate your experience.

These are some common experiences of being in an emotional flashback. You feel little, fragile and helpless. Everything feels too hard. Life is too scary. Being seen feels excruciatingly vulnerable. Your battery seems to be dead. In the worst flashbacks an apocalypse feels like it will imminently be upon you.

When you are trapped in a flashback, you are reliving the worst emotional times of you childhood. Everything feels overwhelming and confusing, especially because there are rarely any visual components to a Cptsd flashback. This is because, as Goleman's work shows, *amygdala hijackings* are intense reactions in the emotional memory part of the brain that override the rational brain. These reactions occur in the brains of people who have been triggered into a 4F reaction so often, that minor events can now trigger them into a panicky state.

—·—

This is a list of 13 practical steps for helping yourself to manage an emotional flashback:

13 Steps for Managing Emotional Flashbacks
[Focus on Bold Print when flashback is active]

1. **Say to yourself: "I am having a flashback".** Flashbacks take you into a timeless part of the psyche that feels as helpless, hopeless and surrounded by danger as you were in childhood. The feelings and sensations you are experiencing are past memories that cannot hurt you now.

2. **Remind yourself: "I feel afraid but I am not in danger! I am safe now, here in the present."** Remember you are now in the safety of the present, far from the danger of the past.

3. **Own your right/need to have boundaries.** Remind yourself that you do not have to allow anyone to mistreat you; you are free to leave dangerous situations and protest unfair behavior.

4. **Speak reassuringly to the Inner Child.** The child needs to know that you love her/him unconditionally– that s/he can come to you for comfort and protection when s/he feels lost and scared.

5. **Deconstruct eternity thinking.** In childhood, fear and abandonment felt endless – a safer future was unimaginable. Remember this flashback will pass as it always has before.

6. **Remind yourself that you are in an adult body** with allies, skills and resources to protect you that you never had as a child. [Feeling small and fragile is a sign of a flashback.]

7. **Ease back into your body**. Fear launches you into "heady" worrying, or numbing and spacing out.

    [a] **Gently ask your body to Relax**: feel each of your major muscle groups and softly encourage them to relax. [Tightened muscles send false danger signals to your brain.]

    [b] **Breathe deeply and slowly**. [Holding your breath also signals danger.]

    [c] **Slow down**: rushing presses your brain's flight response button.

    [d] **Find a safe place** to unwind and soothe yourself: wrap yourself in a blanket, hold a pillow or a stuffed animal, lie down on your bed or in a closet or in a bath; take a nap.

    [e] **Feel the fear in your body without reacting to it**. Fear is just an energy in your body. It cannot hurt you if you do not run from it.

8. **Resist the Inner Critic's Drasticizing and Catastrophizing**.

    [a] **Use thought-stopping** to halt the critic's endless exaggerations of danger, and its constant planning to control the uncontrollable. Refuse to shame, hate or abandon yourself. Channel the anger of self- attack into saying "NO" to your critic's unfair self-criticism.

    [b] **Use Thought-substitution & Thought-correction** to replace negative thinking with a memorized list of your qualities and accomplishments.

9. **Allow yourself to grieve**. Flashbacks are opportunities to release old, unexpressed feelings of fear, hurt, and abandonment. Validate and soothe your child's past experience of helplessness and hopelessness. Healthy grieving can

turn your tears into self-compassion and your anger into self-protection.

10. **Cultivate safe relationships and seek support**. Take time alone when you need it, but don't let shame isolate you. Feeling shame doesn't mean you are shameful. Educate your intimates about flashbacks and ask them to help you talk and feel your way through them.

11. **Learn to identify the types of triggers that lead to flashbacks**. Avoid unsafe people, places, activities and triggering mental processes. Practice preventive maintenance with these steps when triggering situations are unavoidable.

12. **Figure out what you are flashing back to.** Flashbacks are opportunities to discover, validate and heal your wounds from past abuse and abandonment. They also point to your still unmet developmental needs and can provide you with motivation to get them met.

13. **Be patient with a slow recovery process**. It takes time in the present to become de-adrenalized, and considerable time in the future to gradually decrease the intensity, duration and frequency of flashbacks. Real recovery is a gradually progressive process [often two steps forward, one step back], not an attained salvation fantasy. Don't beat yourself up for having a flashback.

My clients, who post this somewhere conspicuous until they memorize the gist of it, typically progress more rapidly in their recovery. You can easily print out a copy from the "13 Steps" page of my website: www.pete-walker.com.

Triggers and Emotional Flashbacks

A trigger is an external or internal stimulus that activates us into an emotional flashback. This often occurs on a subliminal level outside the boundaries of normal consciousness. Recognizing what triggers us can therefore be difficult. Nonetheless, becoming increasingly mindful of our triggers is crucial because it sometimes allows us to avoid flashback-inducing people, situations and behaviors.

External triggers are people, places, things, events, facial expressions, styles of communication, etc., that remind us of our original trauma in a way that flashes us back into the painful feelings of those times. Here are some examples of powerful and common triggers: revisiting your parents; seeing someone who resembles a childhood abuser; experiencing the anniversary of an especially traumatic event; hearing someone use a parent's shaming tone of voice or turn of phrase.

Many triggers however are not so explicit. Sometimes all unknown adults can trigger us into fear even when there is no resemblance to our original abuser[s]. I still occasionally feel triggered when I come across a group of teenagers, because I grew up in a neighborhood where there were many violent ones. For this reason, my son who is quite empathic joked that he will not become a teenager when he grows up.

Sometimes someone looking at us, or even noticing us, can trigger us into fear and toxic shame. One of my clients once came in intensely triggered because a cat was staring at him. Other common triggers include making a mistake, asking for help, or having to speak in front of a group of people. Moreover, simply feeling tired, sick, lonely or hungry can sometimes trigger a flashback. Any type of physical pain can also be a trigger.

For many survivors, authority figures are the ultimate triggers. I have known several survivors, who have never gotten so much as a parking ticket, who cringe in anxiety whenever they come across a policeman or a police car.

It took me decades to overcome my intense performance anxiety about teaching. Nothing could trigger me more than an upcoming teaching engagement. Fortunately I was unwilling to give up this activity, because I enjoyed it most of the time once I got going. I did not make any real progress, beyond learning to "white-knuckle it," until I recognized my performance anxiety as a flashback to the danger of talking at family dinner time. This recognition allowed me to see that I was unconsciously terrified that my parents were going to show up and scoff at me in public.

At first, I [my critic] labeled this a preposterous idea, but when I started to imagine and practice aggressively defending myself against them on the drive to my teaching engagement, I soon experienced an enormous reduction in my anxiety. This experience lead to me formulating Step 6 in the flashback management steps above, as well as my ideas about angering against the critic, which will be explored in the next chapter.

The Look: A Common Trigger of Emotional Flashbacks

Early on in working with this model, I was surprised that certain clients with relatively moderate childhood abuse were plagued by emotional flashbacks. Most of them in fact were quite sure that they had never even been hit. Many of them however would talk about how they hated it when their parents gave them the look.

The look, in most cases, is the facial expression that typically accompanies contempt. Contempt is a powerful punishing visage backed up by an emotional force-field of intimidation and disgust. A raised voice can be added intermittently to the look to amp up its power.

When a parent gives the look to a child, she is "telling" him that he is not only in serious jeopardy, but that he is also "a sorry excuse for a human being". Over time, the look can make the recipient feel terrified and repugnant, as it drives him into an emotional flashback of fear and shame.

When the look is used to control an older child, it commonly flashes her back to an earlier, pre-memory time when the look was empowered by traumatizing punishment. The look rarely terrifies a child into obedience unless it has previously been paired with hitting or other dire consequences. Years of working at Parental Stress Services convinced me that most young children ignore the look unless it was previously accompanied by traumatizing punishment.

Typically, the look is empowered via a psychological process called *conditioning*. Here is a classic example of aversive conditioning. Technicians deliver an electric shock to an animal in a cage at the same time that they ring a bell. The animal of course has a fearful and distressed response to the shock. It does not, however, take many repetitions of pairing the sound with the shock before the sound alone elicits the same upset response in the animal.

This is analogous, I believe, to how a child learns to be terrified of the look. With enough pairings of the look with physical punishment or extreme abandonment, the parent can eventually delete the smack and get the same results with just the look. With enough repetitions in early childhood, this pairing can last a lifetime, so that the parent can control the child forever with the look. In my hospice work, I have seen several dying, ninety-pound mothers still able to put the fear of god into their huge sons with the look.

The look then is a powerful trigger for making adult survivors flashback to the fear and humiliation of their childhoods. Once again, many of my clients do not remember this because the punishment only had to accompany the look for a few months while they were toddlers before it became permanently wired as a trigger. Moreover, it is the rare person who has any memory before he is three or four years old.

Unfortunately the look can continue to work even after the parent dies. There are at least two reasons for this.

First, we internalize our parents in a way that they can subliminally appear in our imaginations and give us the look whenever we are less than perfect. This includes "imperfections" in thought, feeling or action.

Sadly, I often see this subliminal look mimicked on the faces of my flashbacked clients as they scowl contemptuously at themselves.

And second, when anyone else looks at us disapprovingly, we can generalize that they are as dangerous as our parents. This is what happened to me in the emotional flashback that I described in chapter 1.

The worst thing about having been traumatized with the look in childhood is that we can erroneously transfer and project our memory of it onto other people when we are triggered. We are especially prone to doing this with authority figures or people that resemble our parents, even when they are not sporting the look.

Internal vs. External triggers

As we move out of early recovery, we begin to observe that internal triggers are even more common than external ones. Such triggers are commonly the nasty spawn of the inner critic. Typically they are thoughts and visualizations about endangerment or the need for perfection. The survivor may, seemingly without reason, visualize someone being abusive. Moreover he can also, seemingly out of the blue, worry himself into a flashback by simply thinking he is not perfectly executing a task that he is undertaking. He can also frighten himself by enumerating the many ways that he might mess up any upcoming task.

When internal triggering is at its worst, small potato miscues and peccadilloes trigger us into a full blown emotional flashback. We then devolve into a polarized process of *negative-noticing* – an incessant preoccupation with defects and hazards. We perseverate about everything that has gone or could go wrong.

As recovery progresses, many survivors are shocked to discover that the majority of their flashbacks are triggered internally by these types of inner critic programs. We will explore below and in the next two chapters the ways we can rescue ourselves from the critic's internal triggering processes.

Progressive Trigger-Recognition

With ongoing recovery, we become more knowledgeable about our triggers, and avoid them when practical. Identifying our triggers also helps us to get into flashback management mode more quickly.

Recognition further aids us to handle unavoidable triggering situations. Forethought allows us to prophylactically practice flashback management before we get activated, as I did in the performance anxiety situation mentioned earlier.

Recognizing the moment of triggering is even more important than recognizing the trigger itself. This is because flashbacks sometimes start out subtly and then progressively become more intense. Early recognition therefore helps us to invoke the steps earlier, and decrease the intensity and duration of the flashback.

Finally, resolving a flashback requires rebalancing significant biochemical changes in the brain and body that take time to subside. For example, over-adrenalization sometimes dramatically morphs into the hangover of adrenalin exhaustion, before the adrenal function can be rebalanced. Decreasing the intensity of a flashback with quick remedial action decreases the time it takes for our physiology to recover.

Signs of Being in a Flashback

We can often find ourselves in a flashback without ever having seen the "flash." There are a variety of clues that we can learn to identify as signs that we are caught in a flashback. This is essential to recovery, as naming our experience "flashback" [step#1 in flashback management] often immediately brings some relief. Even more importantly, it points us in the direction of working the other 12 steps of flashback management.

One common sign of being flashed-back is that we feel small, helpless, and hopeless. In intense flashbacks this magnifies into feeling so ashamed that we are loath to go out or show our face anywhere. Feeling fragile, on edge, delicate and easily crushable is another aspect of this. The survivor may also notice an evaporation of whatever self-esteem he has earned since he left home. This is a flashback to the childhood years where implicit family rules forbade any self-esteem at all.

Another common clue that we are flashing back is an increase in the virulence of the inner or outer critic. This typically looks like increased drasticizing and catastrophizing, as well as intensified self-criticism or judgmentalness of others. A very common example of this is lapsing into extremely polarized, all-or-none thinking such as only being able to see what is wrong with yourself and/or others.

In my own mid-level recovery, I learned that when I was feeling especially judgmental of others, it usually meant that I had flashed back to being around my critical parents. The trigger was usually that some vulnerability of mine was in ascendancy. In response, I then over-noticed others' faults so that I could justify avoiding them and the embarrassment of being seen in a state of not being shiny enough.

Another clue that we are in a flashback occurs when we notice that our emotional reactions are out of proportion to what has triggered them. Here are two common instances of this: [1] a minor upset feels like an emergency; [2] a minor unfairness feels like a travesty of justice.

In the first instance, you drop a book that you are carrying and launch into an angry, self-berating tirade that lingers for hours. In the second instance, another driver's relatively harmless, un-signaled lane change triggers you into rageful indignation that reverberates in your psyche for hours.

When we are not mindful at such times, we can erupt against ourselves in self-disgust and self-hatred, or we can unfairly explode out against the relatively innocent other.

On the other hand, we can choose healthy flashback management once we recognize these examples as flashbacks to the real emergencies and injustices of our childhood. Furthermore, we can harvest recovery out of these unpleasant flashbacks by seeing them as proof that we were traumatized. When we do the latter, we can morph our anger into healthy indignation about the outrageously unfair conditions of our upbringing.

More on Self-Medication

Another clue about being in a flashback is an increased use of primitive self-soothing techniques. Many survivors learn early in life to manage their painful feelings with food, distracting activities or mood-altering substances. Over time self-medication can become habitual and devolve into substance or process addictions.

With self-medication, I believe there is a continuum of severity that stretches from occasional use on one end to true addiction on the other. For many survivors, self-medication is a matter of degree. An especially strong urge to use more substance or process than normal is a powerful clue that you are in a flashback. With practice, mindfully noticing a sudden upsurge in craving can be interpreted as the need to invoke the flashback management steps. Moreover, I see many survivors gradually decrease their self-medicating habits by effectively using these steps.

Flashbacks in Therapy Sessions

This section is for survivors who are in therapy or contemplating starting it. Over the years, I have noticed that as survivors feel safe enough with me, opportunities arise more frequently for working with flashbacks during sessions. Sometimes it even seems that some part of them "schedules" their flashbacks to occur just prior to or during our session. It is as if they are looking for "on the job training" in flashback management. Some therapists describe this as regression in the service of building the healthy ego.

I recently experienced this with a client who rushed into my office five minutes late, visibly flushed and anxious. She opened the session by exclaiming: "I'm such a loser. I can't do anything right. You must be sick of working with me." This was someone who had, on previous occasions, been moved by my validation of her ongoing accomplishments in our work.

Based on what she had uncovered about her mother's punitive perfectionism in previous sessions, I was certain that being late had triggered her into an emotional flashback. In this moment, she was experiencing right-brain emotional dominance and a decrease in left-brain rational thinking. As so often happens in a flashback, she temporarily lost access to her post-childhood knowledge and understanding. This appears to be a mechanism of dissociation, and in this instance, it rendered my client amnesiac of my high regard for our work together.

I believe this type of dissociation also accounts for the recurring disappearance of previously established trust that commonly occurs with emotional flashbacks. As we progress in our recovery, we learn that flashbacks can cause us to forget that our proven allies are in fact still reliable. With enough practice, however, we can learn to interpret feelings of distrust with proven friends as evidence that we are in a flashback. We are flashing back to our childhoods when no one was trustworthy.

Grieving Resolves Flashback [Step # 9]

Returning to the above vignette, I wondered out loud to my client, "Do you think you might be in a flashback?" Because of the numerous times we had previously identified her emotional upsets as flashbacks, she immediately recognized this and let go into deep sobbing. She dropped into profound grieving.

Her crying combined tears of relief with tears of grief. Her tears of relief came from being able to take in my empathy. Her tears of grief were the feelings of her abject childhood pain being released. Her tears of relief also came from once again remembering the source of this previously confusing and overwhelming pain.

My client continued to cry and released more of the pain of her original trauma. Further tears were about being stuck so often in flashbacks. As her tears subsided, she recalled a time as a small child when she literally received a single lump of coal in her Christmas stocking. Mean mom had "scrooged" her as punishment for being ten minutes late to dinner. Her tears then morphed into healthy anger about this abuse, and she felt herself returning to an empowered sense of self. Grieving brought her back into the present and broke the amnesia of the flashback.

She then remembered to invoke her instinct of self-protection. We had gradually been rebuilding it with role-plays and assertiveness training. She angrily vented about her parents' destruction of her right to defend herself against abuse and unfairness. She started cheekily chanting "That's not fair!" as if to show her parents they could no longer attack her for saying it.

She then moved further into reiterating her right to have boundaries. She mocked mom and dad as poor excuses for parents. And then she turned her anger onto the critic with a resounding refrain of saying "no". "No, you cannot judge me. No, you cannot pick me apart anymore. No you cannot waste my time with all your stupid worries!"

Finally, I reminded her to reinvoke her sense of safety by recognizing that she now inhabited an adult body. She was now free of parental control. She had many resources to draw on: intelligence, strength, resilience, and a growing sense of community. She lived in a safe home. She had the support of her therapist and two friends who were her allies and who readily saw her essential worth.

I also observed that she was making ongoing progress in managing her flashbacks which were occurring less often and less intensely.

After about forty minutes, she was released from the flashback. I have witnessed this restorative power of grieving on innumerable occasions. The intricacies of therapeutic grieving will be explored in chapter 11.

Managing the Inner Critic [Step # 8]

When Cptsd survivors come of age and launch from the traumatizing family, they are often unaware that their minds are dominated by an inner critic. In assisting others to manage flashbacks, the most common help I offer is to encourage them to challenge the alarmist and perfectionistic programming of the inner critic.

This type of scenario arises frequently in my practice. A client, in the midst of reporting an inconsequential mistake, suddenly launches into a catastrophizing tale. He reports from his critic's nightmarish fantasy that his life is deteriorating into a cascading series of disasters. He is flashing back to the way he was continuously over-punished in childhood.

One of my client's drasticizing sounded like this: "My boss looked at me funny when I came back from my bathroom break this morning and I know he thinks I'm stupid and lazy and is going to fire me. I just know I won't be able to get another job. My girlfriend will think I'm a loser and leave me. I'll get sick from the stress, and with no money to pay my medical insurance and rent, I'll soon be living out of a shopping cart." It's disturbing how many drasticizing inner critic rants end with up with an image of homelessness. What a symbol of abandonment!

Recovering requires being able to recognize inner-critic catastrophizing so that we can resist it with *thought-stopping and thought-correction*. In this case, I reminded my client of the many times we had caught his critic "freaking out" about every conceivable way his life could go down the tubes. I then encouraged him to refuse to indulge this process, and to angrily say "no" to the critic every time it tried to scare or demean him.

Finally, I reminded him of all the positive experiences he actually had with his boss [thought-correction]. I also helped him enumerate his many successes at work, at school and at life in general.

The inner critic not only exacerbates flashbacks, but eventually grows into a psychic agency that triggers them. Reversing the damaging effects of the critic is the subject of the next two chapters

ADVANCED FLASHBACK MANAGEMENT

Waking Up in the Abandonment Depression

As recovery progresses, you notice more subtlety in the triggering process. As you do, you become more mindful of your inner critic's hard-to-detect triggers. You also discover that some triggers are indiscernible. This is especially true of triggering that occurs during sleep.

Advanced flashback management, then, involves learning how to manage the disconcerting experience of falling asleep feeling reasonably put together and waking up in a flashback. Typically this occurs because a dream has triggered you into a flashback. If you remember the dream, you can sometimes figure out why it triggered you. With growing mindfulness you may even understand which events from the previous day triggered your dream.

The most difficult situation to manage is when you cannot remember the dream. This type of flashback can feel particularly unfair and discouraging. It is rich fodder for the critic, which can declare that you are not only getting nowhere in his recovery, you are getting worse.

Flashbacks as the Inner Child's Plea for Help

With undetectable triggers, I find that it is most helpful to see a flashback as a communication from the child that you were. The child is reminding you that he woke up feeling desolate innumerable times in that house that was not a home. He woke up daunted by the prospect of once again having to reenter the poisonous milieu of your family. The child is now asking you to meet his unmet need of having someone to go to for comfort when he wakes up feeling wretched. It is as if he is saying: "See! This is how bad it was – this is how overwhelmed, ashamed and miserable I felt so much of the time."

Managing the pain of waking up in the abandonment depression is one of the most difficult, long term challenges in recovery. Sleep seems to be a regressive, right-brain dominant experience. It is not uncommon to wake up with a temporary loss of access to the left-brain cognitive functions that control our more sophisticated understandings of our present-day reality. Without the latter, flashback management often reverts to the critic and our early childhood attempts to cope. This creates a fruitful ground for the critic to explode its arsenal of self-pathologizing programs [enumerated in the next chapter].

Years ago, I customarily responded to awakening in flashback with hypochondriasizing ruminations about my health: "What's happening to my energy? Something must be seriously wrong with me. I feel like death warmed over. That ache in my back is probably a tumor. I lost two pounds this month. I just know its cancer! I wish I could just die and get it over with."

This kind of drasticizing could and did sometimes go on for hours – even days. Moreover, it typically pulled me out of the abandonment depression by creating so much anxiety, that I was forced out of bed into busyholic rushing. I would then hurry through the day unconsciously rushing to outdistance myself from this awful thinking process, as well as the abandonment pain underlying it.

Because of a great deal of practice, I now quickly realize that hypochondriasizing means that I am in a flashback. Accordingly, I work to shift the focus of my thought processes to the theme of generating love and kindness to the child within me. I dedicate this work to my historical child who woke up countless times feeling horribly abandoned in my love-impoverished family of origin. For me, this is now my most practiced flashback management process: breaking my merge with the critic to concentrate on caring for myself.

There is another type of flashback message that seems to come from my inner child. It is that I have slipped back into my old habit of neglecting him. Often it occurs when I ignore him by regressing into overusing my flight response. My flashback then seems to be his clamoring for some proof that my compassion for him is not merely empty rhetoric. And typically when I slow down and go inside, I find that old pain of self-abandonment - that old pain that I now think of as "being lonely for myself." Often this brings up some tears. Almost as often, crying initiates a release from my flashback.

Flexible Use of the Flashback Management Steps

Helen started her session in a deep state of self-alienation: "I am just such a hopeless case! For no reason at all, I got myself stuck in a terrible flashback yesterday. And it wasn't one of those impossible-to-figure-out, waking up-flashbacks you keep telling me about. I was fine all morning, and then Bam! I was in it up to here, and there wasn't any stupid trigger. Nothing caused it. It's just me. Hopelessly screwed up! Mentally defective!"

Discerning the trigger of a flashback is a slippery slope. Seeing the trigger can often rescue us from blaming and hating ourselves for the flashback, but there is not always an identifiable trigger. In such situations, looking for the trigger can quickly deteriorate into self-pathologizing vivisection. This slippery slope can quickly become a cliff as we plummet deeper into the abyss of the flashback.

It is almost always a matter of perspective. Am I trigger-searching from a place of being on my side or a place of fault-finding? When it is the latter, it is best to abandon the search and move toward invoking self-acceptance, as there will always be triggerings that are unfathomable. The process of self-support needs to trump the healthy urge to "figure it ALL out" at such times.

The process of self-acceptance also needs to trump any of your efforts to fix the flashback when this striving becomes tainted with self-irritation and self-disappointment. Sometimes, as described above, the best understanding you can achieve is an overarching one that your inner child is feeling profoundly abandoned. She is cowering from a humiliating attack from your critic and needs for you to switch gears and demonstrate that you will care for her no matter what.

Existential Triggers

Many psychologists use the term *existential* to describe the fact that all human beings are subject to painful events. These are normal recurring afflictions that everyone suffers from time to time. Horrible world events, difficult choices, illnesses and periodic feelings of abject loneliness are common examples of existential pain. Existential calamities can be especially triggering for survivors, because we typically have so much family-of-origin calamity for them to trigger us into reliving.

Another particularly triggering existential phenomenon is the fact that we all suffer invisible, unpredictable mood shifts. Good moods sometimes inexplicably deteriorate into bad ones. As novelist, David Mitchell wrote "Good moods are as fragile as eggs... and bad moods as fragile as bricks".

Unpredictable shifts in your emotional weather are typically problematic in Cptsd. These shifts can quickly trigger you into a full-fledged flashback. This is usually because you were punished or abandoned in the past for showing your full complement of feelings. So now, out of old habit, you automatically dissociate when your emotional weather is inclement.

The inner child often experiences this as you reverting to the pre-recovery adult who had no time for feelings. The child then feels that he is once again trapped in the past where he was so devastatingly abandoned. Perhaps, the resultant flashback is his only way to really get your attention. This is, again, why I try to make my default position turning to myself and my inner child with unconditional positive regard as much as possible.

Later Stage Recovery

When your recovery matures sufficiently, you realize that much of the emotional pain of your flashbacks is appropriate but delayed reactions to your childhood abuse and neglect. You process your feelings in a way that resolves flashbacks, and also builds an increasingly healthy, sense of self.

This, in turn, leads to an ongoing reduction of the unresolved childhood pain that fuels your emotional flashbacks. Flashbacks then become less frequent, intense and enduring. Eventually, you learn to invoke your self-protective instinct as soon as you realize that you are triggered. As flashbacks decrease and become more manageable, the defensive structures built around them (narcissistic, obsessive-compulsive, dissociative and/or codependent) are more readily deconstructed.

At this stage of your recovery, you may now experience an ironically satisfying experience when you come out of a flashback. You may sense on many levels of your awareness that life as a child in your parents' house was even worse than you realized. Simultaneously, you may feel a corresponding sense of relief that you are now freer from your parents' life-spoiling influence than ever before.

HELPING KIDS MANAGE EMOTIONAL FLASHBACKS

This list is for social workers, teachers, relatives, neighbors and friends to help children from traumatizing families. It is adapted from the steps at the beginning of this chapter. Depending on the age of the child, some steps will be more appropriate than others. Even if you are not in a position to help other kids, please read this list at least once for the benefit of your own inner child.

1. Help the child develop an awareness of flashbacks [inside "owies"]: "When have you felt like this before? Is this how it feels when someone is being mean to you?"
2. Demonstrate that "Feeling in danger does not always mean you are in danger." Teach that some places are safer than others. Use a soft, easy tone of voice: "Maybe you can relax a little with me." "You're safe here with me." "No one can hurt you here."
3. Model that there are adults interested in his care and protection. Aim to become the child's first safe relationship. Connect the child with other safe nurturing adults, groups, or clubs.
4. Speak soothingly and reassuringly to the child. Balance "Love & Limits:" 5 positives for each negative. Set limits kindly.
5. Guide the child's mind back into her body to reduce hypervigilance and hyperarousal.
   a. Teach systemic relaxation of all major muscle groups
   b. Teach deep, slow diaphragmatic breathing
   c. Encourage slowing down to reduce fear-increasing rushing

    d. Teach calming centering practices like drawing, Aikido, Tai Chi, yoga, stretching

    e. Identify and encourage retreat to safe places

6. Teach "use-your-words." In some families it's dangerous to talk. Verbal ventilation releases pain and fear, and restores coping skills.

7. Facilitate grieving the death of feeling safe. Abuse and neglect beget sadness and anger. Crying releases fear. Venting anger in a way that doesn't hurt the person or others creates a sense of safety.

8. Shrink the Inner Critic. Make the brain more user-friendly. Heighten awareness of negative self-talk and fear-based fantasizing. Teach thought-stopping and thought substitution: Help the child build a memorized list of his qualities, assets, successes, resources.

9. Help the child identify her 4F type & its positive side. Use metaphors, songs, cartoons or movie characters. Fight: Power Rangers; Flight: Roadrunner, Bob the Builder; Freeze: Avatar; Fawn: Grover.

10. Educate about the right/need to have boundaries, to say no, to protest unfairness, to seek the protection of responsible adults.

11. Identify and avoid dangerous people, places and activities. [Superman avoids Kryptonite. Shaq and Derek Jeter don't do drugs.]

12. Deconstruct eternity thinking. Create vivid pictures of attainable futures that are safer, friendlier, and more prosperous. Cite examples of comparable success stories.

CHAPTER

SHRINKING THE INNER CRITIC

This chapter explores what one of my clients calls the "nasty and sneaky tricks of the critic."

ORIGIN OF THE CPTSD CRITIC

A flashback-inducing critic is typically spawned in a danger-ridden childhood home. This is true whether the danger comes from the passive abandonment of neglect or the active abandonment of abuse. When parents do not provide safe enough bonding and positive feedback, the child flounders in anxiety and fear. Many children appear to be hard-wired to adapt to this *endangering* abandonment with perfectionism.

A prevailing climate of danger forces the child's superego to over-cultivate the various programs of perfectionism and endangerment listed below. Once again, the superego is the part of the psyche that learns parental rules in order to gain their acceptance.

The inner critic is the superego gone bad. The inner critic is the superego in overdrive desperately trying to win your parents' approval. When perfectionist striving fails to win welcoming from your parents, the inner critic becomes increasingly hostile and caustic. It festers into a virulent inner voice that increasingly manifests self-hate, self-disgust and self-abandonment. The inner critic blames you incessantly for shortcomings that it imagines to be the cause of your parents' rejection. It is incapable of understanding that the real cause lies in your parents' shortcomings.

As a traumatized child, your over-aroused sympathetic nervous system also drives you to become increasingly hypervigilant. *Hypervigilance* is a fixation on looking for danger that comes from excessive exposure to real danger. In an effort to recognize, predict and avoid danger, hypervigilance is ingrained in your approach to being in the world. Hypervigilance narrows your attention into an incessant, on-guard scanning of the people around you. It also frequently projects you into the future, imagining danger in upcoming social events. Moreover, hypervigilance typically devolves into intense performance anxiety on every level of self-expression.

Like the soldier overlong in combat, ptsd sets in because you feel as if you are constantly under attack. Unfortunately, internal attack is now added to external attack, and you become locked into hypervigilance and sympathetic nervous system arousal.

A traumatized child becomes desperate to relieve the anxiety and depression of abandonment. The critic-driven child can only think about the ways she is too much or not enough. The child's unfolding sense of self [the healthy ego], finds no room to develop. Her identity virtually becomes the critic. The superego trumps the ego.

In this process, the critic becomes increasingly virulent and eventually switches from the parents' internalized voice: "You're a bad boy/girl" to the first person: "I'm a bad boy/girl." Over time, self-goading increasingly deteriorates: "*I'm* such a loser. *I'm* so pathetic... bad... ugly...worthless...stupid...defective."

This is unlike the soldier in combat who does not develop a toxic critic. This process whereby the superego becomes carcinogenic is a key juncture where ptsd morphs into Cptsd. The cruel, totalitarian inner critic is a key distinguishing feature of Cptsd.

One of my clients grief-fully remembered the constant refrains of his childhood: "If only I wasn't so needy and selfish...if only my freckles would fade...if only I could pitch a perfect game...if only I could stop gagging on the canned peas during dinner...if only I could pray all the time to get mom's arthritis cured, then maybe she'd stop picking on me, and then maybe dad would play catch with me."

———•——

In my work with survivors, I am continuously struck by how often the inner critic triggers them into overwhelming emotional flash-backs. The Cptsd-derived inner critic weds our fear of abandonment to our self-hate about our imperfections. It then tortures us with the entwined serpents of perfectionism and endangerment. *Endangerment* is the process of constantly projecting danger onto safe enough situations.

Your recovering depends on learning how to recognize and confront the 14 inner critic attacks listed below. When this process of recovering is bypassed, these deeply engrained programs continue to send you tumbling back into the overwhelming fear, shame and hopelessness of your childhood abandonment.

14 COMMON INNER CRITIC ATTACKS

[Each attack/program is paired with a therapeutic *thought-correction response]*

Perfectionism Attacks

1. Perfectionism. *My perfectionism arose as an attempt to gain safety and support in my dangerous family. Perfection is a self-persecutory myth. I do not have to be perfect to be safe or loved in the present. I am letting go of relationships that require perfection. I have a right to make mistakes. Mistakes do not make me a mistake. Every mistake or mishap is an opportunity to practice loving myself in the places I have never been loved.*

2. All-or-None & Black-and-White Thinking. *I reject extreme or over-generalized descriptions, judgments or criticisms. One negative happenstance does not mean I am stuck in a never-ending pattern of defeat. Statements that describe me as "always" or "never" this or that, are typically grossly inaccurate.*

3. Self-Hate, Self-Disgust & Toxic Shame. *I commit to myself. I am on my side. I am a good enough person. I refuse to trash myself. I turn shame back into blame and disgust, and externalize it to anyone who shames my normal feelings and foibles. As long as I am not hurting anyone, I refuse to be shamed for normal emotional responses like anger, sadness, fear and depression. I especially refuse to attack myself for how hard it is to completely eliminate the self-hate habit.*

4. Micromanagement/Worrying/Obsessing/Looping/Over-Futurizing. *I will not repetitively examine details over and over. I will not jump to negative conclusions. I will not endlessly second-guess myself. I cannot change the past. I forgive all my past mistakes. I cannot make the future perfectly safe. I will stop hunting for what could go wrong. I will not try to control the uncontrollable. I will not micromanage myself or others. I work in a way that is "good enough", and I accept the existential fact that my efforts sometimes bring desired results and sometimes they do not. "God grant me the serenity to accept the things I cannot change, the courage to change the things I can, and the wisdom to know the difference." - The Serenity Prayer*

5. Unfair/Devaluing Comparisons to others or to your most perfect moments. *I refuse to compare myself unfavorably to others. I will not compare "my insides to their outsides". I will not judge myself for not being at peak performance all the time. In a society that pressures us into acting happy all the time, I will not get down on myself for feeling bad.*

6. Guilt. *Feeling guilty does not mean I am guilty. I refuse to make my decisions and choices from guilt. Sometimes I need to feel the guilt and do it anyway. In the inevitable instances when I inadvertently hurt someone, I will apologize, make amends, and let go of my guilt. I will not apologize over and over. I am no longer a victim. I will not accept unfair blame. Guilt is sometimes camouflaged fear: "I feel guilty and afraid, but I am not guilty or in danger."*

7. "Shoulding". *I will substitute the words "want to" for "should" and only follow this imperative if it feels like I want to, unless I am under legal, ethical or moral obligation.*

8. Over-productivity/Workaholism/Busyholism. *I am a human being not a human doing. I will not choose to be perpetually productive. I am more productive in the long run, when I balance work with play and relaxation. I will not try to perform at 100% all the time. I subscribe to the normalcy of vacillating along a continuum of efficiency.*

9. Harsh Judgments of Self & Others/ Name-Calling. *I will not let the bullies and critics of my early life win by joining and agreeing with them. I refuse to attack myself or abuse others. I will not displace the criticism and blame that rightfully belongs to my dysfunctional caretakers onto myself or current people in my life. "I care for myself. The more solitary, the more friendless, the more unsustained I am, the more I will respect myself". - Jane Eyre*

Endangerment Attacks

10. Drasticizing/Catastrophizing/Hypochondriasizing. *I feel afraid but I am not in danger. I am not "in trouble" with my parents.*

I will not blow things out of proportion. I refuse to scare myself with thoughts and pictures of my life deteriorating. No more home-made horror movies and disaster flicks. I will not turn every ache and pain into a story about my imminent demise. I am safe and at peace.

11. Negative focus. *I renounce over-noticing and dwelling on what might be wrong with me or life around me. I will not minimize or discount my attributes. Right now, I notice, visualize and enumerate my accomplishments, talents and qualities, as well as the many gifts that life offers me, e.g., nature, music, film, food, beauty, color, friends, pets, etc.*

12. Time Urgency. *I am not in danger. I do not need to rush. I will not hurry unless it is a true emergency. I am learning to enjoy doing my daily activities at a relaxed pace.*

13. Disabling Performance Anxiety. *I reduce procrastination by reminding myself that I will not accept unfair criticism or perfectionist expectations from anyone. Even when afraid, I will defend myself from unfair criticism. I won't let fear make my decisions.*

14. Perseverating About Being Attacked. *Unless there are clear signs of danger, I will thought-stop my projection of past bullies/critics onto others. The vast majority of my fellow human beings are peaceful people. I have legal authorities to aid in my protection if threatened by the few who aren't. I invoke thoughts and images of my friends' love and support.*

———

Critic attacks like most things are not all-or-none. They can vary in intensity and duration. Most of the case examples that follow are on the intense end of the spectrum. I chose them because they are more illustrative of how the critic operates. Once you become proficient at identifying intense critic attacks, you typically develop the mindfulness necessary to notice more subtle attacks. This is essential because most survivors spend tremendous amounts of time barely conscious of how incessantly self-critical they are.

As with the flashback management steps, memorizing these rebuttals to the critic and using them like mantras is especially helpful in critic shrinking.

Critic-initiated Flashbacks

The inner critic commonly increases the intensity of a flashback via a barrage of the attacks listed above. Flashbacks can devolve into increasingly painful levels of the abandonment depression. One attack can repetitively bleed into another and tumble us further down a spiral of hopelessness. It is awful enough to take a single punch in a fight, but when the punches keep coming, the victim is severely thrashed.

Once again, Cptsd flashbacks do not typically have a visual component. However, it is not unusual for a survivor to sometimes flash on a snapshot of a parent's contemptuous face at the moment of triggering.

My client, Dmitri, began his session by telling me that he was contentedly puttering around his kitchen when he accidentally knocked over a glass of water. He immediately pictured his father and a loud internal voice blurted: "I'm such a world class spaz!"

Retrospectively, he realized that he then plummeted instantly into a flashback. Anxiety quickly overwhelmed him and he was soon lost in a tirade of self-attacking diatribes emanating from the critic. "Spaz" is an example of the name-calling that the critic specializes in. It is a combination of critic attacks # 1, 3 and 9 above.

The attacks soon deteriorated into a full scale laundry listing of all his imperfections. These were characteristically blown out of proportion, and often not reality based. The critic screamed: "I'm so clumsy. I never do anything right [#2 all-or-none thinking]. "I could f*ck up a free lunch!"

Quickly, Dmitri's thinking was totally dominated by a negative focus[#11] that merged with drasticizing [#10], and culminated in attack fantasies [#14] that made him cancel his plans to go out.

This example is only a micro-portion of the unending onslaught that can accompany a major flashback. After enduring many, many more elaborations of this process, Dmitri became entrenched in the ultimate abandonment catastrophization [#10]: "No wonder I don't have a partner or any friends; who could tolerate being around such a loser" [#2: He actually had two good friends].

Dmitri's felt-sense of abandonment then morphed into self-abandonment. Primitive self-soothing behaviors reemerged as he self-medicated by binging on an enormous amount of junk food. He then retreated into his bedroom to dissociate further into a long morning nap.

All this in reaction to the tiny faux pas of a spilled glass of water!

I must emphasize here that Dmitri was not crazy or defective because his critic made a hell out of a spilled glass of water. *All this* was a re-visit via flashback to the real traumatic experiences of being profoundly rejected by his parents for trivial mistakes. His father had contemptuously told him he could f*ck up a free lunch innumerable times.

As Dmitri resolved and harvested the learning potential of this flashback, he said to me: "Pete, I can't tell you how horrible they were. Life at home was one no-win, mind-f*ck situation after another. F*cked if I did, and f*cked if I didn't. It's no wonder I've been stuck all these years with this ball and chain code: 'Don't ever let down your guard!' Something's just moved in me and I swear I'm gonna start cutting myself some slack!"

Thoughts as Triggers

Rejecting parents typically make the child believe that his opinions and feelings are dangerous imperfections. In worst case scenarios the mere impulse to speak triggers fear and shame. How could anything the child says not reveal his stupidity and worthlessness? Opening his mouth invariably leads to deeper rejection and trouble.

As ongoing neglect and abuse repetitively strengthen the critic, even the most innocuous, self-interested thought or musing can trigger a five alarm fire of intense emotional flashback. To maintain the illusive hope of someday winning parental approval, the child's perfectionistic striving escalates, and may become obsessive/compulsive. Even an imagined mistake can then initiate a flashback.

The Critic as the Shaming Internalized Parents

Not infrequently, a client comes into a session and shamefully confesses something that sounds like this: "I called myself a f*ckwit over and over last night. I must really be inherently messed up, because I know my mother never said that. As bad as she was, she never swore and I doubt she ever even heard that word."

The explanation for this is that the critic is essentially a process. It is an ever developing process that co-opts our creativity and funnels it into "new and improved" ways of imitating our parents' disparagement.

Parental contempt is the key piece of the emotional abuse that creates toxic shame. Toxic shame is the emotional matrix of the abandonment depression. It is also the glue that keeps us stuck helplessly in flashbacks. As such, toxic shame is the affect or emotional tone of the inner critic. Shame besmirches us as it emotionally intensifies each of the 14 assaults described above.

In main stream psychology, shame is often described as a social emotion. Normal shame is a somewhat healthy, self-regulating emotional reaction that arises when someone witnesses us acting in an unfair, offensive, or hurtful way.

This is not the case with toxic shame however. Many Cptsd survivors in recovery soon realize that they do not need a witness to suddenly be catapulted into a shame attack.

Dmitri was all alone when he knocked over the glass.

Or was he? There is an invisible social context to toxic shame attacks. Toxic shame is social because the inner critic came into existence through pathological interactions with our parents. Moreover, toxic shame is social in the moment of the solitary flashback, because at the time it is as if we are in the presence of our parents.

For me, the strongest evidence of this occurs when I am on my own and trying to do something difficult. If I make a mistake or do not accomplish my task as efficiently as possible, I often feel very anxious as if I am being watched and criticized.

I believe this phenomenon corresponds with an internalization of our parents. Our parents were such formative and formidable presences in our developing life, that we have strong representations of them in our psyches. These representations include their beliefs and condemnation about us. Until we work on shrinking their influence, our internalized parents exist in our psyches as the key controlling force of our lives.

Facing the Stubbornness of the Critic

The work of shrinking the critic is one of the most essential processes of recovery. As obvious as its value may seem as you read this, embracing the task of renouncing the critic is much more challenging than it may seem at first blush.

The critic's programs are not only burned deeply into our psyches by our parents, but we also unknowingly emblazon them into our minds by mimicking our parents. We are now the key reinforcing agents of their toxic legacy. With little mindfulness of it, we injure ourselves with countless angry, self-disgusted repetitions of their judgments. Recovery now depends on you withdrawing your blind allegiance to this terrible process of only noticing yourself negatively.

The task of diminishing these self-negating patterns is daunting. It is typically lifetime work – often negotiable only at the rate of two-steps-forward, one-step backward. And oh how unfair it is that the step backward often feels more like six!

Yet recent findings in neuroscience [*The General Theory of Love; The Talking Cure*] have shown that biologically ingrained mental patterns can be diminished and replaced with new ones through long term repetitive work. I believe this is analogous to adding or subtracting girth to parts of your physique, which typically takes seemingly innumerable repetitions of a given exercise.

In the last couple of decades my brain has gone from being my own worst enemy almost all the time to being very reliably on my side. I have also seen similar gains with many of the clients I have worked with long-term.

Perfectionism and Emotional Neglect

As stated earlier, perfectionism also seems to be an instinctual defense for emotionally abandoned children. The existential impossibility of perfection saves the child from giving up, unless or until lack of success forces her to retreat into a dissociative freeze response or an anti-social fight response.

Perfectionism also provides a sense of meaning and direction for the powerless and unsupported child. Striving to be perfect offers her a semblance of a sense of control. Self-control is also safer to pursue because abandoning parents typically reserve their severest punishment for children who are vocal about their negligence.

As the quest for perfection fails over and over, and as parental acceptance and nurturing remain elusive, imperfection becomes synonymous with shame and fear. Perceived imperfection triggers fear of abandonment, which triggers self-hate for imperfection, which expands abandonment into self-abandonment. This in turn amps fear up even further, which in turn intensifies self-disgust, etc. On and on it goes in a downward spiral of fear and shame-encrusted depression. It can go on for hours, days, weeks, and for those with severe Cptsd, can become their standard mode of being.

More on Endangerment

The importance and magnitude of the critic's endangerment programs cannot be overstated. I have worked with numerous "well-therapized" people who were relatively free from perfectionism, but still seriously afflicted with the critic's addiction to noticing potential danger. Said another way, I have seen survivors eliminate much of their perfectionist, self-attacking thinking without realizing that the critic was still flooding their minds with fear-inducing thoughts and images.

I learned to disidentify from perfectionism long before I learned to stop perseverating on my critic's harrowing snapshots of danger. In fact, I became quite adept at morphing these snapshots into feature long films about my imminent demise.

Permanent abandonment, public humiliation, lethal illness, lonely death, imminent attack, and penniless homelessness are common endangerment themes of many survivors. One of my clients identified his inner critic endangerment process as: "My critic, the horror movie producer". This made me think: "My critic the terrorist".

If I had to describe the two most key processes of the critic, I would say this. First, the critic is above all a self-perpetuating process of extreme negative noticing. Second the critic is a constant hypervigilance that sees disaster hovering in the next moment about to launch into a full-court-press.

Using Anger to Thought-Stop the Critic

Thought-stopping is the process of using willpower to disidentify from and interrupt toxic thoughts and visualizations. Sometimes visualizing a stop sign at the same time can help strengthen thought-stopping.

Since traumatizing parents cripple the instinctive fight response of their child, recovering the anger of the fight response is essential in healing Cptsd. We need the aid of our fight response to empower the process of thought-stopping the critic.

I cannot over-encourage you to use your anger to stop the critic in its tracks. We can re-hijack the anger of the critic's attack, and forcefully redirect it at the critic instead of ourselves. We can then silently and internally say "No!" or "Stop!" or "Shut Up!" to short-circuit drasticizing and perfectionistic mental processes.

Angrily saying "No!" to the critic sets an internal boundary against unnatural, anti-self processes. It is the hammer of self-renovating carpentry that rebuilds our instinct of self-protection. Furthermore recovery is deepened by directing our anger at anyone who helped install the critic, as well as at anyone who is currently contributing to keeping it alive.

I recently received this e-mail from a website respondent who read some of my writing about angering at the critic: "Another explanation I really liked is for people that don't have much of the FIGHT response to start using it to stop the inner critic. I am a huge fan of self-compassion which has really helped me recently (loving-kindness) and I continually just accept all the messages and just let them flow by. When I heard your comments about saying NO and rejecting them, I was like 'Yeah- I guess Pete maybe hasn't found it all yet.' I was being close minded. A couple days later I tried it out and Oh My Gog has it helped. I get mad now and it just shuts down my anxiety and turns shame into blame/anger. It feels much better for me! After all it wasn't messages I would have given to myself, and they are all messages from my parents."

———·•·———

Successful critic-shrinking usually requires thousands of angry skirmishes with the critic. Passionate motivation for this work often arises when we construct an accurate picture of our upbringing. Natural anger eventually arises when we really get how little and defenseless we were when our parents bullied us into hating ourselves.

Most trauma survivors were blank slates who were brainwashed into accepting the critic as their primary identity. To the degree that a family is Cptsd-engendering, to that degree is it like a mini-cult. Cults demand absolute loyalty to the leader's authority and belief system. In early thought-stopping work, most survivors need to empower their efforts with a healthy rage against their parents for destroying their self-loyalty and their self-individuation. However, with enough practice, the survivor's healthy observing ego can use willpower alone to disidentify from the critic.

———·•·———

My son's birth graced me with an enormous boost in my motivation to practice thought-stopping on the critic. Witnessing the many miracles of his ongoing development moved me to increasingly deepen my emotional bonding with him. This was quite disconcerting to my critic which began working overtime on its endangerment programs.

The critic warned me interminably about the danger of my rapidly expanding attachment to him. It was trying to protect me from the devastation that would ensue if my loving emotional investment turned out as badly as it did with my parents. What if untrustworthy "Life" let him die or rendered him a "bad seed."

The critic manufactured the most dreadful horror movies of accidents, diseases, kidnapping, mental illness, oedipal betrayals, etc. Had I not known how to recognize, interpret and refuse to indulge these catastrophizations, I am sure that my capacity to bond with him would have been seriously compromised. Moreover, had I not been able to use my outrage to disidentify from the critic, thought-stopping by itself would not have been a powerful enough tool.

I particularly like this way of challenging the critic. "I'm not afraid of you anymore, mom and dad. You were the critic, and you put the critic in me. I renounce your toxic messages. Take back your shame and disgust. I am disgusted at your shameful job of parenting."

One of my clients shared with me a phrase that spontaneously came to her while she was fighting her critic at home. "You totally ruined my childhood, and I'm not going to let you get away with ruining my life now." She reported that this perspective emblazoned in her consciousness, and now often helps to fire her up to fire the critic.

Shame is Blame Unfairly Turned against the Self

The great psychologist, Erik Eriksen, gave us a great tool when he formulated this emotional mathematics equation. "Shame is blame turned against the self". Our parents were too big and powerful to blame, so we had to blame ourselves instead. Now, however we are free of them, and we can cut off the critic's shame supply by redirecting unfair self-blame back to our parents.

You can redirect the anger of the critic's blaming messages away from you. You can direct the anger onto the installers of the critic, or sideways onto the critic itself. You can give shame back by allowing yourself to feel angry and disgusted at the image of your parent bullying you. You can rage at them for overwhelming you with shame when you were too young and small to defend yourself.

An inner critic that has dominated us since childhood, however, does not give up its rulership of the psyche easily. It stubbornly refuses to accept the updated information that adulthood now offers the possibility of increasing safety and healthy attachment. It is as if the critic has worn a flashback-inducing groove in the brain the size of the Grand Canyon. Now, any of the thinking patterns listed earlier can hair-trigger an amygdala-hijacking that dumps us into the abandonment mélange.

Progress in critic-shrinking is often infinitesimally slow and indiscernible at first. Our brains have become addicted to only noticing what is wrong and what is dangerous. And as with most addictions, breaking this deeply entrenched habit may require life-long management.

In early recovery work, we need to challenge the critic's monocular negative focus over and over with all the ferocity we can muster. Eventually with practice we can find a part of ourselves that is mad about how grossly unfair our parents' bullying and indifference was. We can find a part of us that is outraged that we were indoctrinated and inculcated into chronically abandoning and bullying ourselves. We can fume that this occurred when we were too young to protest or even know what was happening to us. We can gradually build our ability to say "No!" and "Shut up!" whenever we catch the critic attacking us.

With enough healthy inner self-defense, the survivor gradually learns to reject her unconscious acceptance of self-abuse and self-abandonment. Her sense of healthy self-protection begins to emerge and over time grows into a fierce willingness to stop unfair criticism - internal or external.

Psychologically speaking, this is part of the process of working through repetition compulsion. Deconstructing repetition compulsion has both an internal and external dimension. On the internal dimension, we decrease the habit of repetitively perpetrating our parents' abuse against ourselves by staunchly confronting the inner critic. This then allows us to become more mindful on the external dimension when others reenact our parents' mistreatment. We can then confront them to stop, or banish them from our lives. With enough practice, we can repudiate our parents' awful legacy of teaching us that love means numbly accepting abuse and neglect.

Further encouragement and guidance for therapeutically angering at the critic can be found in *Soul Without Shame,* by Byron Brown, and *Healing Your Emotional Self* by Beverly Engel.

Embracing the Critic

In my experience, until the fight response is substantially restored, the Cptsd client benefits little from CBT, psychodynamic or mindfulness techniques that encourage us to accept the critic. In later recovery, when the survivor has removed the venomous stinger from the critic, these techniques can be quite valuable. Then, and only then, are we able to reconnect with the helpful side of healthy self-criticism [see Stone and Stone's book *Embracing Your Inner Critic*].

A typical indication that the critic has mellowed into being functional is that it speaks to us in a kind and helpful voice. It reminds us dispassionately to adjust our behavior when we can and ought to be doing something better. If, however, it blasts us for imperfection, it is giving itself away as the toxic critic that was installed by our parents.

A left-brained, objective approach of embracing the critic is rarely helpful unless it is balanced with a subjective, right-brained capacity for assertive self-protection. Perhaps this is because the inner critic appears to operate simultaneously with hyper-emotional right-brain flashback dynamics. Perhaps toxic inner critic processes are so emotionally overwhelming that efforts to resist them rationally and dispassionately are too weak to be effective.

THOUGHT-SUBSTITUTION AND THOUGHT-CORRECTION

Thought-substitution, especially in the form of thought-correction, is another essential tool for empowering the work of thought-stopping the critic. Many years ago, I sensed that my critic became as tough as a body-builder's bicep through myriad repetitions. I guessed that similarly exercising self-protective responses to the critic would build my thought-correction muscles. It did in fact, and my instinct to protect myself almost always arises automatically now when I am triggered into a flashback. I believe I am not exaggerating when I say that tens of thousands of positive thought-substitutions have rewarded me with a psyche that is fairly consistently user-friendly.

Accordingly, I encourage you to immediately confront the critic's negative messages with positive ones like those in the list at the beginning of the chapter. This is essential in Cptsd recovery, because a single unconfronted toxic thought can act like a virus and rage infectiously out of control into a flu-like mélange of shame, fear and helplessness.

Moving quickly into thought-stopping and thought correction often obviates a headlong tumble into the downward spiral of a flashback. This is essential in critic-work, as the critic typically attacks us more viciously once it has gotten up a head of steam. At such times, the critic can hypocritically scorn us for falling back into self-criticism when we "should" know better. This is the time then, more than ever, to "thought-correct and not self-berate," as my last intern liked to say to her clients.

Additionally, I encourage you to write out a list of your positive qualities and accomplishments to read it to yourself if you get lost in self-hate. Toolbox 5 in chapter 16 is a practical exercise to help you elaborate this list in a multidimensional way.

Making a written record of your positive attributes is especially helpful as flashbacks often create a temporary amnesia about your essential worthiness and goodness. Flashbacks seem to involve a temporary loss of access to more current left-brain learning. MRI's show greatly reduced left-brain activity in hyper-aroused Cptsd survivors. In my experience, memorizing your list enhances your capacity to dissolve that amnesia.

Reciting part or all of your list over and over like a mantra can also help you during those times when the critic is particularly severe and relentless. If you have trouble making the list or filling out Toolbox 5, ask a friend or a therapist for their input. Additionally, please let me remind you that qualities do not have to be perfect or ever-present to qualify as qualities. If it is true of you most of the time then, it is a quality.

Finally, *positive visualization* can be a powerful adjunct to thought-substitution. Some survivors gradually learn to short-circuit the fear-mongering processes of the critic by invoking images of past successes and accomplishments, as well as picturing safe places, loving friends or comforting memories. There are also a variety of CD's available at places like Amazon.com that contain guided meditations that use positive language and imagery in a way that enhances deactivation and relaxation.

Perspective-Substitution & Correction

The most important thought correction of all is a switch in the perspective of our thinking.

Perspective-substitution is a broadening of our overall perspective. It moves our viewpoint from the critic's narrow, negative focus to the more balanced and accurate focus of the observing ego – the mindful self.

Perspective-substitution helps us to dethrone the critic from its life-negating point of view. This resembles the firing of a bad manager or inept coach – one with a distorted view who dwells so much on what is wrong that he cannot see anything that is right.

As stated in chapter 1, perspective-substitution can be enhanced with the spiritual practice of gratitude. In this vein, gratitude is a type of mindfulness that looks for empirical proof that life is essentially good even though it is also quite difficult at times.

Perspective-Substitution and Gratitude

Gratitude is a delicate subject to write about because many survivors have been abused by shaming advice to "just be grateful for what you have". Consequently many survivors totally reject the concept of gratitude and throw the baby out with the scorn-sodden bathwater. Once again, this is quite understandable when you legitimately had little to be grateful for in your childhood.

Moreover, the concept of gratitude is damagingly used by some psychologists to support the psychological defense of denial. They tout gratitude as a fast track that can bypass traumatic pain. This is worse than absurd when applied to Cptsd survivors. It is in fact shamefully abusive to survivors because profound, extended trauma cannot be resolved until it is fully understood and worked through.

Gratitude is nevertheless a wonderful natural experience that can recurrently enhance the quality of your life. You can cultivate a perspective that is open to noticing what there is to be grateful about as long as you do not do it with the intention of creating a permanent feeling of gratitude. Over time an attitude of gratitude can gradually increase authentic gratefulness.

This can best be illustrated with the example of love. While it is of course healthy to adopt a cognitive attitude of love toward our friends and chosen family, it is impossible to feel loving all the time. If I expect that of myself, I give my inner critic endless fodder to attack me for not feeling loving enough. Similarly if I expect myself to feel grateful all the time, I keep the critic's prodigious program of self-disappointment hale and hearty.

Nonetheless, aligning with attitudes like love and gratitude is generally therapeutic. When I am temporarily stuck in a flashback feeling alienated from life, remembering what I am *usually* grateful for in life can sometimes pull me out of the polarized negative thinking that helps keep the flashback alive.

Invoking gratitude is particularly difficult, and often impossible at first, because flashbacks typically strand us in an emotional overwhelm that cancels out our ability to feel anything good about life. Reminding ourselves of what is worthwhile in our lives does not seem to help much in the early phases of using this tool. However, with enough practice of positive-noticing, we can sometimes relax out of a flashback by invoking our memories of gratitude.

When I experience this at the end of an especially long flashback, positive-noticing sometimes arises spontaneously and brings with it sweet tears of gratitude. These are also typically tears of relief, and tears of an achieved sense of belonging.

These tears typically arise unbidden, seemingly out of the blue. Typically they are positively triggered by experiences of beauty or connection, such as when flowers authentically strike me as beautiful once again, or when my appreciation of music returns and deeply moves my soul, or when I suddenly fully feel how much I love my wife, my son, my friend or my client.

After a painful lapse in being able to emotionally enjoy these experiences, this return brings these gratitude-laden tears which on really momentous occasions can vacillate between crying and laughing as I resurface into authentically being grateful to be alive.

———•——

Once again, my experience is that the more I practice the thought substitution of focusing on what I am grateful for, the sooner genuine gratitude returns to me on the occasions that I lose touch with it.

A powerful way to practice perspective-correction is as follows. After you go to bed at night, list at least ten positive happenings of the day. More often than not these will not be peak experiences, but rather basic and simple pleasures and appreciations. They may be as simple as a catchy tune, an engaging color, a sweet scent, an enjoyable food serving of the day, a new flower in a local garden, a satisfying TV show, a neighbor's hello, a feeling of fitness climbing the stairs, soothing words from a favorite author, or a pleasant encounter with a pet.

Decades of this practice have helped me immeasurably to upgrade the sour perspective I inherited from my parents. Alignment with this function of the healthy observing ego provides us with a more balanced and accurate perception of life and other people.

The Neuroplasticity of the Brain

I am repeatedly heartened to read the accumulating evidence from neuroscience research that proves the neuroplasticity of the brain. *Neuroplasticity* means that the brain can grow and change throughout our life. Old self-destructive neural pathways can be diminished and new healthier ones can replace them. *A General Theory of Love* by Thomas Lewis inspiringly explicates this fact. This fact helps me to remember that the critic can indeed literally be shrunk via long-term, frequent and dedicated use of the thought-stopping, thought-substitution and thought-correction practices.

———

As recovery progresses, you notice the critic sooner before its attack becomes multidimensional. This then allows you to take more immediate self-protective action. Moreover, Cptsd flashbacks can be utilized as evidence of, and in later stages of recovery, proof of your childhood traumatization. Flashbacks point irrefutably to the fact that your parent's abandonment forced you to habituate to hypervigilance and negative noticing.

CHAPTER 10

SHRINKING THE OUTER CRITIC

THE OUTER CRITIC: THE ENEMY OF RELATIONSHIP

In Cptsd, the critic can have two aspects: inner critic and outer critic. The inner critic is the part of your mind that views you as flawed and unworthy. The outer critic is the part that views everyone else as flawed and unworthy. When the outer critic is running your mind, people appear to be too awful and too dangerous to trust.

When she was stuck in an outer critic attack, one of my clients would often rant like this: "Everybody s*cks. People are so selfish and scary. They either f*ck you over or they let you down." She eventually named this an "I'm-moving-to-another-planet flashback."

The *outer critic* is the counterpart of the self-esteem-destroying inner critic. It uses the same programs of perfectionism and endangerment against others that your inner critic uses against yourself.

Via its all-or-none programming, the outer critic rejects others because they are never perfect and cannot be guaranteed to be safe.

As with the inner critic, outer critic attacks are usually internal and silent, unless you are a fight type as we will see below.

When we regress into the outer critic, we obsess about the unworthiness [imperfection] and treacherousness [dangerousness] of others. Unconsciously, we do this to avoid emotional investment in relationships.

The outer critic developed in reaction to parents who were too dangerous to trust. The outer critic helped us to be hyperaware of the subtlest signal that our parents were deteriorating into their most dangerous behaviors. Over time the outer critic grew to believe that anyone and everyone would inevitably turn out to be as untrustworthy as our parents.

Now, in situations where we no longer need it, the outer critic alienates us from others. It attacks others and scares them away, or it builds fortresses of isolation whose walls are laundry lists of their exaggerated shortcomings. In an awful irony, the critic attempts to protect us from abandonment by scaring us further into it.

If we are ever to discover the comfort of soothing connection with others, the critic's dictatorship of the mind must be broken. The outer critic's arsenal of intimacy-spoiling dynamics must be consciously identified and gradually deactivated.

4F TYPES AND OUTER CRITIC/INNER CRITIC RATIOS

Depending on your 4F type, you may gravitate to either the inner or the outer critic. Different 4F types generally have different ratios of outer and inner critic dynamics, and some polarize extremely to one or the other.

Freeze and Fight types are often polarized to the outer critic. Fawn types tend to be dominated by the inner critic. Flight types can have the most variance in inner and outer critic ratio. Your sub-type can also have a big influence on this.

The Freeze type can judgmentally denounce the entire outside world to justify her all-or-none belief that people are dangerous. The Flight type can use his own perfectionistic striving to excel so that his outer critic can judge everyone else as inferior. The Fawn type uses inner critic self-hate to self-censor and avoid the fear of being authentic and vulnerable in relationship. The Fight type, in a paradoxical twist, controls others through the outer critic to prevent them from abandoning him while at the same time using prickliness to not let them get too close.

Fight types can also leave at the first sign that the other can-not be controlled. One flight-fight type, who I worked with briefly, told me with great upset about a recent betrayal. His new partner "insisted" on replacing the empty toilet paper roll so that the new roll unwound from the bottom instead of the top. He asked her once to do it his way and felt so betrayed when she did not comply, that he broke up with her. I could not help feeling that she was fortunate that she got away.

Unfortunately, this client was not able to take in that the lion's share of his upset was a flashback. He had flashed back to his rig-idly controlling mother frightening him into believing that the toilet paper must unwind from the top. She had punished him into believ-ing that this was a universal truth. Perfectionism, in the hands of the outer critic, can be paranoiacally picayune.

————————

Finally it is not unusual for survivors, who have significantly shrunk their dominant critic mode, to experience a reciprocal increase in the virulence of its opposite counterpart. This came as a disap-pointing shock to me at a time when I was congratulating myself that my inner critic was a mere shadow of its former self. Soon thereafter, I noticed that I was plagued by a new judgmentalness that seemed out of character. Curiosity and a growing mindfulness about this development lead me to a lot of the insights that I share in this chapter. With enough mindfulness, this shift in critic mode can then become an opportunity to further shrink the overall combined agency of the outer and inner critic.

PASSSIVE-AGGRESSIVENESS AND THE OUTER CRITIC

Children are initially wired to respond angrily to parental abuse or neglect. Outside of the fight types, most traumatized children learn early that protesting parental unfairness is an unpardonable offense. They are generally forced to repress their protests and complaints. This then renders their anger silent and subliminal. This anger however, does not disappear. It percolates as an ever accumulating sea of resentment that can fuel the outer critic's obsession for finding fault and seeing danger in everyone.

Viewing all relationships through the lens of parental abandonment, the outer critic never lets down its guard. It continuously transfers unexpressed childhood anger onto others, and silently scapegoats them by blowing current disappointments out of proportion. Citing insignificant transgressions as justification, the survivor flashes back into outer critic mode, and silently fumes and grumbles in long judgmental ruminations. To bastardize Elizabeth Barrett Browning: "How do I find thee lacking? Let me count the ways."

When silently blaming the wrong person becomes habitual, it manifests as *passive-aggressiveness*. Common examples of passive aggression are distancing yourself in hurt withdrawal, or pushing others away with backhanded compliments. Other examples include poor listening, hurtful teasing disguised as joking, and the withholding of positive feedback and appreciation. Chronic lateness and poor follow through on commitments can also be unconscious, passive-aggressive ways of expressing anger to others.

Refusing to Give Voice to the Critic's Point of View

The outer critic is the author of this intimacy-spoiling program: *Being honest to a fault*. In the guise of honesty, the outer critic can negatively notice only what is imperfect in another. Under the spell of perfectionism, the outer critic can tear the other apart by laundry-listing his normal weaknesses and foibles. When challenged about this many fight types will respond that: "I was just trying to be honest!"

The inner critic has its own version of excessive honesty which I sometimes call "beating you to the punch." Afraid of being criticized [as in childhood], the inner critic can launch the survivor into a "confession" of her every defect in hopes of short-circuiting anyone else from bringing them up. Sometimes hearing the criticism from yourself feels less hurtful than hearing it from someone else. After all, it's old news to you and your critic.

I subscribe to authenticity as one of my highest values, but it does not include sharing my outer critic's view of you or exposing my inner critic's unfair judgments of me.

As stated earlier, the toxic critic is not an authentic part of us. We were not born with it. We were indoctrinated with it by parents who viewed us in an extremely negative and jaundiced way. Because of this, we need to protect our intimates from its distorted and destructive judgments. Just as importantly, we need to protect ourselves from alienating people by presenting ourselves as if we are so defective that we do not deserve to be loved.

OUTER CRITIC-DOMINATED FLASHBACKS

Holly, an elderly client and a flight-fight type, was suffering minor, age-related memory loss. She started her session chuckling: "I was reading your article on the Outer Critic again last night. I didn't really get it when I read it three years ago, but I get it now and I think it's because my memory deterioration has a silver lining.

"So, you know how I'm always blaming my husband whenever anything goes wrong at home. Well I'm starting to get that it's an all-or-none, outer critic process that I get stuck in.

"I've been blaming him for misplacing or not putting things away for decades but I've started to notice that it's me who often misplaces things. I was cooking a meal last night and looking for the food scissors that I use to cut up leafy vegetables. It wasn't on the magnetic wall strip where I insist that we keep it, and I immediately started feeling very angry at him - and more and more angry as I searched in various drawers to no avail.

"The longer I searched, the more exasperated I got, and sure enough, I found myself laundry-listing all his faults. My resentment rapidly escalated and peaked with me deciding that I really was going to leave him this time. As I continued to amass evidence that he was a terrible loser and that this was a wise decision, I went back to the stove and found the scissors where I'd left them five minutes ago. I could see the scraps of spinach still on them from when I'd cut it up over the pot!

"What a mortifying epiphany I had! - Especially since a similar thing had happened with the tooth paste the night before. I forgot I had put it in the medicine cabinet in one of my organizational upgrades, and I was convinced Frank had moved it from its proper place. I started reading him the riot act so intensely, that he pretended he had to get something out of the car. And then, when I went to the medicine cabinet for some aspirin, there it was where I had placed it myself!

"Oh my god, that outer critic did an instant about face into becoming the inner critic. And then when it had contemptuously lambasted me to tears, I suddenly had another epiphany about how I would let any mistake on his part launch me into a two volume history of his past mistakes. I'd get so stuck in that negative noticing that I couldn't call to mind a single good thing about this good enough husband that I've had for thirty-five years."

Holly and I spent a great deal of time fleshing this out. She could see that the outer critic typically triggered her into a very old feeling and belief that "People are so unreliable – they always let you down –they just can't be trusted!"

We then moved into exploring her childhood, looking for clues as to where this belief that people were so untrustworthy began. She closed her eyes, took a few deep breaths, and when she opened them tears trickled down her face. "It was Father – Daddy - that incredibly selfish, alcoholic a-hole. Please pardon my French. No matter where I'd hide my baby-sitting money he'd always find it, and come home drunk later, crying about how sorry he was and how he'd never do it again. He'd even let me go off on him! Oh my God, just like poor Frank! Just sit there and take it. Only poor Frank [more tears], he's never done anything like that to me. He's pretty reliable in most ways, except for not being as organized as me."

OUTER CRITIC MODELLING IN THE MEDIA

Outer critic entrenchment is also difficult to dislodge because its parlance is normalized, and worse, celebrated in our society. Skewering people seems to be standard practice in most TV comedies. Moreover, many influential, seemingly healthy adults model a communication style that is rife with judgmentalness, sarcasm, negativity, fear-mongering and scapegoating.

Giving control of our social interactions to the outer critic prohibits the cultivation of the vulnerable communication that makes intimacy possible. We must renounce unconscious outer critic strategies such as: [1] "I will use angry criticism to make you afraid of me, so I can be safe from you"; [2] "Why should I bother with people when everyone is so selfish and corrupt" [all-or-none thinking]; [3] "I will perfectionistically micromanage you to prevent you from betraying or abandoning me"; [4] "I will rant and rave or leave at the first sign of a lonely feeling, because 'if you really loved me, I would never feel lonely'".

The Critic: Subliminal B-Grade Movie Producer

The outer critic typically arises most powerfully during emotional flashbacks. At such times, it transmutes unconscious abandonment pain into an overwhelmingly negative perception of people and of life in general. It obsessively fantasizes, consciously and unconsciously, about how people have or could hurt us.

Over the years these fantasies typically expand from scary snapshots into film clips and even movies. Without realizing it, we can amass a video collection of real and imagined betrayals that destroy our capacity to be nurtured by human contact.

"Don't trust anyone", "Proud to be a loner", "You can only depend on yourself", "Lovers always leave you", "Kids will break your heart", "Only fools let on what they really think", "Give them an inch and they'll take a mile", are titles of video themes survivors may develop in their quest for interpersonal safety.

These defensive and often subliminal daydreams are analogs of the critic-spawned nightmares that also shore up the "safety" work of frightening us into isolation. Over time, with enough recovery, intrusive anti-intimacy reveries become clues that we are actually in a flashback, and that we need to invoke our flashback management skills.

The dynamics of the outer critic are often obscured by minimization and denial. Its obsessions and "daymares" often occur just below the level of our awareness. They become subliminal via their repetitiveness like the sound of waves at the beach - like the sounds of traffic in the city - like the sound of the critic repetitively calling you or someone else a jerk, a loser, a dumbsh*t!

Watching the News as a Trigger

Sometimes the outer critic's penchant for raising false alarms ensnares us with an insatiable hunger for listening to the news. When we do not resist this junk food feeding of our psyches with a news "service" that exults so thoroughly in the negative, we can be left floundering in a dreadful hypervigilance.

The critic can then work overtime to amass irrefutable proof that the world is unforgivably dangerous. Isolation, and minimal or superficial relating, is therefore, our only recourse. At such times any inclination to call a friend triggers images of rejection and humiliation before the phone can even be picked up. When flashbacks are particularly intense, impulses to venture out may immediately trigger fantasies of being verbally harassed or even mugged on the street.

In worse case scenarios, outer critic drasticizing deteriorates into paranoia. At its worst paranoia deteriorates into fantasies and delusions of persecution. I remember one horribly, humiliating experience that occurred in my early twenties on an occasion when I was very sleep-deprived. I was sitting on a park bench struggling to concentrate on the book I was reading. I had read the same short paragraph four times and barely registered a word of it. At the same time, I was becoming more and more aware of a group of people who had sat down behind me. I started feeling ashamed because they were having a great time while I sat there painfully self-conscious and despondent.

Suddenly I realized they were talking disparagingly about me. I was too scared to turn around. Their comments became steadily more insulting. Their loud laughter became increasingly mocking. In my mind's I eye I could see them all staring and pointing at me: "Look at that sorry-ass loser. He's pretending he's not even listening!" Finally, in desperation, I turned around and croaked out a weak "What's going on?"

I was shocked and even more mortified at the same time. They were not even looking at me. They were so immersed in their joyful banter that they did not even notice that I turned around and spoke. It became immediately obvious to me that it was a terrible figment of my imagination. I slunk away in shame and had to wait decades to understand how my Cptsd and the outer critic had manufactured this terrible paranoia.

INTIMACY AND THE OUTER CRITIC

As stated earlier, Cptsd typically includes an attachment disorder that comes from the absence of a sympathetic caregiver in childhood. When the developing child lacks a supportive parental refuge, she never learns that other people can soothe loneliness and emotional pain. She never learns that real intimacy grows out of sharing all of her experience.

To the degree that our caretakers attack or abandon us for showing vulnerability, to that degree do we later avoid the authentic self-expression that is fundamental to intimacy. The outer critic forms to remind us that everyone else is surely as dangerous as our original caretakers. Subliminal memories of being scorned for seeking our parents' support then short-circuit our inclinations to share our troubles and ask for help.

Even worse, retaliation fantasies can plague us for hours and days on the occasions when we do show our vulnerabilities. I once experienced this after being very honest and vulnerable in a job interview with a committee of eight. Over the next three insomnia-plagued nights, my outer critic ran non-stop films featuring my interviewers' contempt about everything I had said, and disgust about all that I had left out. Even after they subsequently and enthusiastically hired me, the outer critic plagued me with "imposter syndrome" fantasies of eventually being exposed as incompetent in the new job.

The No-Win Situation

While scaring us out of trusting others, the outer critic also pushes us to over-control them to make them safer. Over-controlling behaviors include shaming, excessive criticism, monologing [conversational control] and overall bossiness. An extreme example of the latter is the *no-win situation*, which is also known as the double bind. It is described in the vernacular as "damned if you do, and damned if you don't."[Only the most severe fight types do this consciously. These types are found on the end of the narcissistic continuum where narcissism turns into sociopathy.]

Sterling was a fight type client of mine who was strongly narcissistic, but not sociopathic. He wanted me to prove that I was meticulously attending to his pause-less monologue by giving him an empathic "un hunh" at about the rate of once a paragraph. He would usually cue me to do this by ending a sentence with "You Know?"

Over time, I could usually tell when he was in a flashback because he would be bothered by the frequency or quality of my "un hunh." He was alternately frustrated if I used too many or too few "un hunhs". In the first instance he fumed: "Haven't you ever heard of a rhetorical question?" In the alternate instance, his frustration flared out at my lack of sympathy because I was not responding with "un hunh" enough.

———·+·———

There is an inner critic version of the no-win situation. Howard came into a session with a 102 temperature and a raging case of the flu. He told me: "I was lying in bed fluctuating between the sweats and the chills, and the critic was kicking my ass. 'You lazy, flakey piece of sh*t! Stop feeling sorry for yourself. Get off your sorry ass and get to your appointment!'"

Howard then told me that he fought this for about fifteen minutes, but the critic finally won and he came. As he sat in my waiting room, the critic started in again: "You are such an idiot. How could you be so stupid to go out feeling like this? You masochistic loser, you're just trying to kill yourself. Why do you even bother trying to get better?"

Scaring Others Away

To avoid the vulnerability of being close, the outer critic can also broadcast from the various inner critic endangerment program. Catastrophizing out loud can be very triggering to others and can be an unconscious way of making them afraid of us.

One of my basketball-playing acquaintances is addicted to listening to a local, doom-and-gloom news station. He has managed to alienate everyone in our gym by his non-stop proselytizing about the catastrophic demise of our times. One of the players joked that he will not pass him the ball anymore because he thinks the guy believes that it is impossible for it to go through the hoop.

Survivors who unnecessarily frighten others by excessively broadcasting about all the possible things that could go wrong rarely endear themselves to others. Moreover, they "force" others to avoid and abandon them when their *negative noticing* reaches a critical mass and becomes noise pollution.

VACILLATING BETWEEN OUTER AND INNER CRITIC

Many Cptsd survivors flounder in caustic judgmentalness, shuffling back and forth between pathologizing others [the toxic blame of the outer critic] and pathologizing themselves [the toxic shame of the inner critic]. They get stuck in endless loops of detailing the relational inadequacies of others, and then of themselves.

My parents' twisted version of this boiled down to: "As f*cked up as we are, we're still way better than you". Karen Horney described this trauma two-step as all-or-none lurching between the polarities of the *grandiose self* and the *despised self*.

When we become lost in this process, we miss out on our crucial emotional need to experience a sense of belonging. We live in permanent estrangement oscillating between the extremes of too good for others or too unlikeable to be included. This is the excruciating social perfectionism of the Janus-faced critic: others are too flawed to love and we are too defective to be lovable.

A verbal diagram of a typical critic-looping scenario looks like this. The outer critic's judgmentalness is activated by the need to escape the "in-danger" feeling that is triggered by socializing. Even the thought of relating can set off our disapproval programs so that we feel justified in isolating. Extended withdrawal however, reawakens our relational hunger and our impulses to connect. This simultaneously reverses the critic from outer to inner mode. The critic then laundry lists our inadequacies, convincing us that we are too odious to others to socialize. This then generates self-pitying persecution fantasies, which eventually re-invites the outer critic to build a case about how awful people are...ad infinitum...ad nauseam. This looping then keeps us "safe" in the hiding of silent disengagement.

When it emanates from the inner critic direction, the vacillating critic can look like this. The survivor's negative self-noticing drives her to strive to be perfect. She works so hard and incessantly at it that she begins to resent others who do not. Once the resentment accumulates enough, a minor faux pas in another triggers her to shift into extreme outer critic disappointment and frustration. She then silently perseverates and laundry lists "people" for all their faults and betrayals. How long she remains polarized to the outer critic usually depends on her 4F type, but sooner or later she starts to feel guilty about this, and suddenly the inner critic is back on line judging her harshly for being so judgmental. The cataloguing of her own defects then resumes in earnest.

A Case Example of the Vacillating Critic

My wife and I have been living together for more than a decade. We have come a long way in negotiating what seems to both of us - most of the time – a fair and flexible approach to handling the innumerable tasks involved in running a household with a young child. But sometimes, when I am experiencing an extended flashback, I start over-noticing imperfections in the general household order.

Where the critic first points the finger varies. If I am triggered into tired survival mode, the inner critic can launch into berating me for my sub-standard contribution. If on the other hand I am triggered into flight mode and have been speed-cleaning, my outer critic can start keeping score. In this latter mode, my outer critic can perseverate about how little my wife is doing compared to me. The comparisons are typically in the areas where I have recently been over-contributing.

But my fawn side is pretty strong and before too long, I can start noticing all the venues where I do not contribute as much as she. And suddenly I am the selfish slacker of the family. As the flashback continues, I may then flip into berating myself for being picky and ungenerous.

In an especially strong flash back, the outer critic will come back sooner or later and start assigning more weight and importance to my contributions, and then belittle her for being, slack, thoughtless, self-involved, etc.

In our early relationship I could loop this loop for quite some time, losing hours even days to feeling disaffected from my wife, and from myself. My peace of mind would deteriorate into an inner battleground of feeling abandoned by her while simultaneously judging myself for abandoning her. In the worst flashbacks, the process did not stay internal, and we would have conflicts about this issue.

These days conflict rarely occurs over chores. Because of what I have learned about the outer critic, internal looping about this has also decreased immeasurably. Mindfulness about my outer and inner critic processes allows me to identify them sooner and rescue myself and my relationship from them much more quickly.

The scenario above is also a typical example of what worrying looks like in a flashback.

THE CRITIC AS JUDGE, JURY AND EXECUTIONER

As noted above, not all survivors hide their outer critic. Fight types and subtypes can take the passive out of passive-aggressive and become quite aggressive. The survivor who is polarized to the outer critic often develops a specious belief that his subjectively derived standards of correctness are objective truth. When triggered, he can use the critic's combined detective-lawyer-judge function to prosecute the other for betrayal with little or no evidence. Imagined slights, insignificant peccadilloes, misread facial expressions, and inaccurate "psychic" perceptions can be used to put relationships on trial. In the proceedings, the outer critic typically refuses to admit positive evidence. Extenuating circumstances will not be considered in this kangaroo court. Moreover any relational disappointment can render a guilty verdict that sentences the relationship to capital punishment. This is also the process by which jealousy can become toxic and run riot.

On another level, the outer critic is skilled at building a case to justify occupying a higher moral ground. From this lofty position, the critic then claims the right to micromanage others. Typically this is rationalized as being for the other's own good. This control, however, is usually wielded on an unconscious level to protect the survivor from any reenactment of early parental abuse or neglect.

Micromanagement of others also devolves into a host of controlling behaviors. Fight types treat others like captive audiences, give them unsolicited performance evaluations, make unreasonable demands for improvement, and control their time schedules, social calendars and food and clothing choices. In worse case scenarios, they dramatically act out their jealousy, often without cause. At its absolute worst, outer critic relating looks like taking prisoners, not making friends.

Scapegoating

Scapegoating is an outer critic process whereby personal frustration is unfairly dumped onto others. Scapegoating is typically fuelled by unworked through anger about childhood abandonment. Displacing anger on the wrong target however, fails to release or resolve old or unrelated hurts.

Scapegoating is often a reenactment of a parent's abusive role. It is blind imitation of a parent who habitually released his frustration by indiscriminately raging. When a fight type parent scapegoats those around him, he enforces a perverse kind of mirroring. He is making sure that when he feels bad, so does everyone else. It is like a bumper sticker I saw the other day: "If Momma ain't happy, Nobody's happy."

I witnessed this common example of scapegoating several times in my childhood. My parents hated anyone who was late. If one of us children were even a minute late for something, they felt absolutely justified in blasting us with their "righteous" indignation. This was true even though we all learned very quickly to be anally punctual. Because of their untreated Cptsd however, their anger was the tip of the iceberg of their unexpressed rage about their own childhood hurts. In this case, they were flashing back to the pain of their parents' chronic lateness and failure to show up to meet their normal childhood needs.

MINDFULNESS AND SHRINKING THE OUTER CRITIC

Reducing outer critic reactivity requires a great deal of mindfulness. This is as essential for fight types who act out aggressively, as it is for those trauma types who internally rant against the entire human group known as "F*cking People!". It is also of great importance for any survivor who is locked into alienation because of the judgmentalness of his outer critic.

Mindfulness, once again, is the process of becoming intricately aware of everything that is going on inside us, especially thoughts, images, feelings and sensations. In terms of outer critic work, it is essential that we become more mindful of both the cognitive and emotional content of our thoughts.

This is the same as in inner critic work, where the two key fronts of critic shrinking are cognitive and emotional. Cognitive work in both cases involves the demolition and rebuilding processes of thought-stopping and thought substitution, respectively. And, emotional work in both instances is grief work. It is removing the critic's fuel supply - the unexpressed childhood anger and the uncried tears of a lifetime of abandonment.

When Mindfulness Appears to Intensify the Critic

In early recovery the outer critic unfortunately seems to become nastier and stronger the more we challenge it. We may even think we are counter-productively stirring it up or making it worse by daring to resist it.

When mindfulness of the critic seems to strengthen it, we are typically flashing back to how our parents rebuked our early protests at their attacks. This is often impossible to remember because our dysfunctional parents typically kill our protest function before our memory function comes on line. Nonetheless, fear of parental reprisal is often the unconscious dynamic that scares us out of challenging our own toxic thinking. This is why survivors in early recovery often need to invoke the instinct of angry self-protection to empower their thought-stopping.

There is another dynamic occurring when critic-work seems to strengthen rather than weaken the critic. As we become less dissociated, we begin to notice critic processes that were there all along under the horizon of our awareness. Our childhood survival was aided by learning to dissociate from these painful critic processes. Consequently, many of us come into recovery barely able to even notice the critic.

Our recovering depends on us using mindfulness to decrease our habits of dissociation. Only then can we see the critic programs that we need to deconstruct, shrink and consciously disidentify from. This typically involves learning to tolerate the pain that comes from discovering how pervasive and strong the critic is. This pain is sometimes a hard pill to swallow because progress in fighting the critic is hard to see at first. And then, even when our shrinking work is effective, progress usually feels disappointingly slow and gradual. This is especially true during a flashback, when the critic can seem to be as strong as ever.

As stated earlier, the critic grew carcinogenically in childhood. It is like a pervasive cancer that requires many uncomfortable operations to remove. Nonetheless, we can choose to face the acute pain of critic-shrinking work because we want to end the chronic pain of having the critic destroy our enjoyment of life. It is the fight of a lifetime.

Thought Substitution & Correction: Supplanting the Critic

Many of us are still developmentally arrested in our need to orient our psyches towards noticing what is good, trustworthy and loveable about others and life in general. In working to shrink the outer critic, thought substitution is the practice of invoking positive thoughts and images of others to help erode the critic's intimacy-spoiling habit of picking them apart.

One helpful thought substitution exercise is to list five recollections of positive interactions with a given friend, as well as five of her attributes. This same technique works well when we self-apply it to help us separate from our inner critic's negative self-image. Toolbox 5, in chapter 16, contains a written exercise to broaden your appreciation of select others who have benefitted you.

Since thoughts typically give rise to speech, I also recommend that you practice the "5 positives to 1 negative" guideline when giving feedback to a loved one. John Gottman's research has shown that this ratio is characteristic of how intimacy-successful couples communicate. This is also key because the outer critic was spawned in childhood by parental modeling that at least reversed this ratio.

GRIEVING SHORTCIRCUITS THE OUTER CRITIC

The role of grieving in shrinking the outer critic is as crucial as it is with the inner critic. As with the inner critic, angering at the outer critic helps to silence it, and crying helps to evaporate it.

We can use the anger of our grief to energize our thought corrections. This helps us to challenge the critic's entrenched all-or-none perspective that everyone is as dangerous as our parents. Moreover, when our grieving opens into crying, it can release the fear that the outer critic uses to frighten us out of opening to others. Tears can also help us realize that our loneliness is now causing us much unnecessary pain. This in turn can motivate us to open to the possibility of finding safe connections.

Defueling the Outer Critic via Working the Transference

Transference [AKA projection; AKA displacement] occurs when unprocessed feelings from the past amplify present time feelings.

A key characteristic of outer critic-dominated flashbacks is that we displace emotional pain from past relationships onto current ones. Transference is the pipeline from the past that supplies the critic with anger to control, attack or disapprove of present relationships.

As a baby thrives on love, so does the outer critic thrive on anger. Like a parasite, the outer critic gorges on repressed anger, and then erroneously assigns it to present-day disappointments.

The most common transferrential dynamic that I witness occurs when leftover hurt about a parent gets displaced onto someone we perceive as hurting us in the present. When this occurs, we respond to them with a magnified anger or anguish that is out of proportion to what they did.

Transference can also grossly distort our perceptions, and sometimes we can misperceive a harmless person as being hurtful. Transference can fire up the critic to imagine slights that do not actually occur. Transference typically runs wild when the outer critic is on a rampage.

Just as the inner critic transmutes unreleased anger into self-hate, the outer critic uses it to control and /or push others away. Unexpressed and unworked through anger about childhood hurt is a hidden reserve that the critic can always tap into. The anger work of grieving the losses of childhood is so essential because it breaks the critic's supply line to this anger.

Grieving out old unexpressed pain about our poor parenting gradually deconstructs the process of transferring it unfairly onto others. This is crucial because love and intimacy are murdered when the critic habitually projects old anger out at an intimate.

Healthy Outer Critic Venting

There are times when venting from the outer critic perspective is healthy, self-protective behavior. Sometimes the outer critic's judgments are accurate. Sometimes people are acting as abusively as our parents did in childhood. In this vein, there are two healthy applications of outer critic aggressiveness. One is to protect ourselves when someone is actually attacking us. The other is in the work of grieving the losses of childhood. As we shall see in the next chapter, survivors benefit immeasurably from angrily judging their parents' atrocious abuse and negligence.

Road Rage, Transference and the Outer Critic

Let us take another look at how the outer critic displaces anger from the past onto present-day relationships.

My client Johnny came in for his session boiling with road rage. Something infuriating had just occurred on his drive to my office. Before his butt hit the couch, he launched away: "That pompous SOB! People are so obnoxious. Everyone drives like they are the only ones on the road. What a jerk. Driving like he owns the whole road. Not giving a sh*t about anybody but himself. Nobody cares about anybody but themselves. Oh god! Don't let me get started on my wife. I don't know why I get out of bed in the morning. This jerk must have forgotten what turn signals are for. I felt like crashing right into that stuck-up bastard and his shiny new Beamer!"

Johnny radiated anger a full 360 degrees. He hated the driver who had cut him off, all the other drivers on the road, his wife, his employees, his neighbors, the government, and last - but thankfully least - his "overcharging therapist" who was always pretending to be "soooo empathetic."

Johnny was a fawn-fight type. Usually he was mostly fawn. In our two years of working together, I had never seen him so enraged, and I was quite taken aback. I was indeed straining to hold an empathic position, but I knew he was in a flashback.

I encouraged him to further ventilate by hitting a tennis racket on a cushion. [This is a classic anger-release work technique for externalizing anger in a non-harmful way]. Johnny beat it like his life depended on it.

When his catharting petered out, I asked him to close his eyes. I then suggested that he ask himself if his feelings of outrage had a trail into the past. After a moment he said: "I'm so mad. I don't want to do anything that you say right now. And it's weird because I know you're fishing for my father, but I keep thinking of my mother. She was such a wimp! She'd never drive like that asshole in the Beamer, and she didn't rant and rave at me like he did, but you know I just feel so pissed at her for putting up with him for all those years, and never once standing up for me or protecting me. It's bad enough I got him for father, but it's even more unfair that I got her too".

Johnny did another round of venting with the tennis racket: "I thought mothers were programmed to stick up for their kids! You know, like that mother bear sh*t. It's so unfair...it's so un-f*cken-believably unfair. I'd just like to shake her out of that numb trance she'd go into. Just shake some freaking sense into her!"

And then the tears came. Shortly after they subsided, the epiphany arrived. It made him laugh. Genuinely. It was the laughter of relief that we sometimes get when we finally understand why something is really bothering us. He said: "You know this sounds pretty far-fetched and like that psychobabble I hate, but it's the goddamn unfairness of life that just pisses me off so much. You know that you-got-the-queen-of-spades bad luck. That bad luck of being the one person in the crowd who gets crapped on by a pigeon. That cursed luck of getting dealt those assholes from the parenting deck. It's so goddamned unfair! Dad and mom's unfairness was f*cking legendary!

"And that jerk on the freeway making a lane change without signaling was unfair too. I mean if I hadn't seen him, I could have gotten into a serious accident. But if I'm honest, it wasn't really all that bad. I had plenty of time to adjust, and would have been a lousy driver myself if I hadn't.

"But, I mean it was still dangerous though. But nothing compared to growing up in that house. Now that was pure, unadulterated danger for you. I guess my rage was mostly about how unfair it was that I had to grow up in that sorry excuse for a home."

———·—

Road rage and the less intense irritations we experience with our fellow drivers are common forms of outer critic transference. When we become more mindful of our driving frustrations or other minor everyday annoyances, we can look below the tip of this iceberg for old unexpressed anger and hurt that it reminds us of.

I encourage you to experiment with this next time you are inordinately angry at some driver for a relatively minor driving mistake. You can try asking yourself: "What is this situation or feeling reminding me of?" In the next chapter, we will explore more deeply the processes of grieving through the old hurts that we discover when we get to the bottom of our flashbacks.

CHAPTER

GRIEVING

Grieving is an irreplaceable tool for resolving the overwhelming feelings that arise during emotional flashbacks. Moreover, grieving is the key process for working through the host of losses that come from growing up in a Cptsd-inducing family.

We grieve the losses of childhood because these losses are like deaths of important parts of ourselves. Effective grieving brings these parts back to life. In this chapter we describe the healing that is available through the four practices of grieving: *angering, crying, verbal ventilating and feeling.*

———————

If you find that crying or angering is inaccessible, does not help, or makes you feel worse, then your recovery work my need to focus more on deconstructing and shrinking your inner critic.

Grieving expands Insight and Understanding

I saw grief drinking a cup of sorrow and called out:
"It tastes sweet doesn't it?"
"You have caught me", grief answered,
"And you've ruined my business
How can I sell sorrow, when you know its blessing?" -RUMI
Insight, as crucially important as it is, is never enough to attain the deeper levels of recovering. No amount of intention or epiphany can bypass a survivor's need to learn to lovingly care for himself when he is in an emotional flashback. It is crucial that we respond to ourselves with kindness when we are feeling scared, sad, mad, or bad.

Grieving aids the survivor immeasurably to work through the death-like experience of being lost and trapped in an emotional flashback. Grieving metabolizes our most painful abandonment feelings, especially those that give rise to suicidal ideation, and at their worst, active suicidality.

Recoverees also need to grieve the death of their early attachment needs. We must grieve the awful fact that safety and belonging was scarce or non-existent in our own families. We need to mourn the myriad heartbreaks of our frustrated attempts to win approval and affection from our parents.

Grieving also supports recovery from the many painful, death-like losses caused by childhood traumatization. Key childhood losses - addressed throughout this book - are all the crucial developmental arrests that we suffered. The most essential of these are the deaths of our self-compassion and our self-esteem, as well as our abilities to protect ourselves and fully express ourselves.

Grieving the Absence of Parental Care

As our capacity to grieve evolves, we typically uncover a great deal of unresolved grief about the deadening absence of the nurturance we needed to develop and thrive. Here are the key types of parental nurturing that all children need in order to flourish. Knowing about these unmet needs can help you to grieve out the unreleased pain that comes from having grown up without this type of support. Moreover, this knowledge can guide you to reparent and interact with yourself more nurturingly.

1. VERBAL NURTURANCE: Eager participation in multidimensional conversation. Generous amounts of praise and positive feedback. Willingness to entertain all questions. Teaching, reading stories, providing resources for ongoing verbal development.

2. SPIRITUAL NURTURANCE: Seeing and reflecting back to the child his or her essential worth, basic goodness and loving nature. Engendering experiences of joy, fun, and love to maintain the child's innate sense that life is a gift. Spiritual or philosophical guidance to help the child integrate painful aspects of life. Nurturing the child's creative self-expression. Frequent exposure to nature.

3. EMOTIONAL NURTURANCE: Meeting the child consistently with caring, regard and interest. Welcoming and valuing the child's full emotional expression. Modeling non-abusive expression of emotions. Teaching safe ways to release anger that do not hurt the child or others. Generous amounts of love, warmth, tenderness, and compassion. Honoring tears as a way of releasing hurt. Being a safe refuge. Humor.

4. PHYSICAL NURTURANCE: Affection and protection. Healthy diet and sleep schedule. Teaching habits of grooming, discipline, and responsibility. Helping the child develop hobbies, outside interests, and own sense of personal style. Helping the child balance rest, play, and work.

My book, *The Tao of Fully Feeling,* contains extensive guidelines and encouragements for identifying and grieving the losses of childhood. Sandra Bloom's article: "The Grief That Dare Not Speak Its Name, Part II, Dealing with The Ravages of Childhood" also identifies childhood losses from trauma in a very specific and compelling way. [You can find the article by searching for the title.]

———·◦·———

It is often difficult to become motivated to grieve losses that occurred so long ago. Many of these losses seem so nebulous that trying to embrace grieving is a bit like trying to embrace dental work. Who wants to go to the dentist? But who doesn't go once the toothache becomes acute?

Soul ache is considerably harder to assign to the losses of childhood, yet those who take the grieving journey described below come to know unquestionably that the core of their soul ache and psychological suffering is in the unworked through losses of growing up with abandoning parents.

These losses have to be grieved until the person really gets how much her caretakers were not caretakers, and how much her parents were not her allies. She needs to grieve until she stops blaming herself for their abuse and/or neglect. She needs to grieve until she fully realizes that their abysmal parenting practices gave her that awful gift that keeps on giving: Cptsd. She needs to grieve until she understands how her learned habit of automatic self-abandonment is a reenactment of their abject failure to be there for her.

Mourning these awful realities empowers our efforts to develop a multidimensional practice of self-care. As we grieve more effectively, our capacities for self-compassion and self-protection grow, and our psyche becomes increasingly user friendly.

GRIEVING AMELIORATES FLASHBACKS

"Pain is excess energy crying out for release." – Gerald Heard

Grieving sometimes seems sacramental to me in its ability to move me out of the abandonment mélange, that extremely painful and upsetting amalgam of fear, shame and depression that is at the emotional core of most flashbacks.

A survivor can learn to grieve himself out of fear - the death of feeling safe. He can learn to grieve himself out of shame - the death of feeling worthy. He can learn to grieve himself out of depression - the death of feeling fully alive.

With sufficient grieving, the survivor gets that he was innocent and eminently loveable as a child. As he mourns the bad luck of not being born to loving parents, he finds within himself a fierce, unshakeable self-allegiance. He becomes ready, willing and able to be there for himself no matter what he is experiencing - internally or externally.

Griefwork also releases you from the impatience and frustration that can arise when you get re-stuck in an inner critic attack. This is especially important during those "monster" flashbacks when the critic can bully you into wanting to give up. At such times, angering and crying at this terrible intrusion from your past can rescue you from forgetting how far you have come and how much safer you are now.

Inner Critic Hindrances to Grieving

The greatest hindrance to effective grieving is typically the inner critic. When the critic is especially toxic, grieving may be counterproductive and contraindicated in early recovery. Those who were repeatedly pathologized and punished for emoting in childhood may experience grieving as exacerbating their flashbacks rather than relieving them.

I have worked with numerous survivors whose tears immediately triggered them into toxic shame. Their own potentially soothing tears elicited terrible self-attacks: "I'm so pathetic! No wonder nobody can stand me!" "God, I'm so unlovable when I snivel like this!" "I f*ck up, and then make myself more of a loser by whining about it!" "What good is crying for yourself – it only makes you weaker!"

This latter response is particularly ironic, for once grieving is protected from the critic, nothing can restore a person's inner strength and coping capacity like a good cry. I have defused active suicidality on dozens of occasions by simply eliciting the suffering person's tears.

Angering can also immediately trigger the survivor into toxic shame. This is often true of instances when there is only an angry thought or fantasy. Dysfunctional parents typically reserve their worst punishments for their child's anger. This then traps the child's anger inside.

Critic management is often the primary work of early stage grief work. This work involves recognizing and challenging the ways the critic is blocking or shaming the processes of grieving. As disidentification from the critic increases, grieving can then best be initiated with low intensity verbal ventilation. Over time verbal ventilation can be allowed to gradually increase in sad and angry intonation.

Once the critic has been sufficiently diminished and once thought-correction techniques have made the psyche more user-friendly, a person begins to tap into grief's sweet relief-granting potential. He learns to grieve in a way that promotes and enhances compassion for the abandoned child he was and for the survivor he is today – still struggling in the throes of painful flashbacks.

Defueling the Critic through Grieving

Fear drives the toxic inner critic. The critic feeds off fear and flashes the survivor back to the frightening times of childhood. She gets stuck seeing herself only through her parents' contemptuous, intimidating or rejecting eyes. She then imitates them and scornfully mocks herself as "defective", "ugly", "unlovable". She scares herself with endangerment scenarios and abhors herself for insignificant imperfections.

Because fear is a core emotional experience, emotional tools are needed to manage the fright that runs haywire during a flashback. Healthy angering and crying can short-circuit fear from morphing into the flashback-triggering cognitions of the critic. I have seen grieving bring the critic's devastating programs of drasticizing and catastrophizing to a screeching halt on thousands of occasions.

It appears that children are hard-wired to release fear through angering and crying. The newborn baby, mourning the death of living safely and fully contained inside the mother, utters the first of many angry cries not only to call for nurturance and attention, but also to release her fear.

In the dysfunctional family however, the traumatizing parent soon eradicates the child's capacity to emote. The child becomes afraid and ashamed of her own tears and anger. Tears get shut off and anger gets trapped inside and is eventually turned against the self as self-attack, self-hate, self-disgust, and self-rejection. Self-hate is the most grievous reenactment of parental abandonment.

Over time, anger also becomes fuel for the critic and actually exacerbates fear by creating an increasingly dangerous internal environment. Anything the survivor says, thinks, feels, imagines or wishes for is subjected to an intimidating inner attack.

Here are some common anger-powered critic attacks. They are presented in the first person voice, which the critic inevitably acquires: "Why did I ask such a stupid question?" "Could I have had an uglier expression on my face?" "Who am I kidding? How could an undeserving loser like me wish for love?" "No wonder I feel like sh*t; I am a piece of sh*t!"

Recovery is enhanced immeasurably by co-opting this anger from the critic and using it for the work of distancing from and shrinking the critic, as we shall see below. As you become proficient at grieving, you will notice that your critic's volume and intensity ebbs dramatically. In fact, without the aid of effective grieving, progress in critic shrinking can only go so far.

THE FOUR PROCESSES OF GRIEVING

Grieving is at its most effective when the survivor can grieve in four ways: *angering, crying, verbal ventilating and feeling.*

1. <u>Angering</u>: Diminishes Fear and Shame

Angering is the grieving technique of aggressively complaining about current or past losses and injustices. Survivors need to anger - sometimes rage - about the intimidation, humiliation and neglect that was passed off to them as nurturance in their childhoods. As they become adept at grieving, they anger out their healthy resentment at their family's pervasive lack of safety. They become incensed about the ten thousand betrayals of never being helped in times of need. They feel rage that there was never anyone to go to for guidance or protection. They bellow that there was no one to appeal to for fairness or appreciative recognition of their developmental achievements.

My first book, *The Tao of Fully Feeling, Harvesting Forgiveness Out Of Blame,* explicates in great detail a safe process for angering out childhood pain in a way that does not hurt the survivor or anyone else. In most cases, survivors do not have to directly anger at and blame their living parents. The key place to direct it is at your internalized parents - the parents of your past. The most common exception to this occurs when a parent is still abusive. This and other exceptions are explored in depth in my first book.

Angering is therapeutic when the survivor rails against childhood trauma, and especially when he rails against its living continuance in the self-hate processes of the critic. Angrily saying "No!" or "Shut Up!" to the critic, the deputy of his parents, externalizes his anger. It stops him from turning this anger against himself, and allows him to revive the lost instinct of defending himself against unjust attack.

Additionally, angering rescues the survivor from toxic shame. It rescues him from blindly letting his parents' venomous blame turn into shame. Angering redirects blame back to where it belongs. It also augments his motivation to keep fighting to establish internal boundaries against the critic.

Angering can be done alone or in the presence of a validating witness, such as a trusted friend or therapist. Over time the vast majority of angering needs to be done silently in the privacy of your own psyche. This is the anger-empowered thought-stopping of shielding yourself from inner critic attacks.

Many survivors are so identified with the critic that it becomes their whole identity. Such survivors typically need to focus on fighting off the critic until they have established the healthy ego function of self-protection.

Angering also serves to rescue a person from the childlike sense of powerlessness that she is flashing back to. It reminds her that she inhabits an adult body with which she can now defend herself.

Through all these functions, angering serves to reduce or antidote fear. It reawakens and nurtures the instinct of self-preservation. With practice it increasingly builds a sense of both outer and inner boundaries. These boundaries increasingly move us out of harm's way. They offer safety from the bullying of others, and safety from the most damaging bully of all – the inner critic.

Finally, angering can also empower the myriad thought corrections and substitutions needed to establish the survivor's belief in her own essential goodness and in the lovability of discriminately chosen others. Angering bolsters her for the long-term, gradual process of wrestling her self-image away from the critic and reeducating the psyche to make it both user- and intimacy-friendly.

Angering Helps Deconstruct Repetition Compulsion

Survivors need to resuscitate their instinctual anger about parental maltreatment or they risk blindly accepting others' reenactments of these behaviors.

A meek, visibly fearful client of mine suffered devastating sexual seductions by trusted male figures on three occasions in her adult life. Over time we traced these back to a childhood betrayal by a trusted uncle, the only seemingly kind caretaker of her childhood. She was emotionally abandoned by her parents, and he preyed upon her loneliness. He gradually took appropriate physical affection, one increment at a time, into contact that became increasingly sexual.

My client was helpless with her uncle because her ability to say "no" was parentally extinguished by the time she was in pre-school. The ability to say "no" is the backbone of our instinct of self-protection. Consequently, she was unable to protest his sexual violations.

On subsequent occasions in her life, a minister, a doctor and then a therapist exploited her via a reenactment of this original scenario. She was so lost in flashback all three times that she did not protest their exploitive betrayals. She could only react to the situations later by turning her anger inward, and blaming and shaming herself for not stopping it.

Eventually during our work together, she was able to engage in the angering process of grieving. After about six months of my witnessing and validating her anger at her various perpetrators, she came in one week glowing with pride. She welled with tears of joy and relief as she described her success in stopping an office predator who was in the early stages of a similar seduction.

This was the stage of seemingly friendly touching. But unwanted pats on the back gradually escalated into mild sexual innuendo, lingering touches on her hand and then her forearm. These were the first inappropriate advances that she had never been able to protest with her previous abusers. She was thrilled – in awe of herself – that she was able to say, in the presence of another worker no less: "Please don't touch me. I don't like it when you touch me, and I don't want you to touch me anymore". The seduction was immediately terminated.

2. <u>Crying</u>: the Penultimate Soothing

In grieving, crying is the yin complementary process to the yang process of angering. When we are hurt, we instinctively feel sad as well as mad. The newborn child, hurt by the loss of the perfect security of the womb, howls an angry cry.

Crying is also an irreplaceable tool for cutting off the critic's emotional fuel supply. Tears can release fear before it devolves into frightened and frightening thinking. In fact, crying is sometimes the only process that will resolve a flashback. I have witnessed my own critic wither into innocuousness hundreds of times after a good cry. On thousands of other occasions, I have seen my clients dissolve their fear, shame and self-abandonment with the solvent of their tears. I have also seen them then surface into a healthily angry place, determined to confront a current unfairness that they now find unacceptable.

A client who left a year-long therapy to move elsewhere recently wrote to me about an experience that she had with crying. She was hospitalized with terrible stomach pain and soon learned that she had cancer. She had wisely cut off contact with a toxic family, but was all alone in her new living situation. She was beside herself with fear, and felt like she was on the verge of a nervous breakdown. She wrote: "I know you think that all that talking you did to me about crying didn't get through. So did I in fact, but at the moment I was feeling the most hopeless, some of your words came back to me, and a rainstorm of tears fell out of me. It scared me at first, but I soon started feeling this amazing sense of relief, and that I would be OK if I let them operate on me. It's now twelve months since then and many tears later [not to mention a bit of barking at God] and I seem to be well and truly in the clear."

Here is another testimony to the power of tears. It is excerpted from an e-mail of a male client who wrote to me six months after we finished a year long course of therapy. "I think it's the tears..... crying so much of late.....you were right! It's great; I love it, tears of sadness, tears at the beauty in the world, tears of grief and loss, and tears of gratitude that my life is finally becoming manageable and even intimate. I've cried more in the past couple of months than I have done the past couple of decades. I am actually opening up to life, it's become less narrow, it's not just pain, shame, guilt.....there's something else, something quite beautiful."

———·—·———

An additional benefit of crying is that unabashed tears stimulate the relaxation response of the parasympathetic nervous system. This counterbalances the excessive sympathetic nervous system hyperarousal we experience in a flashback.

As we learn to grieve effectively, we allow ourselves to mourn about the lack of positive parental attention in our childhoods. We feel sorrow about the horrible reality that parental attention was typically negative and dangerous. As recovering progresses, we also cry for the child who was not appreciated and reflected as special, worthy, and easy to love.

Crying and Self-compassion

When we greet our own tears with self-acceptance, crying awakens our develop- mentally arrested instinct of self-compassion. Once we establish self-compassion through consistent and repeated practice, it becomes the cornerstone of an increasing sense of self-esteem. When an attitude of self-compassion becomes habitual, it can instantly anti-dote the self-abandonment that so characterizes a flashback.

Moreover self-compassion creates a foundation from which we can build authentic, intimacy-enhancing compassion for others. The depth of our ability to be there for an intimate generally depends on the depth of our capacity to practice unwavering allegiance to ourselves.

Crying and Angering in Concert

Crying and angering are the two key emotional tools for releasing the pain of the abandonment mélange. Typically we need both processes to attain full release.

Crying and angering together differs from whining. Whining is a type of emoting that gives grieving a bad name. Whining is a delicate subject because many people who complain and/or cry in a healthy manner are pathologized as "whiners." Dysfunctional whining however is often an unhealthy mixture of angering and crying, where either the anger or sadness is repressed but leaks through in a grating manner.

Here are two examples of this. When a hurt person only knows how to express anger, his repressed sadness unconsciously seeps into his anger in a way that makes him sound like a martyr or someone with delusions of persecution. Because there is no substantial release of his sadness, no amount of whining brings him relief, and he can angrily whine endlessly in a way that exhausts his listener's empathy. Similarly when a hurt person is only able to cry, repressed anger tinges her sadness and makes it sound like irritable and interminable bellyaching. One of my clients calls this "anger coming through a very small hole."

Many of us suffer from a socialization process that relegates angering to men and crying to women. From an early age boys are shamed for crying while girls are treated similarly for angering. Hence boys become men who can only vent their emotional pain through angering. Sadness then must morph into an irritable mood, aggravated whining or angry catharsis. Similarly, some women unconsciously try to squeeze their anger out by whining or crying in a way that devolves into feeling stuck in helplessness and self-pity.

Many men also rely on anger to carry all of their emotional expression. They get mad when they are scared, humiliated or feel down. Many women, on the other hand, can only try to cry out these feelings. This typically results in a very incomplete release. The full motion of emotion is arrested. Half of the normal emotional release process is then stymied in each gender.

Without complete emoting of his hurt, a survivor can become stuck in moodiness. His unexpressed emotion deteriorates into a stagnant and lingering mood. This moodiness can range from festering resentment to a shame-tainted self-pity that is anything but self-compassionate. Blocked anger can degenerate into bitter sullenness, and blocked sadness can deteriorate into melancholic self-indulgence.

How this contrasts with the healthy grieving of my six-year old son, who has to periodically grieve the loss of his narcissistic entitlement. Less and less does he get to be what Freud called: "His majesty the baby".

As his previously apt entitlement lessens, he mildly bawls at new rules that are age-appropriate for him to learn. Bawling is the evolution of the baby's angry cry, and it releases pain through angry crying. He howled a bit this afternoon about the "unfairness" of having to do his homework after school before he could play some more.

As we climbed the 37 stairs to our home, he punctuated his crying with a flurry of angry condemnations: "I don't like you daddy. You're not fair. I'm not going to be your friend". I am grateful for this healthy grieving, and still somewhat amazed that I can so calmly "hold" it as I help him metabolize this latest loss of early childhood narcissistic privilege.

By the time we get to the top of the stairs he opens the door and genuinely peals out a guileless laugh: "Daddy, look! Picachu fell off the table. Daddy can we play Pokémon after I practice writing my letters?"

Grieving has almost instantly delivered him from painful loss into eager apprehension of what is fun about life and what there is to look forward to. How frequently, I see my clients reemerge into remembering their real, present-day resourcefulness once they have grieved through a painful flashback.

When we can both anger and cry while re-experiencing our early abandonment in a flashback, we can obtain a more complete release from the abandonment mélange. Each survivor does well to assess whether his angering or crying is blocked or stultified, and to then work at recovering it.

There are of course numerous men and women who are reverse examples of the gender polarization mentioned above. Moreover, there are many survivors in whom both angering and crying are blocked. They also benefit inordinately from rescuing the healing balm of both anger and tears from the stultifying prohibitions of the critic.

If you are unable cry or feel angry, focusing on your breath may help you to emote. This is especially true if you attend to the sensations in your abdominal region as it expands and contracts during respiration. Deep, slow and rhythmic breathing stretches and expands various visceral muscles and internal organs in ways that sometimes bring feelings into awareness.

If this does not help, Holotropic Rebirthing and Reichian therapy employ special breathing techniques to help free stuck emotions. I know many survivors who first reclaimed their capacity to emote through these techniques.

3. <u>Verbal Ventilation</u>: the Golden Path to Intimacy

"Joy shared is doubled. Sorrow shared is halved." - Old Chinese saying

Verbal ventilation is the third process of grieving. It is the penultimate resolver of emotional flashbacks. Verbal ventilation is speaking or writing in a manner that airs out and releases painful feelings. When we let our words spring from what we feel, language is imbued with emotion, and pain can be released through what we say, think or write. As our grieving proficiency increases, we can verbally ventilate about our losses, using shame-dissolving language to tell the story of how we were unfairly deprived of our birthright to be welcomed into a family that cherished us.

My favorite technique to enhance verbal ventilation is to encourage the survivor to talk in an uncensored manner about whatever comes to his mind while he focuses on his feelings. If his feelings are not in awareness, focusing on bodily sensations can provide rich grist for verbally venting.

Verbal Ventilation is therapeutic to the degree that a person's words are colored by and descriptive of the anger, sadness, fear, shame and/or depression she feels. Ventilation that is liberally punctuated with actual crying or angering is especially powerful.

Theoretical Neuroscience of Verbal Ventilation

Verbal ventilation is a tool that can remediate brain changes that are caused by Cptsd. Susan Vaughan's MRI research demonstrates that emotional flashbacks over-activate the emotionally oriented right-brain and under-activate the thinking-oriented left-brain. With this hemispheric polarization, there is an overwhelming reemergence of childhood pain that is emotionally remembered by the memory-oriented right-brain. At the same time, the survivor loses access to the higher cognitive functions of her left-brain. This temporary loss of cognitive perspective explains why it is so hard for a survivor to realize that she is only flashing back, and not really lost in the danger, helplessness and hopelessness of the past.

Verbal ventilation, at its most potent, is the therapeutic process of bringing left-brain cognition to intense right-brain emotional activation. It fosters the recoveree's ability to put words to feelings, and ultimately to accurately interpret and communicate about his various feeling states. When this process is repeated sufficiently, new neural pathways grow that allow the left- and right-brain to work together so that the person can actually think and feel at the same time.

The corpus callosum is the part of the brain that connects the left and right hemispheres. Research shows that the corpus callosum is smaller in some Cptsd survivors. Further research shows that the brain can generate new neurons and new neuronal connections to remedy this situation.

Thinking and Feeling Simultaneously

When a survivor becomes proficient at verbal ventilation, she heals a crucial developmental arrest. She learns to think about feeling states in a way that creates healthy, helpful and appropriate responses to feelings. These responses are characteristically respectful to herself and to whomever she is with. In his book, *Emotional Intelligence,* Daniel Goleman writes that this is a core trait of emotional intelligence.

With continued practice, verbal ventilation coordinates the left and right hemispheres of the brain so that whenever the right-brain is hyper-activated in flashback, the left-brain is also fully engaged [this also can be seen in an MRI]. With the left-brain back on line, the survivor can remember to use the flashback management steps to successfully help manage a flashback.

As with angering and crying, verbal ventilation is only effective when it is liberated from the critic's control. In early recovery, verbal ventilation can easily shift into verbal self-flagellation. Verbally ventilating from the self-attacking or drasticizing perspective of the critic is rarely effective grieving. Instead it typically triggers or intensifies flashbacks, which in turn frequently generates self- and intimacy-injuring behavior.

Many survivors in early recovery are unable to notice their unconscious shifts into over-identifying with the critic's point of view. When this is the case, they usually need the help of a therapist or sufficiently recovered intimate to help them recognize and neutralize the critic.

Verbal Ventilation is an especially transformative grieving process. It not only promotes the same type of fear-release and shame-dissolution as angering and crying, but also helps to expose the manifold guises of the critic's self-attack and fear-arousal programs. Verbal ventilation also helps us to identify and communicate about needs that have long been unmet because of our childhood abandonment.

Verbally Ventilating Alone

Verbally venting alone, where no one else can hear you, is a helpful therapeutic technique. Untraumatized children do it frequently in their play, much to their great benefit. If your room is not private, you can drive your car to somewhere that is.

Typically it takes considerable silencing of the critic to regain this therapeutic tool. This tool is so powerful and restorative that it is worth many skirmishes with the critic to reclaim it for your Cptsd toolbox.

One of my clients kept an 18" length of rubber hose and a phone book on the passenger seat of her car. During the year that she was doing the lion's share of her anger work, she would hit the hose loudly on the phonebook whenever her brainwashing, abusive father came up in her mind. She would of course pull over for this, and found over time that she could do it inconspicuously in places with surprisingly limited privacy. It was remarkable to me how much critic-shrinking she did in that year.

Dissociation Deadens Verbal Ventilation

It is important to differentiate verbal ventilation from dissociative flights of fantasy and obsessive bouts of unproductive worrying. Dissociation is a defense that children develop to distract and protect themselves from the overwhelming pain of their abandonment. As unsupported children, we have to dissociate because we are not able to effectively grieve. We have to protect ourselves by not allowing the full brunt of our pain into awareness.

As we saw in chapter 6, there are two common types of dissociation: right-brain dissociation and left-brain dissociation.

Right-brain dissociation can be seen as classical dissociation and as the defense most common to freeze types. It is the right-brain process of numbing out against intense feeling or incessant inner critic attack. Dissociation is once again a process of distraction. Survivors commonly experience it as getting lost in fantasy, fogginess, TV, tiredness or sleep.

Verbally reporting from a place of self-distraction is in fact the opposite of verbal ventilation. Getting lost in daydream-like descriptions of improbable salvation fantasies is a common way that clients avoid their pain in a therapy session. Another common example is recounting long elaborate dreams that are devoid of emotional content or serious attempts at introspection.

Early in my career, I worked briefly with a freeze-fight type client who was stuck in an avoidance process of endlessly monologing about her dreams. Dina recalled them in lifeless, excruciating detail. In fact, her deadened delivery was emblematic of the way she talked about almost everything.

Dina was an intern-therapist who locked up her vulnerability with a belief that dream work was the *piece de resistance* of therapy. My attempts to guide her into exploring her deeper underlying experience were routinely met with the hackles of her fight response. I was unfortunately not experienced enough at the time to help her see that this was a dissociative defense that she had constructed as a child to protect herself from a very intrusive mother. Sadly, she left therapy disgruntled and still trapped in the isolation that was born of alienating others with her distant, abstract and non-interactive dissertations.

Left-brain dissociation

Left-brain dissociation is obsessiveness. Commonly, this ranges in severity from dwelling on a singular worry... to repetitively cycling through a list of worries... to panicky drasticizing and catastrophizing. This type of dissociation from internal pain strands the survivor in unhelpful ruminations about issues that are unrelated or minimally related to the true nature of her suffering.

This is an example of this. Your friend complains incessantly about the bad weather or the unfairness of people who do not use their turn signals. He cannot stop grumbling because no amount of complaining about the wrong thing releases the real pain that is driving his obsessive grievance. If he were able to look deeper at what is really troubling him, he might learn that his wife's constructive feedback is continuously flashing him back into the fear and shame he felt when his mother verbally abused him.

Left-brain dissociation can also be a process of *trivialization*. This occurs when the survivor over-focuses on superficial external concerns to distract himself from upsetting inner experience. Becoming overly preoccupied with sports statistics or the lives of Hollywood celebrities are common examples of this. This is not, of course, to say that such interests are not worthwhile when they are pursued with moderation.

Finally, left-brain dissociation can also be seen in intellectualization. This is what the novelist, Ian McEwan, called the "high-walled fortress of focused thinking". Some survivors over-rely on reasoning and lofty dialogue to protect themselves from the potentially messy and painful world of feeling. Even the highest levels of creative thinking can deteriorate into an obsessive defense when they are excessively engaged.

Verbal Ventilation Heals Abandonment

When we share what is emotionally important to us, we learn to connect with others in a meaningful and healing way. This applies to sharing concerns that excite and please us, as well as those that frighten or depress us. Perhaps there was no more detrimental consequence of our childhood abandonment than being forced to habitually hide our authentic selves. Many of us come out of childhood believing that what we have to say is as uninteresting to others as it was to our parents.

We must repudiate this damaging legacy of the past. Verbal ventilation is *the* key way that people make friends. It parallels the way tender touch, soothing voice, and welcoming facial expressions helps infants and toddlers establish bonding and attachment. When we practice the emotionally based communication of verbal ventilation in a safe environment, we repair the damage of not having had this need met in childhood. This in turn opens up the possibility of finally attaining the verbal-emotional intimacy that is an essential lifelong need for all human beings.

Committing to this type of practice typically requires courage and perseverance. Authentic sharing can be triggering, and sometimes flashes the survivor back to being punished or rejected for being vulnerable. Therapy, individual or group, can help greatly to overcome and work through these obstacles to vitalizing your self-expression.

Verbal Ventilation and Intimacy

Reciprocal verbal ventilation is the highway to intimacy in adult relationships. Sufficient practice with a safe enough other brings genuine experiences of comforting and restorative connection. For me and many of my clients, such experiences are more alleviating of loneliness than we had ever thought possible.

Nowhere is this truer than with mutual commiseration. *Mutual commiseration* is the process in which two intimates are reciprocally sympathetic to each other's troubles and difficulties. It is the deepest most intimate channel to intimacy – profounder than sex. Mutual commiseration also typically promotes a spontaneous opening into many levels of light-hearted and spontaneous connecting.

———·•·———

As deep and meaningful connection with another becomes more available and frequent, the survivor increasingly experiences the shrinking of his abandonment depression.

I must reiterate here that some popular bodywork approaches to trauma belittle the usefulness of talk therapy. While somatic work is a vital tool of recovery, it alone cannot shrink your toxic critic or resuscitate your self-expression. Cognitive work, especially that which is empowered by verbal ventilation, is fundamental to Cptsd recovery.

With that said, we will move on to Feeling, the fourth grieving process – a process that is a type of body work. Feeling is a way of focusing on somatic experience that enables us to reclaim our ability to experience full, relaxed and vital inhabitancy of our bodies.

4. <u>Feeling</u>: Passively Working Through Grief

"Feeling is the antithesis of pain...the more pain one feels, the less pain one suffers"
   – Arthur Janov

Ongoing engagement in the active grieving processes of angering, crying and verbal ventilation can help us to discover the fourth grieving process: Feeling.

Feeling is a subtler, passive process than emoting. It is best illustrated by contrasting the concepts of emoting and feeling. Emoting is when we cry, anger out, or verbally ventilate the energy of an inner emotional experience. Feeling, on the other hand, is the inactive process of staying present to internal emotional experience without reacting. In recovery then, feeling is surrendering to our internal experiences of pain without judging or resisting them, and without emoting them out.

Feeling is a kinesthetic rather than a cognitive experience. It is the process of shifting the focus of your awareness off of thinking and onto your affects, energetic states and sensations. It is the proverbial "getting out of your head" and "getting into your body."

As a grieving process, feeling involves consciously reversing the learned survival mechanism of clamping down on pain to banish it from awareness.

Feeling "occurs" when we direct our attention to an emotionally or physically painful state, and surrender to this experience without resistance. When we relax acceptingly into our pain, we can learn to gently absorb it into our experience. Feeling then functions as if our awareness is a solvent that dissolves and metabolizes the affect, energy and sensation of our emotions.

Feeling Can Heal Digestive Problems

The practice of feeling is also similar to healthy food digestion whereby a relaxed digestive tract allows us to effectively assimilate nutrients. If, however, we suppress or repress our feelings, our bodies typically armor and tighten, especially along the alimentary canal.

I believe digestive tract-tightening can create the types of digestive problems that frequently co-occur with Cptsd. Diarrhea, for instance, is sometimes an emotionally-caused, physical response to intense danger. When this occurs, fear triggers the sympathetic nervous system into further triggering an immediate evacuation of the bowels. Nausea can operate similarly. Constipation, on the other hand, is sometimes a tightening in the alimentary canal that hampers the peristaltic motion necessary for healthy evacuation.

The Emotional-Physical Connection

There is often a close relationship between emotion and physical sensation. Physical sensations in the body often co-occur with feelings. Moreover, sensations of tightness and tension can develop as a defense against feelings. As unexpressed feelings accumulate, a greater degree of muscular tension is necessary to keep them under wraps.

A child who is repeatedly punished for emoting learns to be afraid of inner emotional experience and tightens [armors] the musculature of her body in an effort to hold feelings in and to banish them from awareness.

Holding your breath is a further manifestation of armoring. It is an especially common way of keeping feelings at bay, as breathing naturally brings your awareness down to the level of feeling.

As my client, Kylie, free associated on the feelings of a particularly intense flashback, she painfully recalled the traumas she underwent trying to avoid her mother's punishments for crying. Her worst memory was of the day in the supermarket, when her mother's scolding rained down upon her as she tried to suppress her rapidly mounting urge to cry. Knowing the worst punishment would ensue if she cried, she held her breath to hold back the tears. She held it so long that she fainted from lack of oxygen and cracked her head open on the floor. Her mother, mortified by what she saw as public humiliation, beat her black and blue when she got home.

It took us two years of trust-building work to bring this incident back into awareness. She then cried her first tears since when it happened, three decades earlier. These were also the first tears she could ever remember that brought relief.

The technique of focusing your awareness on physical sensations in your body can help you to become more proficient at the practice of "feeling". With enough practice, paying attention to tightness in your face, throat, heart or belly area brings feelings into awareness, where they can simply be *felt through*. However, in your early experiences of focusing on sensations, feelings may come up so strongly that you will benefit from allowing yourself to emote them.

Balancing Feeling and Emoting

When we become more mindful of the subtle sensations of feelings, the passive grieving process of feeling through them complements the active processes of grieving them out. We are typically in advanced recovery when we can both <u>emote out</u> and <u>feel through</u> our anger, sadness, fear, shame and depression.

Furthermore, *feeling* also helps us to bring emotions into awareness that need to be grieved out through active, cathartic emoting. Thus, grieving is especially profound when we can fluidly shift between feeling and emoting. Sometimes we will only need to fully feel and accept the sensations of our pain. Other times we will want to verbally ventilate about our pain with someone who gives us full permission to color our words with angering and tears.

Learning to Feel

As a survivor becomes more adept at angering and crying, fear of his feelings will decrease, and opportunities to learn to simply feel will present themselves. He can engage these opportunities by passively attuning to the more subtle sensations of his anger and sadness.

Over time this practice will build his ability to stay passively present to the sensations of his deeper feelings – to his fear, shame and depression. But in early stages, this awareness will often morph into the need to actively emote them out – to grieve himself out of the abandonment mélange. Eventually, however, his abandonment mélange feelings will also be digested and worked through purely with the solvent of awareness. This also applies to anxiety which is often fear just below the level of awareness. With sufficient practice, anxiety can often be felt through passively. We will explore this process in greater depth in the next chapter.

An Exercise in Feeling

Here is an exercise to help you enhance your ability to feel and grieve through pain. Visualize yourself as time-traveling back to a place in the past when you felt especially abandoned. See your adult self taking your abandoned child onto your lap and comforting her in various painful emotional states or situations. You can comfort her/him verbally: "I feel such sorrow that you were so abandoned and that you felt so alone so much of the time. I love you even more when you are stuck in this abandonment pain – especially because you had to endure it for so long with no one to comfort you. That shouldn't have happened to you. It shouldn't happen to any child. Let me comfort and hold you. You don't have to rush to get over it. It is not your fault. You didn't cause it and you're not to blame. You don't have to do anything. Just let me hold you. Take your time. I love you always and care about you no matter what."

I highly recommend practicing this even if it feels inauthentic, and even if it requires a great deal of fending off your critic. Keep practicing and eventually, you will have a genuine experience of feeling self-compassion for the traumatized child you were. When that occurs, you will know that your recovery work had reached a deep level.

Techniques to Invite and Enhance Grieving

Tears were hard to come by after my first breakthrough cry in early adulthood. I would often long for the incredible relief I felt on that occasion, but unlike angering, I could not force my crying. I have come to learn that this is typical of many people. My friend Malcolm, suffering the same frustration, wanted to cry so badly, that he squeezed lemon juice into his eyes. He was able to laugh about it later, but solemnly warned me to never try such a thing.

This is a list that evolved out of our ongoing discussions about how to coax out the tears of a good cry. As with all the advice in this book, please feel free to use only the ones that seem to fit, and in whatever order seems best. Moreover, different combinations may enhance either crying or angering, or both together. Finally, sometimes nothing works, but I encourage you to try techniques that intuitively seem like they may work more than once.

1. Find a safe and comfortable place where you won't be heard.
2. Close your eyes and remember a time when you felt compassionate towards someone. This can be from real life, or from reading a book or a poem, or from watching a movie or moving news item.
3. Invoke self-compassion via the memory of someone who was kind to you, or imagine someone you think would be kind to you. I would be kind to you.
4. Verbally ventilate about what is bothering you in a journal or aloud to a real or imagined friend or to me.
5. Imagine yourself being comforted by a Higher Power. See yourself in the lap of a kind higher power or actual person who seems kind. [Santa Claus once worked well for one of my clients].
6. Remember a time when you felt better from crying or angering, or seeing someone else cry in real life or in a movie.
7. Remember a time when being angry, or when someone else being angry, saved you from harm.
8. Imagine your anger forming a protective fiery shield around you.
9. Imagine your tears or anger carrying any fear, shame or depression up and out of you.
10. Imagine holding your inner child compassionately. Tell the child it's normal and okay to feel sad or mad about feeling bad or hurt.
11. Tell the child you'll protect him/her from being criticized.
12. Breathe deeply, fully and slowly.
13. Put on some moving or evocative music.
14. Watch a movie that is poignant.
15. Watch a movie that portrays "enviable" anger release.

An elaborating note on technique #15: Several clients told me that the scene in the 1976 movie *Network* where the main character yells out a window: "We're not taking it anymore", helped them to bring up and ventilate their anger.

———•——

Finally, if reading this book does not begin to release the critic's stranglehold on your ability to grieve, please consider working with a therapist or support group to help you work through the shame that the critic uses to spoil your ability to grieve.

CHAPTER

THE MAP: MANAGING THE ABANDONMENT DEPRESSION

Cptsd burdens us with a hair-trigger susceptibility to painful emotional flashbacks. Flashbacks, as we have seen, are layers of defensive reactions to the abandonment depression. These reactions include physical, behavioral, cognitive, emotional and relational responses to the reemerging sense of danger and despair that plagued our childhood abandonment.

This chapter presents a map of these layered, defensive reactions to abandonment pain. This map shows you which reactions are most important to work on at any given time. It includes a strategy for reducing harmful reactions that are no longer necessary. This strategy involves self-compassionately soothing yourself when you are trapped in fear and/or depression, so that you do not launch into intensified fear, toxic shame, critic attacks, or self-damaging 4F reactions.

Cycles of Reactivity

This section presents a verbal diagram of the layering of our reactions in an emotional flashback. Experiences of depression and abandonment trigger us into fear and shame, which then activates panicky inner critic thinking, which in turn launches us into an adrenalized fight, flight, freeze or fawn trauma response.

This is how that reactivity takes place in a flashback. A survivor wakes up feeling depressed. Because childhood experience has conditioned her to believe that she is unworthy and unacceptable in this state, she feels anxious and ashamed. This in turn activates her inner critic to scare her with perfectionistic rants: "No wonder no one likes me. I've got to get my lazy, worthless ass out of bed or I'll end up like that homeless, bag lady in the park!"

Retraumatized by her own inner voice, she then launches into her most habitual 4F behavior. She either lashes out domineeringly at the nearest person [Fight] – or she launches busily into anxious productivity [Flight] – or she flips on the TV and foggily tunes out or dozes off again [Freeze] – or she self-abandoningly redirects her attention to figuring out how to fix a friend's problem [Fawn].

All this typically happens so quickly that we do not notice the fear and shame, or the inner critic. The first thing that we usually begin to notice in early recovery is that suddenly we are engaged in our most typical 4F response. As recovery progresses we become aware of the critic. Eventually this promotes mindfulness of the fear and shame that fuel the critic. And finally in later recovery, we become aware of the abandonment depression itself.

—————

Unfortunately this dynamic also commonly operates in reverse. This can occur in early recovery when you suddenly notice that you have slipped back into a dysfunctional 4F behavior. This then triggers you into new self-attacking criticism, which then amps up your fear and shame. This in turn increases your abandonment depression *as the process of self-abandonment runs riot.*

Desperate to escape the deathlike feelings of the abandonment depression, the initial cycle revs up again. Depression creates fear and shame which fuels venomous critic attacks and launches you into fighting, fleeing, freezing or fawning.

Survivors can careen back and forth through these layered reactions creating perpetual motion cycles of internal trauma.

I believe this process also accounts for the spiraling down feeling that many survivors report having during intense flashbacks.

This is a diagram of these dynamics:

ABANDONMENT DEPRESSION ⟷ FEAR & SHAME ⟷ INNER CRITIC ⟷ 4Fs

Let us look at a case example of how triggering works in the reverse direction. My mega-perfectionistic, flight-type client, Mario, came into our session five minutes late. It was the first time he had been late in two years of therapy.

Mario was in full-fledged flight, sweating from racing up the hill from his parking space a block away. He told me he just could not sit on the couch today. Could he please just pace in front of the couch. "I hate being late. I won't tell you - please don't ask – just how fast I was driving on the freeway!"

Mario compulsively paced, but this driven-ness was nothing compared to the speed of his obsessing, as he rattled off many versions of most of the inner critic attack programs listed in chapter 9.

To him, his being late was merely the tip of the iceberg of his defectiveness. As his rant against himself amped up, he increasingly scared himself with his own words, and shamed himself with his parents' disgust.

Finally, seemingly exhausted, Mario collapsed on the couch, and launched into the first suicidal ideation I had ever heard from him. He had just landed in the pit of the abandonment mélange [depression encrusted with fear and shame] and was sinking to the bottom into a despairing depression of helplessness and hopelessness. This was the real helplessness and hopelessness that had so characterized his childhood.

Fortunately, I had been diligently planting seeds about his need to grieve over the last two years. For the first time since early childhood, the tears came, and it was the most moving monsoon I had witnessed in ages. He cried for the little forsaken boy he had been. He came home, via his pain, to being on his side. The long exile into self-abandonment was temporarily over for the first time that he could remember.

We were then able to look at the cycle of reactivity that had turned into a cyclone. Triggered by a traffic jam into the "terrible danger" of being late, Cptsd launched him into his flight response as he raced to get to my office. The flight response also immediately triggered the inner critic to attack him for his lateness and to catastrophize about the consequences. As it did he fell deeper and deeper into shame and fear, and then ultimately into the abandonment depression itself.

This time however, Mario broke the flashback with his tears, as his crying released his fear and shame. This in turn defueled his critic and allowed his body to begin releasing the hyperarousal of his flight response.

Had he not been able to do this, he most likely would have continued attacking himself with shame-fueled perfectionism and fear-fueled drasticizing. He would then have launched out of the session back to obsessively and compulsively racing through his day driven by his infinite to-do list.

The Layers of Dissociation in the Cycle of Reactivity

All the layered reactions in the cycle of reactivity are defenses against the abandonment depression. Each layer is also a defense against all of the other layers beneath it. As such, each layer is a type of dissociation. When we are triggered and lost in a 4F response, we fight, flee, freeze or fawn to *dis*associate ourselves from the painful voice of the critic. On a deeper layer, the critic is also distracting and disassociating us from our emotional pain. Moreover, fear and shame dis-associate us from the bottom layer - the terrible abandonment depression itself. Dissociation [the psychological term for disassociation], then, is the process of rendering all these levels less conscious or totally unconscious.

As recovery progresses and we learn to stay present enough to the critic to begin shrinking it, we become increasingly aware of the fear and shame that underlies it. With sufficient feeling into fear and shame, we notice that fear and shame cover up the deadened feelings of the abandonment depression itself. Learning to stay self-supportingly present to the feelings of this depression is the deepest level, bottom-of-the-barrel work of recovery. When we are able to do this, our recovering has reached a profound level.

Parental Abandonment Creates Self-Abandonment

Once again, we had to dissociate with these layered defenses because we were not developmentally capable of managing the pain of being abandoned. We could not tolerate feeling the fear, shame and inconsolableness of it. We could not use our anger and tears to release this shame and fear. We could not bear to stay tuned in to the incessantly persecutory critic, over which we were powerless. We could only fight, flee, freeze or fawn. Over time this elaborate cycle of self-abandonment became habitual.

Chronic emotional abandonment devastates a child. It naturally makes her feel and appear deadened and depressed. Functional parents respond to a child's depression with concern and comfort. Abandoning parents respond to the child with anger, disgust and/

or further abandonment, which in turn exacerbate the fear, shame and despair that become the abandonment mélange.

Deconstructing Self-abandonment

Because of our parents' rejection, the mildest hint of depression, no matter how functional or appropriate, can instantly flash us back into our original abandonment depression. The capacity to self-nurturingly weather any experience of depression, no matter how mild, remains unrealized. Our original experience of parental abandonment has morphed into habitual self-abandonment.

We can gradually deconstruct the self-abandoning habit of reacting to depression with fear and shame, inner critic catastrophizing, and 4F acting out. The mindfulness processes described below awaken the psyche's innate capacity to respond with compassion to depression. Mindfulness also helps us metabolize the fear and shame that we were forced to feel about being depressed.

Ending our reactivity to depression is typically a long difficult journey. This is because our culture routinely humiliates us for any expression of depression. It pathologizes us as if we are violating our patriotic duty to be fully engaged in "the pursuit of happiness."

Taboos about depression even emanate from the psychological establishment, where some schools strip it of its status as a legitimate feeling. For them, depression is nothing more than a waste product of negative thinking. Other schools reduce it simplistically to a dysfunctional state that results from the repression of somewhat less taboo emotions like sadness and anger. This is not to say that these factors cannot cause depression. It is to say that depression is a legitimate feeling that often contains the helpful and important information described below.

Depressed Thinking versus Feeling Depressed

Healing progresses when we learn to distinguish depressed thinking [which we need to eliminate] from depressed feeling [which we sometimes need to feel]. Occasional feelings of listlessness and anhedonia [inability to enjoy our usual pleasures] are normal and existential. A modicum of ennui and dissatisfaction are part of the price of admission to life.

Moreover, depression is sometimes an invaluable herald of the need to slow down for rest and restoration. When depression is most helpful, it gives us access to a unique spring of intuition, such as that which informs us that a once valued job or relationship is no longer healthy for us. In such instances we feel depressed because some irreparable change has rendered some central thing in our lives detrimental to us. This functional depression is signaling us to let it die and move on.

Overreaction to depression essentially reinforces learned toxic shame. It reinforces the person's belief that he is unworthy, defective and unlovable when he is depressed.

Sadly this typically drives him deeper into abandonment-exacerbating isolation.

Mindfulness Metabolizes Depression

Deep level recovery from childhood trauma requires a normalization of depression, a renunciation of the habit of reflexively reacting to it. Central to this is the development of a self-compassionate mindfulness. Once again, mindfulness is the practice of staying in your body – the practice of staying fully present to all of your internal experience.

The practice of mindfulness cultivates our ability to stay acceptingly open to our emotional, visceral and somatic experience without retreating into the cycle of reactivity. Steven Levine's beautiful book, *Who Dies,* is an enlightening, jargon-less and easily accessible guide book on learning the practice of mindfulness.

Somatic Mindfulness

Because depression in Cptsd commonly morphs instantly into fear, early mindfulness work involves staying present to the physical sensations of fearful hyperarousal. This technique is also known as *sensate focusing* and it is the practice of *feeling* we explored in the last chapter. Mild sensations of fear are muscular tightness or tension anywhere in the body, especially in the alimentary canal. Tension in the jaw, throat, chest, diaphragm or belly also often correlates with fear. More intense sensations of fear are nausea, jumpiness, feeling wired, shortness of breath, hyperventilation, and alimentary distress.

Mindfulness also involves noticing the psyche's penchant to dissociate from these uncomfortable sensations. Once again, dissociation can be the classical right-brain distraction of spacing out into reverie or sleep, or the left-brain, cognitive distraction of worrying and obsessing.

Over and over, the survivor will need to rescue himself from dissociation, and gently bring his awareness back into fully feeling the sensations of his fear. Although sensations of fear sometimes feel unbearable at first, persistent focusing with non-reactive attention dissolves and resolves them as if awareness itself is digesting and integrating them.

Somatic Awareness can therapeutically Trigger Painful Memories

Somatic awareness and sensate focusing sometimes opens up memories and unworked through feelings of grief about your childhood abuse and neglect. This phenomenon provides invaluable, therapeutic opportunities to more fully grieve the losses of child-hood. If more pain comes up then you can digest on your own, please consider getting someone more experienced to help you with this process.

With considerable practice, you can begin to exhume from your fear an awareness of the underlying sensations of depression. These are *hypo-aroused* sensations that are subtle and barely perceptible at first. They may include heaviness, swollenness, exhaustion, emptiness, hunger, longing, soreness, or deadness.

These sensations are initially as difficult to stay present to as those of fear. With ongoing practice however, focused attention also digests them as they are integrated into consciousness. One of the biggest challenges of mindfully focusing on depression is to not dissociate into sleep. Sitting up straight in a comfortable chair can help to keep you awake and focused on fully feeling and metabolizing your depression.

As practice becomes more accomplished, these feelings and sensations of depression can morph into a sense of peace, relaxation and ease. On special occasions, they sometimes open to an under-lying, innate *core emotional experience* of clarity, well-being and belonging.

Introspective Somatic Work

I began my journey of learning how to feel by devoting a half hour daily to feeling the sensations of my fear.

This was extremely difficult because I had survived my child-hood with ADHD-like busyness. I had run daily marathons of activity to keep myself one step ahead of my fear and my shame-saturated depression. As an adult, I reduced this to half-marathons but I was still a busyholic, despite my relaxed persona. Tuning into how wired I was, was daunting. In my attempts to become more mindful, I was often exasperated by how frequently my awareness fled my body and went back into thinking or daydreaming.

In the first few months, my focus wavered wildly between feeling the tense sensations of my fear and being disrupted by inner critic thinking. I was assailed by a plethora of catastrophizing thoughts and visualizations. My critic repeatedly misinterpreted my fear as if I were still entrapped in my hazardous family.

My critic goaded me incessantly to launch into flight-mode. I was so itching to get going that I had strange tantalizing fantasies of cleaning my apartment, normally one of my least favorite things to do. In the first year of this practice, I frequently had to white-knuckle the handles on my chair to stay somatically present to my feelings. Otherwise, I would have been off and running into self-medicating with excessive adrenalization.

Dissolving Depression by Fully Feeling it

Gradually, my focused awareness began to metabolize my fear. Many months later, I was typically able to relax the tense fearful sensations of a flashback within ten minutes. As I became more successful at digesting my fear, I experientially discovered the rock bottom underlying core sensations of my abandonment depression itself.

Mindful merging with the subtle emotions and sensations of depression is the finishing tool of deconstructing self-abandonment. Over and over I focused on the sensations of my depression. Occasionally these sensations were intense, but more often they were very subtle. Often it was difficult to resist the urge to fall asleep, and many times I could not.

At other times, I noticed how instantly my depression scared me back into fear. Simultaneously the sensations of depression also triggered me into toxic shame. Often, I would witness myself echoing my parents' contempt: "...bad, lazy, worthless, good-for-nothing, stick-in-the-mud, etc."

Blessedly, with ongoing practice, I gradually learned to dis-identify from the toxic vocabulary of the critic. I also learned to stay awake most of the time. I then found myself more accurately naming these revisited childhood feelings: "Small, helpless, lonely, unsupported, unloved." Over time, this in turn rewarded me with a profound sense of compassion for the abandoned child I was.

Moreover, I made the wonderful discovery that sensate focusing, when it has been well practiced and developed, is the ultimate thought-stopping technique. When the critic is especially loud and persistent, shifting your awareness from thinking to feeling your sensations is a potent way of coming home to a safer place. It is, as one survivor told me, "coming home to rest in the mother of your body."

In my current recovery work, I most commonly apply this mindfulness technique to experiences of survival-mode depression. For me this low grade manifestation of the abandonment depression typically gets triggered by a few nights of poor sleep, which often decreases my energy level and dulls my ability to concentrate. Most of my life, this feeling experience provided rich fodder for my critic. Over the years however, increased mindfulness allows me to see that I typically function well enough no matter how tired or introverted I feel. These days, I am sometimes even able to authentically welcome the most exhausted of these experiences as a chance to take a break from my less essential routines. I have learned how to resist my critic's all-or-none *productivity program,* and be satisfied with days of getting less done.

Hunger as Camouflaged Depression

Feelings of abandonment commonly masquerade as the physiological sensations of hunger. Hunger pain soon after a big meal is rarely truly about food. Typically it is camouflaged emotional hunger and the longing for safe, nurturing connection. Food cannot satiate the hunger pain of abandonment. Only loving support can. Geneen Roth's book offers powerful self-help book on this subject.

Even after a decade of practice, I still find it difficult to differentiate this type of attachment hunger from physical hunger. One often reliable clue is that the sensation of longing for the nourishment of attachment is usually in my small intestine, while physical hunger's locus is a little higher up in my stomach. When I can take the time to meditate on this lower abdomen sensation, I often become aware that I am in a low level flashback. Feeling through this uncomfortable sensation typically resolves both the flashback and my false hunger.

I believe this type of emotional hunger is at the core of most food addictions. One of the reasons food addictions are so difficult to manage is that food was the first source of self-comforting that was available to us. With the dearth of any other comfort, there is little wonder that we came to over-rely on eating for nurturance.

In fact, like Gabor Mate, I believe that attachment hunger is at the core of most addictive behavior, even process addictions. An example of the latter is the sex and love addict's desperate pursuit of high intensity relating. Perhaps all addictive behavior is our misguided attempts to self-medicate deeper abandonment pain and unmet attachment needs.

Pseudo-Cyclothymia

On a parallel with false hunger, feeling tired is sometimes unrelated to sleep deprivation. It is instead an emotional experience of the abandonment depression. I believe that emotional tiredness comes from not resting enough in a safe relationship with yourself or with another. This emotional exhaustion often masquerades as physiological tiredness. Unfortunately, over time, the two can become confusingly intertwined.

When our abandonment depression is unremediated, either kind of tiredness can trigger us into fear. This then activates the inner critic which then translates "tired" into "endangering imperfection," which in turn triggers us into a 4F response.

Ironically, over-reacting to emotional tiredness eventually creates real physical exhaustion via a process I call The Cyclothymic Two-Step. *The cyclothymic two-step* is the dance of flight types or subtypes who habitually overreact to their tiredness with workaholic or busyholic activity. Self-medicating with their own adrenalin, they "run" to counteract the emotional tiredness of the unprocessed abandonment depression.

Eventually however, many exhaust themselves physically, and become temporarily too depleted or sick to continue running. At such times, they collapse into an accumulated depression so painful, that they re-launch desperately into "flight-speed" at the first sign of replenished adrenalin. Survivors with this pattern sometimes misdiagnose themselves as bipolar because of their abrupt vacillations between adrenalin highs and abandonment-exacerbated lows.

Also noteworthy here is the futile journey that many survivors undergo treating emotional tiredness with physiologically-based methods. The limited efficacy of such an approach however typically augments their shame: "What's wrong with me. I've changed everything in my diet and in my sleep and exercise regimen. I've taken every available supplement and seen every type of practitioner imaginable, and I still wake up feeling dead tired."

There is a healthy way out of this cul-de-sac of misdirected striving. It lies in cultivating self-kindness during those inevitable times when you feel tired, bad, lonely, or depressed. In this regard, the notable AA 12 Step acronym, HALT - Hungry, Angry, Lonely, Tired – can be helpful. Accordingly, I recommend that you focus inside to see if you have flashed back into the abandonment depression whenever you experience a HALT feeling. If you have, you can then work to generate the internal, self-compassionate attention described above.

Separating Necessary Suffering from Unnecessary Suffering

You can sometimes gain motivation for this difficult work by seeing your depressed feelings as messages from your inner child who is feeling as abandoned as he ever was. Perhaps this time you can come to him with your remothering-self in a more comforting and protective way. Through such practice, you can gradually achieve the healing that Buddhists call separating necessary suffering [normal fear and depression] from unnecessary suffering [unconscious self-abandonment to helplessness, toxic shame, Cptsd fear, retraumatizing inner critic *acting in*, and 4F *acting out*].

Recovery is Progressive

I begin this section by repeating the chapter 4 section: "Stages of Recovery." This section outlines the overall course of recovery. Hopefully you will notice, since you began reading this book, that your understanding of Cptsd has been significantly enhanced. I also hope that you sense a greater sense of self-compassion and direction in your recovery process.

"Although we often work on many levels of recovering at the same time, recovering is to some degree progressive. It begins on the cognitive level when psychoeducation and mindfulness helps us understand that we have Cptsd. This awakening then allows us to learn how to approach the journey of deconstructing the various life-spoiling dynamics of Cptsd.

Still on the cognitive level, we take our next steps into the long work of shrinking the critic. Some survivors will need to do a great deal of work on this level before they can move down to the emotional layer of work, which is learning how to grieve effectively.

The phase of intensely grieving our childhood losses can last for a couple of years. When sufficient progress is made in grieving, the survivor naturally drops down into the next level of recovery work. This involves working through fear by grieving our loss of safety in the world. At this level, we also learn to work through our toxic shame by grieving the loss of our self-esteem.

As we become more adept in this type of deep level grieving, we are then ready to address the core issue of our Cptsd – the abandonment depression itself. The final task here involves releasing the armoring and physiological reactivity in our body to the abandonment depression via the somatic work discussed in this chapter. This work culminates with learning to compassionately support ourselves through our experiences of depression.

Finally, as we will see in the next chapter, many survivors need some relational help in achieving the complex tasks involved in deconstructing each layer of our old pain-exacerbating defenses."

A Swiss Army Knife Approach to a Flashback

This is a final example of addressing all the layers of reactivity in resolving a flashback.

When I started this work over three decades ago, I ate very poorly and did not know how to soothe and nurture myself with healthy food.

After some years of recovery work however, I deeply intuited that I needed to cook more in order to take self-nurturance to the next level. I had not cooked more however because I hated to cook. Luckily I embraced cooking anyway as a labor of love. Nonetheless cooking was, for a long time, a very trying and unpleasant experience for me. [This was, in fact, much like my many years of struggling to get the upper hand on the critic].

But back to cooking which became a central piece of my self-remothering work. It was not until I understood more about the dynamics of my flight response that I realized how much I rushed around when I was cooking. Via increased mindfulness, I discovered that the smallest unforeseen obstacle could set off what felt like a small electric shock in my chest. Examples of these obstacles include something spilled, a lid too tight to open, an extra unanticipated task, or the clock showing me that I was behind schedule. In an instant, anyone of these normal hindrances could send me rushing around the kitchen in a low grade panic. Whenever this occurred, I would then inhale my meal as soon as it was ready just to get the ordeal over with.

This is an example of what a common, everyday flashback looks like in adulthood. It is so often minor daily frustrations that trigger us into flashbacks, rather than incidents that repeat the gross insults and ordeals of our childhoods.

With ongoing recovery work, I realized that anything to do with food could easily flash me back to the family dinner table - the battlefield of my dysfunctional family.

Many productive grieving sessions came out of this. They lead me to an epiphany that doing anything intricate with lot of steps to it also flashed me back to feeling picked apart by my parents. I subsequently discovered that angering at my parents, whenever I was triggered by doing something complicated, significantly reduced my fear.

There was, however, a huge part of my food trauma that I could not shrink until I started the somatic work described in this chapter.

Since then, years of practicing somatic mindfulness has greatly reduced my hair-triggerable anxiety around cooking. This is however still a work in progress. In terms of the cycles of reactivity, my occasional flashbacks around food and food preparation can look like this. I have thirty minutes to cook and eat my breakfast before I leave for work. I come into the kitchen and... "Oh No, The sink is full of the dishes that I forgot to clean last night!" I immediately notice that I am about to launch into frenzied dish washing, when Flashback Management Step# 1 rises to the front of my conscious-ness. "I am having a flashback."

I go directly to Step# 7 and attempt to "ease back into my body." I sit in my favorite stuffed chair, close my eyes, and bring my aware-ness to my abdomen, where my anxiety typically makes its most strident charge. I can feel tightness in and just below my diaphragm. I feel afraid and get a picture of my father's big hand squeezing my small intestines.

I start to hypochondriasize about the possible long term effects of having this tension in my abdomen. My mindfulness instantly alerts me to invoke the thought-correction of Step# 8. I slowly repeat my current favorite anti-endangerment mantra: "I am safe; I am relaxing."

I slow and deepen my breath, and feel the muscles in my belly as much as I can. I feel the slow cycle of these muscles relaxing and contracting with the ebbing and flowing of my breath. The cycle gradually becomes more fluid as I attend to it.

After about fifty inhalations, I feel a swollen sensation of tired-ness diffusing like ink throughout my body. My gut momentarily retightens to ward off that awful deadening feeling of the abandon ment depression.

But I surrender to the deadness. I do this because I know the tight feeling is fear and that it will soon morph into the screaming critic excoriating me about being late. I say no to the critic's Siren call of "you can do this if you hurry," tempting me back into flight.

I stay with the deadened, tired, lifeless feeling and try to feel it more, welcoming it. I sense myself beginning to become one with the depressed sensation.

Because I am so well practiced, the depression starts to gradu-ally morph into a widening sense of relaxation. It spreads through-out my body, and my body begins to feel like an easy-chair.

I look at my watch and it has taken twenty minutes of my "precious time." I realize my critic is trying to sneak back in and is goading me with the remark "it has taken twenty minutes of my precious time."

I disidentify from the critic and shift into my refathering self and thought-correct the critic. "It's ok Pete, this is all small potatoes. You are not in danger [Step# 2], and this is definitely no emergency."

I take a moment with the angering part of grieving [Step#9] and reinforce my boundaries against my internalized parents. "Screw you Helen [mom] and Charlie [dad] for frightening me so much about making mistakes that I freak out when things don't go perfectly!

"Ooh, that got a few nice tears. What a relief. How many times have I been stuck in that driven-ness and not known how to stop?!"

I return to thought-correction. "So, like I was saying Pete, it's ok. You always show up at your office an hour early anyway. You can take 20 minutes off the routine. You can stay in this relaxed state a bit longer and still have time to get everything done in a relaxed manner."

I feel the sense of triumph I sometimes see in my clients when they have worked hard to successfully manage and resolve a flashback. "It worked!" This time I broke the cycle and did not let my triggered flight response get much further than some momentary rushing.

I stopped the cycle of reactivity from devolving into an inner critic diatribe against myself. I didn't indulge the outer critic and let it make me try to pin the undone dishes on my wife. I chose to stay with the depression. I bypassed the shame and fear that I have gotten stuck in ten thousand times before when I could not accept my current state of being. I refused to abandon myself like the sinking ship I thought I was – like Helen and Charlie abandoned me as a kid on a daily, hourly, yearly basis.

I am also happy to report that I now cook regularly, and triggering is relatively rare. I have even gotten to enjoy my own cooking so much that I rarely eat out.

CHAPTER

A RELATIONAL APPOACH TO HEALING ABANDONMENT

This chapter is a reworking of a professional article I wrote to guide therapists in their Cptsd work. I have kept that point of reference in many sections of this chapter in the hope that it will help you know what it is reasonable to expect from a therapist.

Further on in this chapter, there is a section on how to find a therapist. I hope this information will help you know what to look for, and ask for, when and if you are shopping for a therapist.

Finally, if therapy is not an option for you, I end the chapter with guidelines on how to create a co-counseling relationship with a friend. If that also is not possible, I list recommendations for online forums where you can interact with others who are sharing about their recovery journeys.

The Relational Dimension of Psychotherapy

Many Cptsd survivors have never had a "safe enough" relationship. Healing our attachment disorders usually requires a reparative relational experience with a therapist, partner or trusted friend who is able to stay compassionately present to their own painful and dysphoric feelings. It is essential that they are comfortable with feeling and expressing their own sadness, anger, fear, shame and depression.

When a therapist has this level of emotional intelligence, she can guide the client to gradually let go of the learned habit of automatically rejecting his feelings. This in turn also helps him to avoid getting lost in the cycles of reactivity we explored in the last chapter.

Safe and empathic eye and voice connection with a therapist who has "good enough" emotional intelligence models to the client how to stay acceptingly present to all her own affects.

Daniel Siegel calls this the "coregulation of affect." Moreover, Susan Vaughan's work demonstrates that this *coregulation of affect* promotes the development of the inner neural circuitry necessary to metabolize overwhelmingly painful feelings.

Furthermore, there is increasing neuroscientific evidence suggesting that this process is physiologically accomplished through the agency of a set of neurons called mirror neurons. In one experiment measuring neural activity in two monkeys, one monkey watched as the other cracked open a nut. The observer's neural activity was identical to the performers. Perhaps mirror neurons are involved when the client learns to be as non-reactive to his painful feelings as the therapist.

RELATIONAL HEALING IN COMPLEX PTSD

[Versions of the following article were first published in *The Therapist* and *The East Bay Therapist*.]

Many traumatologists see attachment disorder as one of the key symptoms of Complex PTSD. In the psychoeducational phases of working with traumatized clients, I typically describe attachment disorder as the result of growing up with primary caretakers who were regularly experienced as dangerous. They were dangerous by contemptuous voice or heavy hand, or more insidiously, dangerous by remoteness and indifference.

Recurring abuse and neglect habituates children to living in fear and sympathetic nervous system arousal. It makes them easily triggerable into the abandonment mélange of overwhelming fear and shame that tangles up with the depressed feelings of being abandoned.

A child, with parents who are unable or unwilling to provide safe enough attachment, has no one to whom she can bring her whole developing self.

No one is there for reflection, validation and guidance. No one is safe enough to go to for comfort or help in times of trouble. There is no one to cry to, to protest unfairness to, and to seek compassion from for hurts, mistakes, accidents, and betrayals.

No one is safe enough to shine with, to do "show and tell" with, and to be reflected as a subject of pride. There is no one to even practice the all-important intimacy-building skills of conversation.

In the paraphrased words of more than one of my clients: "Talking to Mom was like giving ammunition to the enemy. Anything I said could and would be used against me. No wonder, people always tell me that I don't seem to have much to say for myself."

Those with Cptsd-spawned attachment disorders never learn the communication skills that engender closeness and a sense of belonging. When it comes to relating, they are often plagued by debilitating social anxiety - and social phobia when they are at the severe end of the continuum of Cptsd.

Many of the clients who come through my door have never had a safe enough relationship. Repetition compulsion drives them to unconsciously seek out relationships in adulthood that traumatically reenact the abusive and/or abandoning dynamics of their childhood caretakers.

For many such clients, we are their first legitimate shot at a safe and nurturing relationship. If we are not skilled enough to create the degree of safety they need to begin the long journey towards developing good enough trust, we may be their last.

Emotional flashback management, therefore, is empowered when it is taught in the context of a safe relationship. Clients need to feel safe enough with their therapist to describe their humiliation and overwhelm. At the same time, the therapist needs to be nurturing enough to provide the empathy and calm support that was missing in the client's early experience.

Just as importantly, the therapist needs to be able to tolerate and work therapeutically with the sudden evaporation of trust that is so characteristic of Cptsd. Trauma survivors do not have a volitional "on" switch for trust, even though their "off" switch is frequently automatically triggered during flashbacks. In therapy, the therapist must be able to work on reassurance and trust restoral over and over again. I have heard too many disappointing client stories about past therapists who got angry at them because they would not simply choose to trust them.

As the importance of this understanding ripens in me, I increasingly embrace an Intersubjective or Relational approach. That means that I believe that the quality of the clients' relationship with me can provide a corrective emotional experience that saves them from being doomed to a lifetime of superficial connection, or worse, social isolation and alienation.

Moreover, I notice that without the development of a modicum of trust with me, my Cptsd clients are seriously delimited in their receptivity to my guidance, as well as to the ameliorative effects of my empathy.

In this regard then, I will describe four key qualities of relating that I believe are essential to the development of trust, and the subsequent relational healing that can come out of it. These are Empathy, Authentic Vulnerability, Dialogicality and Collaborative Relationship Repair.

1. EMPATHY

I used to assume that the merits of *empathy* were a given, but I have sadly heard too many stories of empathy-impoverished therapy. In this regard, I will simply say here that if we are hard and unsympathetic with our clients, we trigger the same sense of danger and abandonment in them that they experienced with their parents.

In terms of a definition, I especially like Kohut's statement that: "Empathy involves immersing yourself in another's psychological state by feeling yourself into the other's experience."

When I delve deeply enough into a client's experience, no matter how initially perplexing or intemperate it may at first seem, I inevitably find psychological sense in it, especially when I recognize its flashback components. In fact, I can honestly say that I have never met a feeling or behavior that did not make sense when viewed through the lenses of transference and traumatology.

Empathy, of course, deepens via careful listening and full elicitation of the client's experience, along with the time-honored techniques of mirroring and paraphrasing which show the client the degree to which we get him.

Noticing my subjective free associations often enhances my empathic attunement and ability to reflect back to the client in an emotionally accurate and validating way. When appropriate, I sometimes share my autobiographical free associations with the client when they are emotionally analogous. I do this to let her know that I really empathize with what she is sharing.

This is an example of this. My client tells me with great embarrassment that she stayed home all weekend because she had a pimple on her nose. She is ashamed of the pimple and of her "vanity" about it. She moans: "How could I be so stupid to let such a little thing bother me?" I suddenly remember cancelling a date once when I had a cold sore. At the time, I also got lost in a toxic shame attack. I share this with her, minus present day shame about it. She tears up and then laughs, relieved as her shame melts away. Months later, she tells me that her trust in me mushroomed at that moment. Guidelines for being judicious about this kind of self-disclosure will be discussed below.

Of the many benefits of empathy, the greatest is perhaps that it models and teaches self-empathy, better known as self-acceptance. To the degree that we attune to and welcome all of the client's experience, to that same degree can the client learn to welcome it in her- or himself.

2. AUTHENTIC VULNERABILITY "Realationship makes healthy relationship"

Authentic vulnerability is a second quality of intimate relating. Authentic vulnerability often begins with emotionally reverberating with the client. I have found that emotional reflection of the client's feelings is irreplaceable in fostering the development of trust and real relational intimacy.

Emotional reflection requires the therapist to be emotionally vulnerable himself and reveal that he too feels mad, sad, bad and scared sometimes. Modeling vulnerability, as with empathy, demonstrates to the client the value of being vulnerable and encourages her to risk wading into her own vulnerability.

I came to value therapeutic vulnerability the hard way via its absence in my own therapy with a therapist who was of the old,

"blank screen" school. She was distant, laconic and over-withhold-
ing in her commitment to the psychoanalytic principle of "optimal
frustration." Therapy with her was actually counter-therapeutic
and shame-exacerbating for me as we reenacted a defective child/
perfect parent dynamic.

Therapeutic Emotional Disclosure

Thankfully, I eventually realized that I had unresolved attachment
issues, and sought out a Relational therapist who valued the use of her
own vulnerable and emotionally authentic self as a tool in therapy.

Her tempered and timely emotional self-disclosures helped me
to deconstruct the veneer of invincibility I had built as a child to
hide my pain. Here are some examples that were especially helpful. "God, the holidays can be awful." "I get scared when I teach a
class too." "I'm so sorry. I just missed what you said. I got a little
distracted by my anxiety about my dental appointment this afternoon." "I feel sad that your mother was so mean to you." "It makes
me angry that you were so bullied by your parents."

My therapist's modeling that anger, sadness, fear, and depression were emotions that could be healthily expressed helped me to
renounce the pain-repressing, emotional perfectionism in which I
was mired. With her, I learned to stop burying my feelings in the
hope of being loved. I renounced my just-get-over-it philosophy and
embraced vulnerability as a way of finally getting close to people.

I needed this kind of modeling, as so many of my clients have,
to begin to emerge from my fear of being attacked, shamed or abandoned for feeling bad and having dysphoric feelings. In order to let
go of my Sisyphean salvation fantasy of achieving constant happiness, I needed to experience that all the less than shiny bits of me
were acceptable to another human being. Seeing that she was comfortable with and accepting of her own unhappy feelings eventually
convinced me that she really was not disgusted by mine.

The therapist's judicious use of emotional self-disclosure helps the client move out of the slippery, shame-lined pit of emotional perfectionism. Here are some self-revealing things that I say to encourage my clients to be more emotionally self-accepting. "I feel really sad about what happened to you." "I feel really angry that you got stuck with such a god-awful family." "When I'm temporarily confused and don't know what to say or do, I..." "When I'm having a shame attack, I..." "When something triggers me into fear, I..." "When my inner critic is overreacting, I remind myself of the Winnicottian concept that I only have to be a 'good enough person.'"

Here are two examples of emotional self-disclosure that are fundamental tools of my therapeutic work. I repeatedly express my genuine indignation that the survivor was taught to hate himself. Over time, this often awakens the survivor's instinct to also feel incensed about this travesty. This then empowers him to begin standing up to the inner critic. This in turn aids him to emotionally invest in the multidimensional work of building healthy self-advocacy.

Furthermore, I also repeatedly respond with empathy and compassion to the survivor's suffering. With time, this typically helps to awaken the recoveree's capacity for self-empathy. She then gradually learns to comfort herself when she is in a flashback or otherwise painful life situation. Less and less often does she surrender to an inner torture of self-hate, self-disappointment, and self-abandonment.

My most consistent feedback from past clients is that responses like these - especially ones that normalize fear and depression – helped them immeasurably to deconstruct their perfectionism, and open up to self-compassion and self-acceptance.

Guidelines for Self-disclosure

What guidelines, then, can we use to insure that our self-disclosure is judicious and therapeutic? I believe the following five principles help me to disclose therapeutically and steer clear of unconsciously sharing for my own narcissistic gratification.

First, I use self-disclosure sparingly.

Second, my disclosures are offered primarily to promote a matrix of safety and trust in the relationship. In this vein my vulnerability is offered to normalize and de-shame the inexorable, existential imperfection of the human condition, e.g., we all make mistakes, suffer painful feelings, experience confusion, etc.

Third, I do not share vulnerabilities that are currently raw and unintegrated.

Fourth, I never disclose in order to work through my own "stuff," or to meet my own narcissistic need for verbal ventilation or personal edification.

Fifth, while I may share my appreciation or be touched by a client's attempt or offer to focus on or soothe my vulnerabilities, I never accept the offer. I gently thank them for their concern, remind them that our work is client-centered, and let them know that I have an outside support network.

Emotional Self-disclosure and Sharing Parallel Trauma History

Since many of my clients have sought my services after reading my somewhat autobiographical book on recovery from the dysfunctional family, self-disclosure about my past trauma is sometimes a moot point. This condition has at the same time helped me realize how powerful this kind of disclosure can be in healing shame and cultivating hope.

Over and over, clients have told me that my vulnerable and pragmatic stories of working through my parents' traumatizing abuse and neglect gives them the courage to engage the long difficult journey of recovering.

Now whether or not someone has read my book, I will – with appropriate clients - judiciously and sparingly share my own experiences of dealing with an issue they have currently brought up. I do this both to psychoeducate them and to model ways that they might address their own analogous concerns.

One common example sounds like this: "I hate flashbacks too. Even though I get them much less than when I started this work, falling back into that old fear and shame is so awful."

I also sometimes say: "I really reverberate with your feelings of hopelessness and powerlessness around the inner critic. In the early stages of this work, I often felt overwhelmingly frustrated. It seemed that trying to shrink it actually made it worse. But now after ten thousand repetitions of thought-stopping and thought-correction, my critic is a mere shadow of its former self."

A final example concerns a purely emotional self-disclosure. When a client is verbally ventilating about a sorrowful experience, I sometimes allow my tears to brim up in my eyes in authentic commiseration with their pain. The first time my most helpful therapist did this with me, I experienced a quantum leap in my trust of her.

3. DIALOGICALITY

Dialogicality occurs when two conversing people move fluidly and interchangeably between speaking [an aspect of healthy narcissism] and listening [an aspect of healthy codependence.] Such reciprocal interactions prevent either person from polarizing to a dysfunctional narcissistic or codependent type of relating

Dialogicality energizes both participants in a conversation. Dialogical relating stands in contrast to the monological energy-theft that characterizes interactions whereby a narcissist pathologically exploits a codependent's listening defense. Numerous people have reverberated with my observation that listening to a narcissist monologue feels as if it is draining them of energy.

I have become so mindful of this dynamic that, in a new social situation, a sudden sense of tiredness often warns me that I am talking with a narcissist. How different than the elevation I sense in myself and my fellow conversant in a truly reciprocal exchange. Again, I wonder if there are mirror neurons involved in this.

I was appalled the other day while perusing a home shopping catalog to see a set of coffee cups for sale that bore the monikers "Designated Talker" and "Designated Listener". My wife and I pondered it for a few minutes, and hypothesized that it had to be a narcissist who designed those mugs. We imagined we could see the narcissists who order them presenting them to their favorite sounding boards as Christmas presents.

In therapy, dialogicality develops out of a teamwork approach – a mutual brainstorming about the client's issues and concerns. Such an approach cultivates full exploration of ambivalences, conflicts and other life difficulties.

Dialogicality is enhanced when the therapist offers feedback from a take-it-or-leave-it stance. Dialogicality also implies *respectful mutuality*. It stands in stark contrast to the *blank screen neutrality and abstinence* of traditional psychoanalytic therapy, which all too often reenacts the verbal and emotional neglect of childhood.

I believe abstinence commonly flashes the client back into feelings of abandonment, which triggers them to retreat into "safe" superficial disclosure, ever-growing muteness and/or early flight from therapy.

Meeting Healthy Narcissistic Needs

All this being said, extensive dialogicality is often inappropriate in the early stages of therapy. This is especially true, when the client's normal narcissistic needs have never been gratified, and remain developmentally arrested.

In such cases, clients need to be extensively heard. They need to discover through the agency of spontaneous self-expression the nature of their own feelings, needs, preferences and views.

For those survivors whose self-expression was especially decimated by their caretakers, self-focused verbal exploration typically needs to be the dominant activity for a great deal of time. Without this, the unformed healthy ego has no room to grow and break free from the critic. The client's healthy sense of self remains imprisoned beneath the hegemony of the outsized superego.

This does not mean, however, that the client benefits when the therapist retreats into extremely polarized listening. Most benefit, as early as the first session, from hearing something real or "personal" from the therapist. This helps overcome the shame-inducing potential that arises in the "One-seen [client] / One-unseen [therapist]" dynamic. When one person is being vulnerable and the other is not, shame has a huge universe in which to grow. This also creates a potential for the client to get stuck flashing back to childhood when the vulnerable child was rejected over and over by the seemingly invulnerable parent.

Consequently, many of my colleagues see group therapy as especially powerful for healing shame, because it rectifies this imbalance by creating a milieu where it is not just one person who is risking being vulnerable.

In this regard, it is interesting to note a large survey of California therapists that occurred about fifteen years ago. The survey was about their therapy preferences, and upwards of ninety percent emphasized that they did not want a blank screen therapist, but rather one who occasionally offered opinions and advice.

For twenty-five years, I have been routinely asking clients in the first session: "Based on your previous experiences in therapy, what would you like to happen in our work together; and what don't you want to happen?" How frequently clients respond similarly to the therapists in the survey!

Moreover, the next most common response I receive is that I don't want a therapist who does all the talking. More than a few have used the exact phrase: "I couldn't get a word in edgewise!"

How I wish there was a way that our qualification tests could spot and disqualify the narcissists who do get licensed and then turn their already codependent clients into sounding boards. This is the shadowy flipside polarity of the blank screen therapist.

Psychoeducation as Part of Dialogicality

Experience has taught me that clients who are childhood trauma survivors typically benefit from psychoeducation about Complex PTSD. When clients understand the whole picture of Cptsd recovery, they become more motivated to participate in the self-help practices of recovering. This also increases their overall hopefulness and general engagement in the therapeutic process. I sometimes wonder whether the rise in the popularity of Coaching has been a reaction to the various traditional forms of therapeutic neglect.

One of the worst forms of therapeutic neglect occurs when the therapist fails to notice or challenge a client's incessant, self-hating diatribes. This, I believe, is akin to tacitly approving of and silently colluding with the inner critic.

Perhaps therapeutic withholding and abstinence derives from the absent father syndrome that afflicts so many Westernized families. Perhaps traditional psychotherapy overemphasizes the mothering principles of listening and unconditional love, and neglects the fathering principles of encouragement and guidance that coaching specializes in.

Too much coaching is, of course, as counter-therapeutic and unbalanced as too much listening. It can interfere with the client's process of self-exploration and self-discovery as described above. At its worst, it can lure the therapist into the narcissistic trap of falling in love with the sound of his own voice.

At its best, coaching is an indispensable therapeutic tool. Just as it takes fathering and mothering to raise a balanced child, mothering and fathering principles are needed to meet the developmental arrests of the attachment-deprived client.

The sophisticated therapist values both and intuitively oscillates between the two, depending on the developmental needs of the client in the moment. Sometimes we guide with psychoeducation, therapeutic self-disclosure and active positive noticing, and most times we receptively nurture the client's evolving practice of her own spontaneously arising self-expression and verbal ventilation.

Once again, I believe that in early therapy and many subsequent stages of therapy, the latter process typically needs to predominate. In this vein, I would guess that over the course of most therapies that I conduct, I listen about ninety percent of the time.

Finally, I often notice that the last phase of therapy is often characterized by increasing dialogicality – a more balanced fluidity of talking and listening. This conversational reciprocity is a key characteristic of healthy intimacy. Moreover, when therapy is successful, progress in mutuality begins to serve the client in creating healthier relationships in the outside world.

Dialogicality and the 4F's

Because of childhood abandonment and repetition compulsion in later relationships, many 4F types are "dying" to be heard. Different types however vary considerably in their dialogical needs over the course of therapy.

The *Fawn/* Codependent type, who survived in childhood by becoming a parent's sounding board or shoulder to cry on, may use her listening defense to encourage the therapist to do too much of the talking. With her eliciting defense, she may even invoke the careless therapist into narcissistically monologing himself.

The *Freeze*/Dissociative type, who learned early to seek safety in the camouflage of silence, often needs a great deal of encouragement to discover and talk about his inner experience.

Psychoeducation can help him understand how his healthy narcissistic need to express himself was never nurtured in his family.

Furthermore, freeze types can easily get lost in superficial and barely relevant free associations as they struggle to learn to talk about themselves. This of course needs to be welcomed for some time, but eventually we must help him see that his flights of fantasy or endless dream elaborations are primarily manifestations of his dissociative defense.

Freeze types need to learn that emotionally disconnected talking is an old childhood habit that was developed to keep them buoyant above their undealt with emotional pain. Because of this, we must repeatedly guide them toward their feelings so that they can learn to express their most important concerns.

The *Fight*/Narcissistic type, who often enters therapy habituated to holding court, typically dodges real intimacy with her talking defense. Therapy can actually be counterproductive for these types as months or years of uninterrupted monologing in sessions exacerbate their sense of entitlement. By providing a steady diet of uninterrupted listening, the therapist strengthens their intimacy-destroying defense of over-controlling conversations. Sooner or later, we must insert ourselves into the relationship to work on helping them learn to listen.

As I write this, I remember Harry from my internship whose tiny capacity to listen to his wife evaporated as my fifty minutes of uninterrupted listening became his new norm and expectation in relationship. I felt guilty when I learned this from listening to a recorded message from his wife about how therapy was making him even more insufferable. I was relieved, however, a few years later when a different client told me that Harry's wife eventually felt happy about this "therapeutic" change. Her husband's increased self-centeredness was the last straw for her and she finally, with great relief, shed herself of him.

A therapist, who is a fawn type herself, may hide in a listening and eliciting defense to avoid the scary work of gradually insinuating herself into the relationship and nudging it towards dialogicality. If we do not nudge the client to interact, there will be no recovering. For more on how to approach this, please see the end of the next section.

The *Flight*/Obsessive-compulsive type sometimes presents as being more dialogical than other types. Like the freeze type, however, he can obsess about "safe" abstract concerns that are quite removed from his deeper issues. It is therefore up to the therapist to steer him into his deeper, emotionally based concerns to help him learn a more intimacy-enhancing dialogicality. Otherwise, the flight type can remain stuck and floundering in obsessive perseverations about superficial worries that are little more than left-brain dissociations from his repressed pain.

It is important to note here that all 4F types use left- or right-brain dissociative processes to avoid feeling and grieving their childhood losses. As dialogicality is established, it can then be oriented toward helping them to uncover and verbally and emotionally vent their ungrieved hurts.

4. COLLABORATIVE RAPPORT REPAIR

Collaborative rapport repair is the process by which relationships recover and grow closer from successful conflict resolution. Misattunements and periods of disaffection are existential to every relationship of substance. We all need to learn a process for restoring intimacy when a disagreement temporarily disrupts our feeling of being safely connected.

I believe most people, if they think about it, realize that their best friends are those with whom they have had a conflict and found a way to work through it. Once a friendship survives a hurtful misattunement, it generally means that it has moved through the fair-weather-friends stage of relationship.

Synchronistic with re-editing this last section, my son uncharacteristically got into a conflict at school. During third grade recess two of his good friends, also uncharacteristically, started teasing him, and when they would not stop he pushed each of them. This earned them all a trip to the principal's office. The principal is a strict but exceptionally wise and kind woman. My son's offense, using physical force to resolve a conflict, was judged as the most serious violation of school policy, but his friends' were also held responsible for their part and given an enlightening lecture on teasing.

My son, not used to being in trouble, had a good cry about it all. He then agreed that a one day loss of recess plus writing letters of apology to his friends were fair consequences. Two days later, I asked him how things were going now between him and the two friends. With a look of surprise and delight, he told me: "It's really funny, daddy. Now, it feels like we're even better friends than we were before."

———•··——

Rapport repair is probably the most transformative, intimacy-building process that a therapist can model. I guide this process from a perspective that recognizes that there is usually a mutual contribution to any misattunement or conflict. Therefore, a mutually respectful dialogical process is typically needed to repair rapport. Exceptions to this include scapegoating and upsets that are instigated by a bullying narcissist. In those situations, they are solely at fault. I have often been saddened by codependent clients who apologize to their bullying parents as if they made their parents abuse them.

In more normal misattunements, I often initiate the repair process with two contiguous interventions. Firstly, I identify the misattunement [e.g., "I think I might have misunderstood you."] And secondly, I then model vulnerability by describing what I think might be my contribution to the disconnection.

Abbreviated examples of this are: "I think I may have just been somewhat preachy...or tired...or inattentive...or impatient...or triggered by my own transference." Owning your part in a conflict validates the normality of relational disappointment and the art of amiable resolution.

Taking responsibility for your role in a misunderstanding also helps to deconstruct the client's outer critic belief that relationships have to be perfect. At the same time, it models a constructive approach to resolving conflicts, and over time leads most clients to become interested in exploring their contribution to the conflict. This becomes an invaluable skill which they can then take into their outside relationships.

As one might expect, fight types are the least likely of the 4F's to collaborate and own their side of the street in a misattunement. Extreme fight types such as those diagnosed with Narcissistic Personality Disorder have long been considered untreatable in traditional psychoanalysis for this reason.

With less extreme fight types, I sometimes succeed in psychoeducating them on how they learned their controlling defenses. From there I try to help them see how much they pay for being so controlling. At the top of the list of debits is intimacy-starvation. Consciously or not, they hunger for human warmth and they do not get it from those whom they control. Victims of fight types are too afraid of them to relax enough to generate authentically warm feelings.

———•·——

Finally, I believe one of the most common reasons that clients terminate prematurely is the gradual accumulation of dissatisfactions that they do not feel safe enough to bring up or talk about. How sad it is that all kinds of promising relationships wither and die from an individual or couple's inability to safely work through differences and conflict. Please see Toolbox 4 in chapter 13 for a list of many pragmatic tools to "Lovingly Resolving Conflict."

Moving through Abandonment into Intimacy: A Case Study

A sweet, freeze-fawn client of mine suffered severe emotional abandonment in childhood. Both his parents were workaholics. They were, by definition, exceedingly unavailable. As the youngest of five children, Frank always finished last in the sibling competition for the paltry caretaking his parents had to offer. His adulthood was unfortunately a reenactment of the relational impoverishment of his childhood.

Childhood trauma left Frank hair-triggered to retreat and isolate. He had never experienced an enduring relationship. As a result of our long-term work, however, he became more motivated to seek a relationship. He successfully dated a healthy and available partner. For the first six months of their relationship, my coaching and her kind nature enabled him to show more of himself. He was rewarded by increasing feelings of relaxation and comfort while relating with her.

When he accepted her request to move in together, however, it became harder to hide his recurring emotional flashbacks. He was more convinced than ever that his feelings of fear, shame and depression were the most despicable of his many fatal flaws.

As we worked with this belief in therapy, he remembered many times when even the mildest dip in his mood triggered his mother to retreat into her home office. He saw that the only times his mother had a bit of time for him was on those rare occasions when he was buoyant enough to lift her spirits. He had a staunch conviction that social inclusion depended on him generating cheerfulness. Gloomy and abashed, he confessed: "That's pretty hard for me, Pete. I'm not much fun to be around."

A codependent defense of being perpetually pleasant and agreeable had been deeply instilled in him. He could not shake off the fear that if he was not upbeat enough, his new partner would be disgusted and abandon him. He reported that his flashbacks at home had increased. Sometimes he felt a desperate need to isolate and hide. His freeze response was so activated, that he increasingly withdrew from his partner into silence. He knew that he was hiding too much in computer activities, excessive sleeping, and marathon TV sports viewing, but he could not stop.

During his most intense flashbacks, his fear and self-disgust became so intense that he invented any excuse to get out of the house. He was besieged by thoughts and fantasies of being single again. His critic was winning the battle. He was sure his partner was as disgusted with his affect as his mother had been. He was on the verge of a literal flight response. He was about to leave, as he had before when the brief infatuation stages of his few previous relationships ended.

We spent many subsequent sessions managing these emotional flashbacks to his original abandonment. He understood more deeply that his silent withdrawals were evidence that he was flashing back. He then committed to rereading and using the 13 steps of flashback management at such times.

With my encouragement and gentle nudging, he grieved over his original abandonment more deeply than ever before. Over and over, he confronted the critic's projection of his mother onto his partner.

At the same time, I encouraged Frank to be more vulnerable with his partner. He practiced doing this in role-plays with me. Encouraged by all this work, he began talking to his girlfriend about his Cptsd. A good-hearted person, she responded with sympathy and support. This eventually helped him to disclose that talking vulnerably made him feel even more afraid and ashamed. To his great relief, she was not only empathic but grateful for his vulnerability. She told him that his vulnerability made her feel safer to share an even deeper level of her own vulnerability. He cried poignant tears of gratitude as he told me this. I commiserated with a welling of sweet tears in my own eyes.

Frank's crowning achievement came some months later when he finally felt brave enough to tell her what he was experiencing while he was actually depressed. This breakthrough further enriched their intimacy. Their love expanded into those special depths of intimacy that are only achieved when people feel safe enough to communicate about anything and everything.

As my client became more skilled at being vulnerable, he was rewarded with the irreplaceable intimacy that comes from mutual commiseration. Over the next year, he and his future wife became such reliable sources of verbal ventilation for each other, that Frank no longer needed my services.

Earned Secure Attachment

In therapy, clients get the most out of their session by learning to stay in interpersonal contact while they communicate from their emotional pain. This gradually shows them that they are acceptable and worthwhile no matter what they are feeling and experiencing.

As survivors realize more deeply that their flashbacks are normal responses to abnormal childhood conditions, their shame begins to melt. This then eases their fear of being seen as defective. In turn, their habits of isolating or pushing others away during flashbacks diminish.

Earned secure attachment is a newly recognized category of healthy attachment. Many attachment therapists believe that effective treatment can help a survivor "earn" at least one truly intimate relationship. Earned secure attachment is the good enough and intimacy-rich attachment discussed throughout this book.

———•+•———

I believe the principles outlined in this chapter are keys to achieving an earned secure attachment. In this vein, good therapy can be an intimacy-modeling relationship. It fosters our leaning and practicing of intimacy-making behavior. Your connection with your therapist can become *a transitional earned secure attachment*. This in turn can lead to the attainment of an earned secure attachment outside of therapy. I have repeatedly seen this result with my most successful clients, and I am grateful to report that my last experience with my own therapy lead me to this reward.

Rescuing the Survivor from the Critic

I will conclude this section with a final note to therapists. The term *rescuing* and what it represents has become taboo in many psychotherapy circles and in the 12-Step Movement (e.g. AA, CODA and ACA). The word "rescuing" is often used in such an all-or-none way that any type of active helping is pathologized. However, I believe that helping survivors out of the abyss of emotional flashbacks is a necessary form of rescuing.

A key place to practice healthy rescuing is in the realm of the critic. I believe there is an unmet childhood need for rescue that I help meet when I "save" my client from the critic, the proxy of her parents. This is the need no one met. The child was not rescued from her traumatizing parent. This was terrible neglect on the part of the other parent, the relatives, the neighbors or teachers who ignored the signs that she was withering from being abused.

Decades of trauma work have taken me to a place where my heart no longer allows me to be silent when someone's inner critic is on the attack. Silence, in my mind, is equivalent to tacit approval. I can no longer sit quietly and not intervene when survivors abuse themselves with their parents' internalized voice.

I am additionally motivated to challenge the client's toxic critic because of the failure of my first long-term experience of psychoanalytic therapy. My "blank screen" therapist let me flounder endlessly in attacking myself with self-hate and self-disgust. Never once did she point out that I could and should challenge this anti-self behavior. UCSF trauma expert Harvey Peskin would call this a failure to bear witness to the traumatization of the child.

I now vocally challenge the critic's lies and slanders, and I try to give the survivor a hand to climb out of the abyss of fear and shame into which the critic has pushed him.

It took me some time to break through the dysfunctional guilt that my early training instilled in me about rescuing. Now, ironically, when I feel guilty, it is sometimes because I have regressed and let the inner critic get away with abusing my friend or my client. This guilt is actually healthy emotional intelligence. It comes from my empathy as a *right action*-call to challenge the critic. At such times, I feel derelict in my human and professional duty if I do not bring attention to how he is hoisting himself on his parents' petard.

Gratefully, I can no longer passively collude with the internalized critical parent by failing to actively notice it like all those other adults did while he was growing up. If an adult does not protest when a child is being attacked with destructive criticism, she is in an unspoken alliance with the critic. The child is forced to assume contempt is normal and acceptable. The witnessing adult has forsaken her/his tribal responsibility to protect the child from parents who perpetrate child abuse.

When I label the traumatizing behavior of the client's parents as contemptible, I begin the awakening of his developmentally arrested need for self-protection. I model to him that he should have been protected, and that he can now resist mimicking their abuse in his own psyche. With most of my clients, this eventually encourages disidentification from the aggressor and weakens the internalization of the attacking parent as the locus of the critic.

In my own case, I felt loved by my grandmother who lived with my family, but she failed to help me see that my parents' vitriolic rages were wrong and not my fault. In retrospect, I believe that her neglect crystallized my belief that I deserved their abuse. The stage was then set for me to morph their contempt into self-loathing. I did this chapter and verse for nearly two decades.

I have also noticed a significant difference in survivors who were helped in childhood to see that it was not their fault that they were being traumatized. When there was one witnessing adult who sufficiently decried what was being done to them, most did not develop such a ferocious, self-annihilating critic. Typically this was the other parent, an enlightened older sibling, a relative, a teacher or a kindly neighbor.

FINDING A THERAPIST

I have as yet to do any therapist trainings in my approach outside of the San Francisco Bay Area, so I cannot make any recommendations for therapists outside this area. However, because my approach is compatible with that of John Bradshaw's, I refer people to a website that lists therapists around the U. S. and the World who report that they embrace his approach. The link to this is www.creativegrowth.com.

I and the Creative Growth Center are however unable to personally endorse these therapists as we are not personally familiar with their work. Nonetheless, I think this is a good place to start. Please begin by first reading the following recommendations for interviewing a therapist.

The purpose of the interview is to ascertain whether your potential therapist is able and willing to work at the levels I describe above. I recommend interviewing and having a trial appointment with at least three therapists, if possible, to determine if their approach is compatible enough with the one I describe above.

A suitable therapist will be happy to answer your question about their approach and generally talk with you on the phone for at least five minutes before scheduling a meeting. Should the therapist respond to you in an aloof, critical or shaming way, I would immediately cross them off your list and keep looking.

Finally, it is important to note that there are many untherapized therapists who are licensed to practice psychotherapy, and my experience is that these types are rarely able to work at the depth required for guiding Cptsd recovery.

I believe it's appropriate to ask a prospective therapist if they have done their own therapy. I would then at least expect from him/her a response that they have and have found it helpful. Ideally, the therapist would also be willing to disclose that they have done their own family of origin work.

————·—·——

Further guidance on how to find a therapist can be found at www. alice-miller.com. Click on "articles" at the top, and then on the next page in the left column, click on "FAQ How to find the right therapist." This is a very helpful website – the website of *"The"* Alice Miller, who wrote the great book: *The Drama of The Gifted Child.*

Good luck in your search. If you live in a reasonable sized city and persevere, I think your chances of finding a "good enough" therapist are good.

Finding an Online or Live Support Group

If you cannot afford or find helpful enough therapy, there are many types of self-help groups that are free and powerfully therapeutic. Moreover, if you are in therapy, your recovery process may be enhanced by using any of the resources that follows. Here are some websites that have been repeatedly recommended to me:

www.outofthefog.website

www.ptsdforum.org

www.coda.org is the URL for Codependents Anonymous, one of my favorites, which can be especially helpful for anyone who is a fawn type or subtype.

www.ascasupport.org for survivors of childhood abuse in general.

www.adultchildren.org provides support for ACA's – Adult Children of Alcoholics.

www.siawso.org is a helpful site for survivors of incest.

www.thehotline.org is a site for those survivors whose childhood abuse has lead them to become victims of domestic violence.

www.nobully.com is a very helpful website for survivors who, because of bad luck or repetition compulsion, are stuck in a job or relationship where they are being bullied.

www.daughtersofnarcissisticmothers.com
www.narcissisticmother.org these last two are for recovering from being raised by a narcissistic mother

Several of these sites also have listings of live meetings that can be attended in person. The Creative Growth Center mentioned at the beginning of the last section also offers groups for recovering from shame and grieving the losses of childhood. They are located in Berkeley CA.

Finally, if none of these recommendations seem suitable, Googling "online support groups for recovering from childhood trauma" brings up a plethora of results.

—————

An important guideline for finding a safe enough online or in-person group: If you find that a leader or member is over-dominating a group through narcissistic behaviors such as monologing, monopolizing the time, pressuring anyone with unwanted advice or shaming anyone in anyway, please allow yourself to leave and try another group.

—————

CO-COUNSELING

If you are not able to find or afford a "good enough" therapist, and/ or if you want to supplement your current therapy as my wife and I do regularly with each other, you can look for a safe partner who is willing to work with you to mutually evolve a co-counseling relationship.

There are many forms of co-counseling. {Google "co-counseling" to learn more.}

My wife and I have a simple structure for establishing a safe and healing co-counseling relationship. We have been using this model for many years and derive great benefit from it. I have similarly benefitted from co-counseling with two wonderful friends in the past. Please feel free, of course to adapt the model to fit your own mutual needs and agreements.

Meet weekly and exchange 30 or 60 minute sessions.

Begin with the counselee talking about all and any of his/her concerns and with the counselor refraining from intervening other than to practice, Active Listening.

Active listening is based on an attitude of "unconditional positive regard". It enhances the counselee's process of full verbal ventilation, and it uses non-directive, non-intrusive verbal feedback to let the counselee know that you are attuned and paying attention to him/her.

Active listening includes responses like "un hunh" and "mmm-hmmm" as well as a technique known as mirroring. *Mirroring* occurs when we repeat key words or phrases that the other person says to let them know that we are paying attention to them.

Advanced mirroring occurs when we paraphrase in our own words what we hear. This is only helpful however if we make an accurate translation of what's been said.

Finally, the use of *open-ended questions* is perhaps the penultimate active listening techniques. Questions such as "Can you tell me more about that?", "What else happened?", and "Do you have other thoughts and feelings about that?" can be very helpful.

Opened ended questions stand in contrast to pointed questions which tend to limit or shape the way the counselee responds. "What do you think or feel about that?" allows the other person greater internal exploration than "Did you feel upset about that?" which may be perceived as a statement rather than a question. It can sound like you are telling them what they should be feeling.

People vary in the amount of active listening they find helpful. Please be open to giving and receiving feedback about how much you or the other person would like.

In order to establish safety and build trust, begin with a commitment to refrain from advice giving, criticism or any kind of unsolicited feedback except active listening. If and when the desire for feedback comes up, it is best to let the counselee determine when, what kind and how much they want. Feedback is best given from a take-it or leave-it perspective

Do not give any feedback unless it is clearly asked for. The counselee often does well to be specific about the type of feedback desired, or the desire to not have any feedback; e.g., "I'd like to just verbally ventilate about my relationship, but don't really want any feedback about it other than active listening." At another point the counselee might like to say: "This is something I would actually like some feedback on. I'd like to know whether it seems that I'm perceiving my boss clearly."

With enough grace, luck, respect, practice and compassion, mutual trust may eventually come so far that you both agree to change the structure to allow for spontaneous feedback at certain times in the session. Don't rush to get there, and always reserve permission to invoke the no-feedback guideline for any given issue, session or indefinite number of sessions.

In this vein, my wife or I might say to each other: "I think I'd just like active listening today. I'd like to just extensively free associate on and explore this anxious feeling in my chest without getting any input about it."

Practice therapeutic confidentiality. Let what is said in a session stay in the session.

I also recommend that both partners read Toolbox 4 in chapter 13, and the section above on the four key qualities of relational healing prior to commencing a co-counseling relationship.

CHAPTER 14

FORGIVENESS:
BEGIN WITH THE SELF

This chapter is a reworking of an article of mine that was published in *Recovering*, November 1991. I wrote it because I was appalled at how much pressure my clients were getting to just forgive and forget. Consequently, many of them were diving right back into denial, and minimizing all the trauma that they had endured. Their recovery processes then, screeched to a halt as their inner critics denigrated them for being so unforgiving.

Because this article was helpful to my clients and because I received so much positive feedback from the recovery community, I was motivated to write my first book, *The Tao of Fully Feeling, Harvesting Forgiveness Out of Blame*. This book explores the complex subject of forgiving past abusers in considerable depth. In this vein, it asserts that some parents were so destructive to us, that they are not forgivable.

There is a lot of shaming, dangerous and inaccurate "guidance" put out about forgiveness in both the recovery community and in many spiritual teachings. Many survivors of dysfunctional families have been injured by the simplistic, black-and-white advice that they must embrace a position of being totally and permanently forgiving in order to recover.

Unfortunately, those who take the advice to forgive abuses that they have not fully grieved, abuses that are still occurring, and/or abuses so heinous they should and could never be forgiven, often find themselves getting nowhere in their recovery process.

In fact, the possibility of attaining real feelings of forgiveness is usually lost when there is a premature, cognitive decision to forgive. This is because premature forgiveness mimics the defenses of denial and repression. It keeps unprocessed feelings of anger and hurt about childhood trauma out of awareness.

Real forgiveness is quite distinct from premature forgiveness. It is almost always a byproduct of effective grieving and no amount of thought, intention or belief can bring it into being without a great deal of emotional work.

Conversely, belief systems that are not open to the possibility of forgiveness sometimes block our access to forgiving feelings, even when such feelings are present.

It might be that the healthiest cognitive position concerning forgiveness is an attitude that allows for the possibility of its occurrence on the other side of extensive grieving. This attitude works best if it includes the condition that feelings of forgiveness will not be forced or falsely invoked to cover up any unresolved feelings of hurt or anger.

In this vein, it is crucial to understand that certain types of abuse are so extreme and damaging to the victim that forgiveness is simply not an option. Examples of this include sociopathy, conscious cruelty, and many forms of scapegoating and parental incest.

———·—

When forgiveness has substance, it is felt palpably in the heart, and is usually an expansion of the emotion of compassion. Compassion is certainly not always the same thing as forgiveness, but it is usually the experience within which forgiveness is born. Often this happens via an intermediate process, where having grieved our childhood losses substantially, we occasionally find ourselves considering the extenuating circumstances that contributed to our parents raising us in neglectful or abusive ways.

Most commonly these extenuating circumstances revolve around two issues. First, our parents often parented us in ways that blindly replicated the ways that they were parented. And second, they were often supported in their dysfunctional parenting by the social norms and values of their times.

Nonetheless, it is once again vitally important that we do not jump into considering their mitigating circumstances until we have significantly worked through the traumatic consequences that their abuse and abandonment had on us.

———·—

When considering our parents extenuating circumstances, we may sometimes "get" that our parents were also quite victimized, and we may consequently find ourselves on occasion feeling sorry (sorrow) for them.

Sometimes this experience of feeling compassion for them becomes profound enough for us to comprehend how similarly awful and unfair their childhoods were. This feeling-based realization may on occasion morph into feeling some forgiveness for them.

However, unless this feeling of forgiveness for our parents is grounded in compassion for ourselves, the above process is an empty mental exercise. Even worse, it may become a great hindrance to doing the fundamental angering work of real recovery.

Premature forgiveness will prohibit us from showing the inner child that she had the right to be angry about her parents' cold-hearted abandonment of her. It will stop us from helping her to express and release those old angry feelings.

Premature forgiveness will also inhibit the survivor from reconnecting with his instinctual self-protectiveness. He may never learn that he can now use his anger, if necessary, to stop present day unfairness.

As real forgiveness is primarily a feeling, it is - like all other feelings - ephemeral. It is never complete, never permanent, and never a done deal.

Forgiveness is governed by the *dynamic* nature of all human feeling experience. Our emotional experience is a frequently changing, unchoosable and unpredictable process of the psyche.

No emotional state can be induced to persist as a permanent experience. As sad as this may be, as much as we might like to deny it, as much as it continuingly frustrates us, and as much as we are pressured to control and pick our emotions, they are still by definition of the human condition, largely outside the province of our wills.

———•·•———

Forgiveness then, like love, remains a human feeling experience that is only temporarily ours. However, when we thoroughly vent our angry feelings about the past, feelings of forgiveness become more accessible. When we learn how to grieve ourselves out of abandonment flashbacks, we reemerge into a feeling of belonging to and loving the world.

Moreover, when we learn to effectively grieve through present day hurts, we quite naturally move back into loving feelings. As our emotional flexibility matures, lost feelings of love and forgiveness return so reliably that they can become consciously chosen values.

Thus, when I occasionally feel hurt by proven intimates, I may not be able to immediately invoke loving or forgiving feelings towards them, but I know that with sufficient communication and non-abusive venting, I will eventually return to an appreciative experience of them.

As much as I can forgive myself, that much can I forgive others. What I often forgive in others is an old pain of mine, released from the disgust of self-hate. It is an old vulnerability of mine that I now love and welcome like a bird with a broken wing. Shame and self-hate did not start with me, but with all my heart, I deign that they will stop with me. I will do unto myself as I would have others do unto me.

Carol Ruth Knox wrote a poem about *loving feelings* and the hide-and-seek game they seem to play with us.

It comes and goes, doesn't it?
Sometimes related
to people and how they
treat us, and sometimes not

Sometimes related
to the moon
to personal finances
to the questions of life
to nothingness
to everything
to the seasons, the time
to the food we ate
to. . . .

It would appear as if the art of loving is not whether you love
or not (we all do in our present way) but whether you trust that
when love leaves, it has a reason and it will return again.
Always.

We humans are instruments for love by design.
(So is the whole universe!)
When love blows across us,
naturally we sing a love song.
And when there is no love wind to blow,
though it leaves us strange
and willow-like,
love has gone to an empty field where it fills its
wind sails again
so that it might return
and blow across our all too hungering instruments
one more time.

What shall we do while we wait?

We shall weep of course -
something as lovely as love
leaves a gaping hole when gone.

We shall remember love in our hearts and wait
tenderly and compassionately
with ourselves
as we wander in question
and doubt
until we remember,
"Love always returns."

CHAPTER

BIBLIOTHERAPY AND THE COMMUNITY OF BOOKS

Bibliotherapy is a term that describes the very real process of being positively and therapeutically influenced by what you read. As stated earlier, when it is at its most powerful, bibliotherapy is also relationally healing. It can rescue you from the common Cptsd feeling of abject isolation and alienation.

Bibliotherapy can play an enormous role in enhancing recovery from Cptsd. I usually find that my clients who make the most progress are those who augment their therapy sessions with reading homework [self-prescribed or recommended by me].

This is especially true of those who further augment their reading with journaling about their cognitive and emotional responses to what they have read. I believe that journaling helps build the new physiological and neuronal brain circuitry that occurs as we effectively meet our developmentally arrested childhood needs. [For more on Journaltherapy, read the section on verbal ventilating in chapter 5 of my first book].

Bibliotherapy is especially helpful for people like me who grew up in dangerous social environments replete with adults who offered little but criticism, intimidation and disgust. It equally serves those whose early lives were devoid of adults who could be looked to for safe support and guidance.

It was not until later in life, after I had quite a few years of group and individual therapy, that I realized that my journey of recovering had actually begun decades before my formal therapy. It began with all the therapeutic reading and writing I had instinctively gravitated to. I unconsciously sought the help of others in the many spiritual and psychological self-help books that I was intuitively drawn to.

Without really understanding it, I gained valuable insights about how to improve the way I treated myself and others. Just as importantly, I subliminally realized that there were a number of good, safe, wise and helpful adults out there who could be trusted and who had a great deal of wise and kind guidance to offer.

I remember my first deeply emotional experience of entering *the community of books*. I was in the library resentfully slogging through the poetry section trying to find a book for my homework in high school English.

I was up to "W "and had found nothing that remotely interested me when I came to an anthology with the picture of a very compelling looking old man on its cover. Walt Whitman! His epic poems *Song of Myself* and *Song of the Open Road* thrilled me and changed my life. He became my hero and the first adult role model that had something useful and important to teach me. His ideas became my *raison d'être* and gave me a hopeful plan for what I would do when I finally escaped my family.

Over time the authors in my community of books seemed like a small tribe of elders who I imagined as people who would have empathy for me if I were to meet them. Eventually when I achieved something of a critical mass of this awareness, I managed to take a frightening leap into the water of therapy. I lucked out and got a good enough therapist to help me take steps in my healing that I could not manage on my own.

So here are some authors [and their works] who have been especially helpful to me on my journey. These are the wise aunts and uncles I never biologically had.

ESPECIALLY RECOMMENDED READING

Alice Miller   The Drama of The Gifted Child {Great book for overcoming denial and understanding the profound impact of growing up poorly parented. Very relevant for fawn types.}
Gravitz & Bowden   Guide to Recovery {Great short, powerful overview of recovery. Oriented to recovering from having alcoholic parents, but very relevant to having traumatizing parents. Read this if you can only read one book.}
L. Davis & E. Bass   The Courage to Heal {Classic on recovering from sexual abuse.}
Jack Kornfield   A Path with Heart {Using meditation to increase self-compassion.}
Steven Levine   Who Dies {Mindfulness and radical self-acceptance.}
Sue Johnson Hold Me Tight {The book, and especially the DVD of the same name, shows how she teaches real couples to use their emotional vulnerability to develop real intimacy and a healthy attachment bond.}
John Bradshaw   Healing The Shame That Binds {Brilliant book on recovering from toxic shame and growing up in a dysfunctional family.}

Judith Herman   Trauma and Recovery {The book in which Herman coins the term Complex PTSD. Last half of book more relevant to recovery.}

Susan Anderson   The Journey from Abandonment to Healing {Oriented toward recovering from divorce, but remarkably relevant to Cptsd recovery.}

J. Middleton-Moz   Children of Trauma {Excellent overall book on recovery.}

Beverly Engel   Healing Your Emotional Self {Advocates angering-at-the-critic work.}

Theodore Rubin   Compassion and Self-hate {Wonderful appeal to self-compassion.}

Susan Forward   Betrayal of Innocence { Good overall book on recovery.}

Byron Brown   Soul Without Shame {Inner critic shrinking with angering-at-the- critic and Mindfulness perspective.}

Susan Vaughan   The Talking Cure {How Therapy and Relational Healing works with very accessible neuroscientific evidence and an enlightened view of therapy.}

Lewis & Amini   A General Theory Of Love {Accessible poetic and scientific argument on the human need for love and attachment.}

Pat Love   The Emotional Incest Syndrome {Great book to heal from codependent entrapment with a narcissistic mother.}

Robin Norwood   Women Who Love Too Much {Early classic on Codependence.}

Gay Hendricks   Learning to Love Yourself

Lucia Capacchione   Recovery of your Inner Child {Great book on Journaltherapy.}

Cheri Huber There is Nothing Wrong with You {Great book for overcoming shame and cultivating self-compassion.}

Christine Lawson   Understanding The Borderline Mother {Healing from having a borderline or narcissistic mother; explores 5 different types.}

Elan Golomb Trapped in The Mirror {Healing from having a narcissistic parent.}

John Gottman   The Seven Principles of Making Marriage Work

CHAPTER

SELF-HELP TOOLS

This chapter is composed of six toolboxes, each with a set of tools to address different recovery issues. Nonetheless, I still value these lists as indispensable adjuncts to my own journey of recovering. I often hand out these lists to clients at appropriate times in their journey. I also give them to students who attend my classes. I have received a great deal of positive feedback about how helpful they have been to enhancing recovery.

My friends and clients whose recovery progresses at the greatest rate are those who supplement their therapy with self-help activities. Those who print out these lists, and carry them around or post them in a conspicuous place until they are deeply ingrained seem to take a quantum leap in their recovery.

I hope that you become immersed in these lists, and that they give you the healing support that I have seen so many others receive from them.

Here's a poem that I found graffitied on a wall. It was signed "Hank," which turns out to be Charles Bukowski's nickname.

> your life is your life
> don't let it be clubbed into dank
> submission.
> be on the watch.
> there are ways out.
> there is light somewhere.
> it may not be much light but
> it beats the
> darkness.
> be on the watch.
> the gods will offer you
> chances.
> know them, take them.
> you can't beat death but
> you can beat death in life,
> sometimes.
> and the more often you
> learn to do it,
> the more light there will
> be.
> your life is your life.
> know it while you have
> it.
> you are marvelous
> the gods wait to delight
> in
> you.

———•·•———

Conclusion

In conclusion, you progress in recovering from the multidimensional wounding of Cptsd:

[1] as increasing mindfulness decreases your unconscious 4F acting out,
[2] as your critic shrinks,
[3] as your brain becomes more user-friendly,
[4] as grieving your childhood losses builds your emotional intelligence,
[5] as your body relaxes and your mind becomes more peaceful,
[5] as your healthy ego matures into a healthy sense of self,
[6] as your life narrative becomes self-compassionate and self-affirming,
[7] as your emotional vulnerability creates authentic experiences of intimacy and
[8] as you attain a "good enough" safe relationship.

And let me reemphasize once again that recovery is not an all-or-none phenomenon. It is a gradual process marked by ongoing growth in any of these arenas, and most especially in a decreasing frequency, intensity and duration of flashbacks.

———•·•———

I hope and pray that much sooner than later you will experience an increasing access to the silver linings I described in chapter 4. I hope you sense the ongoing resolution of your developmental arrests. I hope you will notice an increasing kindness to yourself and a pride in the beautiful uniqueness of yourself. I hope you become as fierce in your allegiance to yourself as you need to be to feel that you safely belong to the world. I further hope that the benefits of your improved emotional intelligence will bring you at least one intimate relationship where you can ongoingly discover the benefits of safe and multidimensional relating.

TOOLBOX 1
SUGGESTED INTENTIONS FOR RECOVERY

Here are normal and safe wants and needs to wish and hope for . . .
to cultivate with mental, spiritual, emotional and physical energy.
As usual, focus on the ones that most appeal to you. Skip the ones
that do not feel right for you or that you do not feel ready for.

1. I want to develop a more constantly loving and accepting relationship with myself. I want an increasing capacity for self acceptance.
2. I want to learn to become the best possible friend to myself.
3. I want to attract, into my life, relationships that are based on love, respect, fairness and mutual support.
4. I want to uncover a full, uninhibited self expression.
5. I want to attain the best possible physical health.
6. I want to cultivate a balance of vitality and peace.
7. I want to attract, to myself, loving friends and loving community.
8. I want increasing freedom from toxic shame.
9. I want increasing freedom from unnecessary fear.
10. I want rewarding and fulfilling work.
11. I want a fair amount of peace of mind, spirit, soul and body.
12. I want to increase my capacity to play and have fun.
13. I want to make plenty of room for beauty and nature in my life.
14. I want sufficient physical and monetary resources.

15. I want a fair amount of help (self, human, or divine) to get what I need.
16. I want God's love, grace and blessing.
17. I want a balance of work, rest and play.
18. I want a balance of stability and change.
19. I want a balance of loving interaction and healthy self sufficiency.
20. I want full emotional expression with a balance of laughter and tears.
21. I want a sense of meaningfulness and fulfillment.
22. I want to find effective and non-abusive ways to deal with anger.
23. I want all this for each and every other being.

TOOLBOX 2

HUMAN BILL OF RIGHTS [GUIDELINES FOR FAIRNESS AND INTIMACY]

1. I have the right to be treated with respect.
2. I have the right to say no.
3. I have the right to make mistakes.
4. I have the right to reject unsolicited advice or feedback.
5. I have the right to negotiate for change.
6. I have the right to change my mind or my plans.
7. I have a right to change my circumstances or course of action.
8. I have the right to have my own feelings, beliefs, opinions, preferences, etc.
9. I have the right to protest sarcasm, destructive criticism, or unfair treatment.
10. I have a right to feel angry and to express it non-abusively.
11. I have a right to refuse to take responsibility for anyone else's problems.
12. I have a right to refuse to take responsibility for anyone's bad behavior.
13. I have a right to feel ambivalent and to occasionally be inconsistent.
14. I have a right to play, waste time and not always be productive.
15. I have a right to occasionally be childlike and immature.

16. I have a right to complain about life's unfairness and injustices.
17. I have a right to occasionally be irrational in safe ways.
18. I have a right to seek healthy and mutually supportive relationships.
19. I have a right to ask friends for a modicum of help and emotional support.
20. I have a right to complain and verbally ventilate in moderation.
21. I have a right to grow, evolve and prosper.

TOOLBOX 3

SUGGESTED INTERNAL RESPONSES TO COMMON CRITIC ATTACKS

The attacks of the critic often operate below the radar of self-awareness. Unless we can identify them, we are at their mercy and helpless to deconstruct them. Once we learn to recognize inner critic attacks, the simple techniques of Thought-Stopping and Thought-Substitution are powerful tools in short-circuiting the critic.

There are two categories of attacks. *Perfectionism* attacks, fueled by toxic shame, create chronic self-hate and self-flagellation. *Endangerment* attacks, fueled by fear, create chronic hypervigilance and anxiety.

PERFECTIONISM ATTACKS

1. Perfectionism. My perfectionism arose as an attempt to gain safety and support in my dangerous family. Perfection is a self-persecutory myth. I do not have to be perfect to be safe or loved in the present. I am letting go of relationships that require perfection. I have a right to make mistakes. Mistakes do not make me a mistake. Every mistake or mishap is an opportunity to practice loving myself in the places I have never been loved.

2. All-or-None & Black-and-White Thinking. I reject extreme or over generalized descriptions, judgments or criticisms. Statements that describe me as "always" or "never" this or that, are typically grossly inaccurate.

3. <u>Self-Hate, Self-Disgust & Toxic Shame</u>. I commit to myself. I am on my side. I am a good enough person. I refuse to trash myself. I turn shame back into blame and disgust and externalize it to anyone who shames my normal feelings and foibles. As long as I am not hurting anyone, I refuse to be shamed for normal emotional responses like anger, sadness, fear and depression. I especially refuse to attack myself for how hard it is to completely eliminate the self-hate habit.

4. <u>Micromanagement/Worrying/Obsessing/Looping/Over-Futurizing</u>. I will not repetitively examine details over and over. I will not endlessly second-guess myself. I cannot change the past. I forgive all my past mistakes. I cannot make the future perfectly safe. I will stop hunting for what could go wrong. I will not try to control the uncontrollable. I will not micromanage myself or others. I work in a way that is "good enough", and I accept the existential fact that my efforts sometimes bring desired results and sometimes they do not. "God grant me the serenity to accept the things I cannot change, the courage to change the things I can, and the wisdom to know the difference."

5. <u>Unfair/Devaluing Comparisons</u> to others or to your most perfect moments. I refuse to compare myself unfavorably to others. I will not compare "my insides to their outsides". I will not judge myself for not being at peak performance all of the time. In a society that pressures us into acting happy all the time, I will not get down on myself for feeling bad.

6. <u>Guilt.</u> Feeling guilty does not mean I am guilty. I refuse to make my decisions and choices out of guilt; sometimes I need to feel the guilt and do it anyway. In the inevitable instance when I inadvertently hurt someone, I will apologize, make amends, and let go of my guilt. I will not apologize over and over. I am no longer a victim. I will not accept unfair blame. Guilt is sometimes camouflaged fear: "I am afraid, but I am not guilty or in danger".

7. "Shoulding". I will substitute the words "want to" for "should" and only follow this imperative if it feels like I want to, unless I am under legal, ethical or moral obligation.

8. Over-Productivity/Workaholism/Busyholism. I am a human being not a human doing. I will not choose to be perpetually productive. I am more productive in the long run, when I balance work with play and relaxation. I will not try to perform at 100% all the time. I subscribe to the normalcy of vacillating along a continuum of efficiency.

9. Harsh Judgments of Self & Others/ Name-Calling. I will not let the bullies and critics of my early life win by joining and agreeing with them. I refuse to attack myself or abuse others. I will not displace the criticism and blame that rightfully belongs to my original critics onto myself or current people in my life. "I care for myself. The more solitary, the more friendless, the more unsustained I am, the more I will respect myself". - Jane Eyre

ENDANGERMENT ATTACKS

10. Drasticizing/Catastrophizing/Hypochondriasizing. I feel afraid but I am not in danger. I am not "in trouble" with my parents. I refuse to scare myself with thoughts and pictures of my life deteriorating. No more home-made horror movies and disaster flicks. No more turning tiny ailments into tales of dying.

11. Negative focus. I will stop anxiously looking for, over-noticing and dwelling on what might go wrong or what might be wrong with me or life around me. Right now, I will notice, visualize and enumerate my accomplishments, talents and qualities, as well as the many gifts life offers me, like music, film, food, beauty, color, books, nature, friends, etc.

12. <u>Time Urgency</u>. I am not in danger. I do not need to rush. I will not hurry unless it is a true emergency. I am learning to enjoy doing my daily activities at a relaxed pace.

13. <u>Disabling Performance Anxiety</u>. I am reducing procrastination by reminding myself not to accept unfair criticism or perfectionist expectations from anyone. Even when afraid, I will defend myself from unfair criticism. I won't let fear make my decisions.

14. <u>Perseverating About Being Attacked</u>. Unless there are clear signs of danger, I will thought-stop my projection of past bullies/critics onto others. The majority of my fellow human beings are peaceful people. I have legal authorities to aid in my protection if threatened by the few who aren't. I invoke thoughts and images of my friends' love and support.

TOOLBOX 4
TOOLS FOR LOVINGLY RESOLVING CONFLICT

This is a list of techniques and perspectives I've gathered over the years to help couples resolve conflict as lovingly as possible. When I give it to couples that I work with, I ask them to take time at home to read it aloud together and to discuss each one as much as necessary to see if they can agree to adopt it as a guideline for handling conflict.

When I first got together with my wife eleven years ago, we spent considerable time on a weekend trip discussing these guidelines one at a time. We aired our concerns, enthusiasms, caveats and reservations about using them. Over subsequent years, we refined our usage of them, and have evolved a communication style around our conflicts that has helped to keep our intimacy healthy and ever growing.

1. Normalize the inevitability of conflict & establish a safe forum for it. Discuss and agree to as many of these guidelines as seem useful.
2. The goal is to inform and negotiate for change, not punish. Punishment destroys trust. Love can open the "ears" of the other's heart.
3. Imagine how it would be easiest to hear about your grievance from the other.
    Say it as it would be easiest for you to hear.
4. Preface complaints with acknowledgement of the good of the other and your mutual relationship.

5. No name-calling, sarcasm or character assassination.
6. No analyzing the other or mind reading.
7. No interrupting or filibustering
8. Be dialogical. Give short, concise statements that allow the other to reflect back and paraphrase key points to let you hear that you are accurately being heard.
9. No denial of the other's rights as outlined in the Bill of Rights above.
10. Differences are often not a matter of right or wrong; both people can be right, and merely different. Be willing to sometimes agree to differ.
11. Avoid "you" statements. Use "I" statements that identify your feelings and your experience of what you perceive as unfair.
12. One specific issue, with accompanying identifiable behavior, at a time. Ask yourself what hurts the most to try to find your key complaint.
13. Stick to the issue until both persons feel fully heard. Take turns presenting issues.
14. No interrupting or filibustering.
15. Present a complaint as lovingly and calmly as possible.
16. Timeouts: If discussion becomes heated either person can call a timeout [one minute to 24 hours], as long as s/he nominates a time to resume. {See 1 below}
17. Discharge as much of any accumulated charge before hand as possible.
18. Own responsibility for any accumulated charge in the anger that might come from not talking about it soon enough.
19. Own responsibility for accumulated charge displaced from other hurts. {See 2 below}
20. Commit to grow in your understanding of how much of your charge comes from childhood abuse/neglect.
21. Commit to recovering from the losses of childhood by effectively identifying, grieving, and reclaiming them.

22. Apologize from an unashamed place. Make whatever amends are possible.

Include your intention to correct your behavior in the future. Explain your extenuating circumstances as evidence – not as an excuse - that you were not trying to be hurtful.

1. More on Timeouts, #16

Two of the most common reasons that relationships break up is irreconcilable differences and irreparable damages. The latter could have been prevented in many cases if couples knew how to use timeouts judiciously.

This is especially true for fight-type trauma survivors, who when flashing back, can easily lose control to the outer critic and say intimacy-destroying things. Survivors benefit greatly from

learning to recognize the signs of being over-activated so that they can then take timeouts to stop the bleeding caused by a critic on the rampage.

Things said in the heat of a flashback can wound deeply and engrave themselves in the psyche of the other in ways that cripple trust. So much of this needless intimacy-destruction will be prevented if both members of the couple agree that either of them can call a time-out whenever they feel too triggered to be lovingly confrontive, or are experiencing the other as flashing back into being overly aggressive.

Timeouts can range from one minute to 24 hours depending on how long it takes either or both partners to achieve good enough flashback management.

Timeouts work best when the person calling them nominates a time to resume conflict resolution, so that timeouts do not become techniques for dodging issues.

Timeouts can be used individually as a time to release any accumulated charge. This can be done by using the safe "angering out" techniques I describe in chapter 5 of my book, *The Tao of Fully Feeling*.

2. More on Transference, #19 & #20

In using this list with couples, I notice that those who are most skilled in conflict resolution, have achieved significant skill with steps 19 through 21. These steps are about learning to handle transference.

For trauma survivors, transference is often a type of flashback whereby we unconsciously react to our significant others as though they were our childhood caretakers. When this occurs, we displace onto them a great deal of our unresolved childhood emotional pain.

One common example of this occurs when a partner's fair and minor complaint triggers a torrent of rage, fear and/or shame that is left over from decades of a parent's overwhelming and rejecting criticism.

Another instance of this occurs when her failure to say what he was hoping to hear stirs up the pain of decades of his aloof, detached mother or father's neglect. All gender combinations can of course fall into this trap.

The composition of most conflicts that I witness in my office eventually seems to be approximately 90% re-experienced pain from the past and 10% actual current pain. Harville Hendrix's

Getting The Love You Want, is a wonderful guide for working through this dynamic in a way that heals childhood wounds and enhances intimacy at the same time.

In my experience, the vast majority of conflicts between consenting adults involve a dynamic where both people play a part and have some responsibility for a disruption in their loving connection.

Truly healing resolutions to conflict typically occur when each partner owns their part and expresses an apology about their contribution to the conflict. For deep level resolution this usually includes an apologetic reference to your transference. A good apology sounds something like this of this: "I'm sorry for the amount of charge I had in expressing my disappointment. While I believe I have a fair complaint, the intensity with which I expressed it was too much. I'm sorry I responded to you as if you were my constantly withholding mother."

325

TOOLBOX 5
SELF-GRATITUDES 12X12

This chart is a self-esteem building exercise and is best approached as a work in progress. Try to think of twelve entries for each category. Resist the critic's all-or-none dynamic, and list something if it is generally true of you a good deal of the time. Work on it when you are not in a flashback. Ask someone who you trust enough to help you with this exercise.

1. Accomplishments

2. Traits

3. Good deeds

4. Peak Experiences

5. Life Enjoyments

6. Intentions

7. Good Habits

8. Jobs

9. Subjects studied

10. Obstacles overcome

11. Grace Received

12. Nurturing memories

GRATITUDES ABOUT OTHERS 12X12

This chart is an exercise for deconstructing the outer critic' program of generalizing that everyone is as dangerous as our traumatizing caregivers. Use the same guidelines as those of the last chart.

1. Friends [past and current]

2. Inspiring people

3. Inspiring authors

4. School friends [whether or not you are still in contact]

5. Circles of friends [past and current]

6. Childhood friends [you do not need to still be in touch with them]

7. Teachers

8. Kindness of strangers

9. Pets & Animals

10. Work friends [past and current]

11. Groups [past and current]

12. Nurturing memories

TOOLBOX 6

I am ending this book with a reiteration of the most essential principles of Cptsd recovering. Please reread these steps to help anchor them in your psyche. Notice also if they reverberate with you more significantly than when you first read them back in chapter 8.

13 STEPS FOR MANAGING FLASHBACKS

1. **Say to yourself: "I am having a flashback".** Flashbacks take you into a timeless part of the psyche that feels as helpless, hopeless and surrounded by danger as you were in childhood. The feelings and sensations you are experiencing are past memories that cannot hurt you now.

2. **Remind yourself: "I feel afraid but I am not in danger!** I am safe now, here in the present." Remember you are now in the safety of the present, far from the danger of the past.

3. **Own your right/need to have boundaries**. Remind yourself that you do not have to allow anyone to mistreat you; you are free to leave dangerous situations and protest unfair behavior.

4. **Speak reassuringly to the Inner Child**. The child needs to know that you love her/him unconditionally– that s/he can come to you for comfort and protection when s/he feels lost and scared.

5. **Deconstruct eternity thinking.** In childhood, fear and abandonment felt endless – a safer future was unimaginable. Remember this flashback will pass as it always has before.

6. **Remind yourself that you are in an adult body** with allies, skills and resources to protect you that you never had as a child. [Feeling small and fragile is a sign of a flashback.]

7. **Ease back into your body**. Fear launches you into "heady" worrying, or numbing and spacing out.

   [a] **Gently ask your body to Relax**: feel each of your major muscle groups and softly encourage them to relax. [Tightened muscles send false danger signals to your brain.]

   [b] **Breathe deeply and slowly**. [Holding your breath also signals danger.]

   [c] **Slow down**: rushing presses your brain's flight response button.

   [d] **Find a safe place** to unwind and soothe yourself: wrap yourself in a blanket, hold a pillow or a stuffed animal, lie down on your bed or in a closet or in a bath; take a nap.

   [e] **Feel the fear in your body without reacting to it**. Fear is just an energy in your body. It cannot hurt you if you do not run from it.

8. **Resist the Inner Critic's Drasticizing and Catastrophizing**.

   [a] **Use thought-stopping** to halt the critic's endless exaggerations of danger, and its constant planning to control the uncontrollable. Refuse to shame, hate or abandon yourself. Channel the anger of self- attack into saying "NO" to your critic's unfair self-criticism.

   [b] **Use Thought-substitution & Thought-correction** to replace negative thinking with your memorized list of your qualities and accomplishments.

9. **Allow yourself to grieve**. Flashbacks are opportunities to release old, unexpressed feelings of fear, hurt, and abandonment. Validate and soothe your child's past experience of helplessness and hopelessness. Healthy grieving can turn your tears into self-compassion and your anger into self-protection.

10. **Cultivate safe relationships and seek support**. Take time alone when you need it, but don't let shame isolate you.

Feeling shame doesn't mean you are shameful. Educate your intimates about flashbacks and ask them to help you talk and feel your way through them.

11. **Learn to identify the types of triggers that lead to flashbacks**. Avoid unsafe people, places, activities and triggering mental processes. Practice preventive maintenance with these steps when triggering situations are unavoidable.

12. **Figure out what you are flashing back to.** Flashbacks are opportunities to discover, validate and heal your wounds from past abuse and abandonment. They also point to your still unmet developmental needs and can provide you with motivation to get them met.

13. **Be patient with a slow recovery process**. It takes time in the present to become de-adrenalized, and considerable time in the future to gradually decrease the intensity, duration and frequency of flashbacks. Real recovery is a gradually progressive process [often two steps forward, one step back], not an attained salvation fantasy. Don't beat yourself up for having a flashback.

BIBLIOGRAPHY

Abrams, Jeremiah (ed). Reclaiming the Inner Child, Los Angeles: Jeremy P. Tarcher, Inc., 1990.

Anderson, Susan. The Journey from Abandonment to Healing, New York: Berkley Books, 2000.

Bach, George and Goldberg, Herb. Creative Aggression, New York: Avon, 1975.

Bass, E.& Davis, L. The Courage To Heal, NY: Harper&Row, 1988.

Beaver, Daniel. Beyond The Marriage Fantasy, New York: Harper & Row, 1982.

Bender, Sheila. Love From The Coastal Route, Seattle: Puckabush Press, 1991.

Bettelheim, Bruno. A Good Enough Parent, New York: A. Knopf, 1987.

Boon, Suzette. Coping with Trauma-related Dissociation

Bradshaw, John. Healing The Shame That Binds You, Deerfield Beach, Florida: Health Communications, Inc., 1988.

_____. Bradshaw On: The Family, Deerfield Beach, Fla: Health Communications, 1988.

Branden, Nathaniel. How To Raise Your Self-Esteem, New York: Bantam, 1987.

Briggs, Dorothy Corkville. Your Child's Self-Esteem, New York: Dolphin, 1975.

Brooks, C. The Secret Everyone Knows, San Diego: Kroc Foundation, 1980.

Brown, Brene. The Gifts of Imperfection, Minnesota: Hazelden, 2010.

Brown, Byron. Soul Without Shame, Boston: Shambala, 1999.

Cameron, Julia. The Artist's Way, New York: Putnam's, 1992

Campbell, Susan. The Couple's Journey, San Luis Obispo, CA: Impact Publishers, 1981.

Covitz, Joel. Emotional Child Abuse: The Family Curse, Boston: Sigo Press, 1986.

Engel, Beverly. Healing Your Emotional Self, NJ: Wiley, 2006.

Faber, Adelle and Mazlish, Elaine. How to Talk So Kids Will Listen & Listen So Kids Will Talk, New York: Rawson, Wade Publishers, 1980.

Forward, Susan. Betrayal of Innocence, New York: Penguin, 1970.

Frey, William H., II, Ph.D., Crying: The Mystery of Tears, New York: Harper & Row, 1987.

Fromm, Erich. The Art Of Loving, New York: Bantam, 1962.

Fromm-Reichmann, F. Principles of Intensive Psychotherapy, Chicago: University of Chicago Press, 1950.

Glendenning, Chellis. My Name Is Chellis & I'm Recovering from Western Civilization, Boston: Shambala, 1994

Golomb, Elan. Trapped in the Mirror, NY: Quill, 1992

Gottman, John. The Seven Principles of Making Marriage Work, NY: Three Rivers Press, 1999.

Gravitz, Herbert and Bowden, Julie. Recovery: A Guide For Adult Children Of Alcoholics, New York: Simon & Schuster, 1985.

Guntrip, H. Psychoanalytic Theory, Therapy, and the Self, New York: Basic Books, 1971.

Hazelden. Hazelden's Meditations, San Francisco: Hazelden, 1985,

Hazelton, Lesley. The Right To Feel Bad, Garden City, New York: The Dial Press, 1984

Hendrix, Gay. Learning To Love Yourself, New York: Prentice Hall Press, 1987.

Herman, Judith. Trauma and Recovery, New York: Basic Books, 1997.

Hoffman, Bob. Getting Divorced from Mother & Dad, New York: E.P. Dutton, 1976.

Huber, Cheri. There Is Nothing Wrong With You, Keep It Simple Books, 2000.

Jeffers, Susan. Feel the Fear and Do It Anyway, San Diego: Harcourt Brace Jovanovich, 1987.

Jung, Carl. Memories, Dreams, and Reflections, Edited by Aniela Jaffe. New York: Random House, 1961.

Kabat-Zinn, Jon. Mindfulness for Beginners, Boulder: Sounds True, 2012.

Kalsched, Donald. The Inner World of Trauma, NY: Routledge, 1999.

Katherine, Anne. Where to Draw the Line, N.Y.: Simon&Schuster, 2000.

Kopp, Sheldon. If You Meet The Buddha On The Road, Kill Him, New York: Bantam, 1981.

Kornfield, Jack. A Path With Heart, New York: Bantam, 1993.

Kubler-Ross, Elizabeth. On Death And Dying, London: Collier-Macmillan, 1969.

Laing, R. D. The Voice of Experience, New York: Pantheon Books, 1982.

Lawson, Christine. Understanding The Borderline Mother, Oxford: Jason Aronson, 2000.

Leech, Peter and Singer, Zeva. Acknowledgement: Opening to the Grief of Unacceptable Loss, Missoula, Mt: Zeva Singer, 1988.

Levine, Stephen. Who Dies, Garden City, NY: Anchor Press, 1982.

_____. Meetings At The Edge, Garden City, NY: Anchor Press, 1984.

Lewis, T., Amini, F., Lannon, R. A General Theory of Love, New York: Vintage,2000.

Love, Patricia. The Emotional Incest Syndrome, New York: Bantam, 1990.

Lowen, Alexander. Bioenergetics, New York: Coward, McCann, 1970.

Marris, Peter. Loss and Change, Garden City, N.Y.: Anchor, 1975.

May, Rollo. Love and Will, New York: W.W. Norton, 1969.

McClelland, W. Robert. God Our Loving Enemy, Nashville: Abingdon, 1982

Meade, Michael, Robert Bly and James Hillman. The Rag and Bone Shop of the Heart, New York: Harper, 1992.

Middleton-Moz, Jane. After the tears: Reclaiming the Personal Losses of Childhood, Deerfield Beach, Florida: Health Communications, Inc., 1986.

Miller, Alice. For Your Own Good, Toronto: Collins Publishers, 1984

_____. Thou Shalt Not Be Aware: Society's Betrayal Of The Child, New York: Farrar, Strauss, & Giroux, 1984

_____. The Drama of the Gifted Child (original title Prisoners of Childhood), New York: Basic Books, 1981.

Mitchell, Stephen. The Enlightened Heart, New York: Harper, 1989.

Missildine, W. Hugh. Your Inner Child of the Past, New York: Simon and Schuster, 1963.

Monroe, Herbie. Wisdoms of a Dog Scholar, Sydney: Unpublished, 1982.

Moore, Thomas. Care of the Soul, New York: Harper Collins, 1992.

Norwood, Robin. Women Who Love Too Much, New York: Pocket Books, 1985.

Peck, M. Scott. The Road Less Traveled, New York: Simon and Schuster, Touchstone, 1978.

Real, Terrence. I Don't Want To Talk About It, NY: Fireside, 1997.

Roth, Geneen. Breaking Free of Compulsive Eating, London: Grafton, 1986.

Roth, S. Psychotherapy: The Art of Wooing Nature, Northvale, NJ: Jason Aronson, 1987.

Rubin, Theodore. Compassion and Self-Hate, New York: Macmillan, Collier, 1975.

_____. The Angry Book, New York: Macmillan, Collier, 1976.

Rubin, Theodore. Compassion & Self-Hate, New York: Ballantine, 1975.

Satir, Virginia. Conjoint Family Therapy, Palo Alto, CA: Science and Behavior Books, 1983.

Schatzman, M. Soul Murder: Persecution in the Family, New York: Jason Aronson, 1973.

Schaef, Anne Wilson. When Society Becomes An Addict, San Francisco: Harper & Row, 1987.

Schutz, Will. Profound Simplicity, New York: Bantam, 1979.

Semrad, E. Semrad, The Heart of a Therapist, ed. S. Rako and H. Mazer. New York: Jason Aronson, 1980.

Shain, M. Hearts That We Broke A Long Time Ago, New York: Bantam, 1982.

Smalley, Stuart. I'm Good Enough, I'm Smart Enough, and Doggone It, People Like Me, New York: Dell, 1992.

Smith, Manuel. When I Say No, I Feel Guilty, New York: Bantam, 1975.

Short, Susanne. "Understanding Our Childhood: The Hidden Secret." Psychological Perspectives, Fall, 1989.

Stein, Robert M. Incest and Human Love: The Betrayal of the Soul, Dallas: Spring Publications, 1973.

Stone, Hal and Sidra. Embracing Your Inner Critic, San Francisco: Harper, 1991.

Vachss, Andrew. "You Carry The Cure in Your Heart", Parade, Aug. 28, 1994.

Viorst, Judith. Necessary Losses, New York: Fawcett Gold Medal, 1986.

Walker, Alice. Her Blue Body Everything We Know, New York: Harcourt Brace Jovanovich, 1991.

Walker, Pete. The Tao of Fully Feeling, Lafayette, CA: Azure Coyote, 1995.

Walker, Pete. The Tao of Existential-Transpersonal Psychology, Oakland: Unpublished Thesis, 1985.

Watts, Alan. In My Own Way, New York: Random House, 1972.

Whitman, Walt. Leaves of Grass, New York: Signet, 1958.

Woodman, Marion. The Pregnant Virgin: A Process of Psychological Transformation, Toronto: Inner City Books, 1985.

Yalom, Irvin. Existential Psychotherapy, New York: Basic Books, 1980.

Made in the USA
Middletown, DE
22 July 2023